A Social History of English

Language and Society Series

General editor

John Spencer

Professor of English,
University of Hong Kong
Formerly Director of the Institute of Modern English Language Studies,
University of Leeds

Loreto Todd   *Pidgins and Creoles*

Michael Gregory and Susanne Carroll   *Language and Situation*

John Oxenham   *Literacy*

A Social History
of English

Dick Leith

Department of English and Foreign Languages
City of Birmingham Polytechnic

Routledge & Kegan Paul
London, Boston, Melbourne and Henley

First published in 1983
by Routledge & Kegan Paul Ltd
39 Store Street, London WC1E 7DD,
9 Park Street, Boston, Mass. 02108, USA,
296 Beaconsfield Parade, Middle Park,
Melbourne, 3206, Australia, and
Broadway House, Newtown Road,
Henley-on-Thames, Oxon RG9 1EN
Set in IBM Press Roman by
Columns, Reading
and printed in Great Britain by
Redwood Burn Ltd, Trowbridge

Library of Congress Cataloging in Publication Data

Leith, Dick, 1947-
A social history of English.
(Language and society series)
Bibliography: p.
1. English language – History. 2. English language –
Social aspects. I. Title. II. Series.
PE1075.L44 1982   420'.9   82-13181

ISBN 0-7100-9260-1
ISBN 0-7100-9261-X (pbk.)

093431

General editor's preface

Languages are part of the history of the peoples who use them, intimately bound up with the changing patterns of the societies they serve. Decade by decade, generation by generation, a language responds to new needs and demands: it will receive an imprint from contact with invaders or immigrants; it will reflect, in new words and turns of phrase, in changes of pronunciation and in grammatical shifts, a community's experience of sustained exposure to other languages or cultures; the rise of new classes may be expected subtly to affect communal attitudes to linguistic behaviour; and the gradual extension of literacy will alter attitudes to linguistic propriety. Somewhere in a language's history there will be a record of almost every major change in circumstance or communicative need of the people who have used it, though the relationship between social cause and linguistic effect is intricate and complex, and often there is insufficient historical detail to allow us to uncover it.

English, the language with which this book is concerned, provides us with texts for almost the whole fifteen hundred year period during which it has existed and developed as a distinct language. For the first seven or eight centuries, however, the texts are relatively scanty. And for much of the whole period the majority of the populations which used it could neither read nor write. Thus we have only vestigial and indirect evidence as to how people spoke, and of the circumstances and needs which shaped everyday spoken discourse at different social levels. Nor is the historian always able to provide the kind of social and cultural detail which might enable us to determine *why* changes in the language occurred.

It is not surprising, perhaps, that histories of English have tended to concentrate on *what* changed, without overmuch reference to social or political factors which might have been responsible for the changes. Not only is the historical record increasingly fragmentary the further back we go; the actual detail of intrinsic change, in phonetic, grammatical, lexical and semantic systems, is in itself complicated enough to unravel. Traditional linguistic history has been primarily concerned to do this, although in the process it has at times engendered the view that languages are organisms; as if, that is, linguistic change and development were determined by tendencies inherent in the languages themselves. This is of course not so, however beguiling the organic metaphor may be. But how far are we able to examine and document the link between social and linguistic change in English over the past fifteen centuries? The answer is that we may be rather better equipped to attempt it than previous generations of scholars, in spite of the absence of much of the evidence.

Contemporary studies of what we may call 'the sociolinguistic equation' have been fruitful for our understanding of languages in many ways. Research on present-day societies has thrown much new light on communal bilingualism in a variety of cultural and political settings; the processes of social communication which give rise to pidginisation, and sometimes ultimately to pidgin and creole languages, are better understood; the impact of literacy on different types of social order has been documented and compared; and we have come to a clearer view of the manifold patterns of relationship which can arise between dominant and suppressed languages, and the complex determinants of language maintenance and language shift. With the aid of these new perceptions we may be able to examine the record again, and see linguistic history within a broader framework.

In this volume Dick Leith offers this broader framework. He has not tried to rewrite linguistic history, rather to fill out the context by introducing sociolinguistic insights, where they are relevant, to complement the established pattern of linguistic evidence. He has done this scrupulously, and with due caution, from a scholarly background which includes both linguistic history and sociolinguistics. This is a rare conjunction, and by the aid of both branches of scholarship the author is able to achieve new insights and raise new questions. Anyone interested in the history of English, or in the complex relationship between language and society, will find this volume lively, thoughtful and illuminating. It also opens up new lines of enquiry, and fresh opportunities for research.

Sociolinguistics is a large and expanding field of interdisciplinary activity, focusing attention in a variety of ways on the interaction of linguistic and social phenomena. For students in a broad range of humane disciplines it can offer new and stimulating perspectives. It is the purpose of this series to offer brief, readable and scholarly introductions to the main themes and topics covered by current sociolinguistic studies.

John Spencer

Contents

Author's preface

This short introduction to the history of English is the product of teaching a subject that is often daunting to the student. It is intended to be as clear and simple as possible and therefore assumes no technical knowledge on the part of the reader.

Inevitably the debt to numerous works of scholarship is too heavy to acknowledge in copious notes and references. The book has drawn extensively on the work of historians of English like C.L. Barber, M.L. Samuels, and Barbara Strang; of linguists and language scholars like A.C. Gimson, Geoffrey Leech, Frank Palmer, Randolph Quirk, and R.A. Waldron; and of sociolinguists like Joshua Fishman, Einar Haugen, William Labov, and Peter Trudgill. And the work of Raymond Williams has proved an invaluable supplement. The more specific contributions of others have been acknowledged in the Notes and Bibliography at the end of the book.

The book is divided into three parts. Parts 1 and 2 trace the history of English within England, first by outlining a 'historical sociology' of the language and then by exploring some case studies of linguistic change. Part 3 concerns the history of English in other areas of the British Isles and in different parts of the world.

Introduction

The English language today is spoken by several hundred million people in five continents. It functions in different kinds of societies as a mother-tongue, a second language, a vehicle of officialdom, a medium of education, and as a language for science, business, and commerce. It is also used widely as a *lingua franca* — a language used among people who have no other tongue in common — and in some areas it has provided a base for pidgins and creoles. It is spoken by people who also use two or three or even more languages in the course of their daily lives, and it has come to symbolise many different and often sensitive issues and institutions in different areas: education, literacy, social mobility, economic advancement, Christianity, and colonial dominance.

These facts are often forgotten by people in England. Most of us tend to associate English with British nationality (the latter is sometimes even defined by it) and since we expect to spend our lives speaking only English it comes as a shock to learn that in other societies quite ordinary and unexceptional people need to be bilingual. When we look at English across the world today we find therefore that it varies enormously in accordance with its wide range of functions, and because it bears the imprints of the languages with which it has made contact. This is something that has also characterised its past — a fact that could be borne in mind when we consider the Asian, West Indian, African, and European languages and dialects that are spoken by schoolchildren in towns and cities of the United Kingdom.

So great is the variation in English that it is often difficult to say whether a certain variety in one place or another should be called English or not. But the demarcation of languages is a perennial problem in linguistics because there is no sure way of determining, on purely linguistic grounds, where one language ends and another begins. In reality there are only linguistic continua: different varieties of English shade off into each other, as English shades off into other languages. It is up to us, as social animals, to decide where to draw the lines; and the chances are that our choices will be governed by social and political considerations rather than linguistic ones. Wherever the line is drawn someone, somewhere, will be upset, since deep emotions are often aroused by issues of language — emotions widely felt, but all too easily ignored in others.

We need not look beyond England itself to find extensive variation in the ways English is used. Language varies because of the wide range of uses to which it is put, and it is a matter of common experience that we speak and write differently in different situations. But English also varies because its speakers come from different backgrounds of region and class, and variations associated with these often function as markers of group identity. Different varieties therefore acquire social values — these are often exploited, for instance, in television commercials — and these values themselves may vary according to the loyalties of different social groups. Most people in England will probably place a high value on the standard variety, but recent research confirms the impression of many that regional and non-standard speech shows little sign of dying out. One reason for this is that varieties of language are intimately involved with issues of power and solidarity. The standard variety constitutes one dimension of the process of political centralisation, and it has recently been suggested that in much of Western Europe and North America that process has by now gone far enough to provoke a counter-reaction of 're-tribalisation', in which language has played a key role. The issue of the Welsh language is a recent example.

Many people argue that since the spread of compulsory education and the mass media there is little justification or excuse for the persistence of speech-forms that we all know lack prestige. But this is to assume that education plays only one role in contemporary society. The education system cannot compensate for a social system that remains fundamentally unequal. The use of the standard variety may be required in certain prestigious occupations, but these are few in number, and people may change their speech-habits only if they consider they have a realistic chance of securing one. Despite the best intentions of many teachers, the education system, instead of engendering a healthy interest in varieties of speech, has often functioned in a way that reproduces and reinforces the ethos of a highly competitive class society. Different varieties of English continue to play a large part in the symbolism of social class.

All these considerations mean that an adequate history of English must respect no national, political, ethnic, cultural, or social boundaries. Neither need we assume that English-speaking communities in the past were any more homogeneous than they are today. Unfortunately, the study of language has been harmed by the divorce of past from present. The historical study of English has developed its own perspectives and methods, but these have been limited in part by the ways in which the subject has been institutionalised in university departments. For most students it has been associated with the translation of Old and Middle English texts, and to many it has had a rather curious preoccupation with the level of linguistic structure which in the past we can know least about − that of sounds. Above all, the emphasis has been on linguistic data, and by presenting linguistic history as moving in stages from Old English (a stage of infancy) through Early Modern English (robust adulthood) to the language of today (creeping senility?) the impression has sometimes been given that language changes by itself.

In this book the users of English have been put first. This helps us to see language as a tool rather than as a commodity or even artefact, and prevents us from seeing its history either as a decline from a Golden Age of elegant eloquence or as progress from the unsophisticated usage of wild Anglo-Saxon tribespeople. A selection of well-known examples of linguistic change have been explored within the general framework of sociolinguistics, and some social and political factors have been suggested to help account for the changes. Much of the book is speculative: lack of evidence has always been a problem in the historical study of language. And rather than propose a general theory of linguistic change the book has been written in the conviction that the historical study of a language cannot itself be an autonomous discipline.

Note: In the interests of simplicity phonetic symbols have been kept to a minimum throughout this book, and length-marks, diacritics, etc. omitted in quotations from the Anglo-Saxon.

Part 1
Emergence and consolidation

Chapter one

Languages in contact

In the Introduction we saw some of the ways in which we need to modify our conception of English as we observe its use in different kinds of communities throughout the world. The same type of adjustment must be made when we look at English across its fifteen centuries of history. In this chapter we shall outline the issues involved in the historical description of a language like English as it has been adapted to changing social functions in different periods, and as it has co-existed with other languages. The period covered is from the earliest records to the end of the Middle Ages. We shall trace the origins of English as the vernacular of certain Germanic tribes on the continent of Europe, at a time when much of that area was dominated by the institutions and language of the Roman Empire. We can use the Latin of that period, with its patterns of contact with other languages, as a model for discussing a major kind of bilingual situation, and also that particular form of standardisation known as diglossia. In describing the Anglo-Saxon settlement of what is now England, we shall see how English came into contact with the Celtic language of the Britons, and how it developed a literature under the influence of Latin. As the various kingdoms of the Anglo-Saxons created institutions and extended literacy, they came to be threatened by the Vikings, who spoke a different though closely related language. There followed two other cases of language-contact, involving different varieties of the same language: Norman-French after the Norman Conquest, followed by the Central French of the Paris area after 1204. Finally, we shall see how an early form of language-loyalty surfaced in the fourteenth century to cause English to become the national language of England.

At no point during the period under discussion was there a standard variety of English accepted as such wherever the language was spoken. Rather we see a growing trend towards dialectal variation, as different centres of power exert their influence over local speech. We are not therefore describing English as a *taught* language; nor is it the case that the bilingual situations we shall discuss were primarily products of the schoolroom. We are dealing with language-learning, and language-contact, in contexts that are more informal, more haphazard, and unplanned: as peoples migrate, as armies occupy new territory, as settlers intermarry. What strikes the modern monoglot speaker of English is the relative ease with which new languages seem to have been acquired or old ones discarded.

Just as there was no norm of language during the first thousand years of England's history, so there was no enduring political centre. Until the late Middle Ages the concept of England itself was a fragile one. The Anglo-Saxon kingdoms were often at war with each other, and for over two centuries they suffered militarily and politically at the hands of the Vikings. The periods of centralisation under Alfred and Athelstan were short-lived; one kingdom, Northumbria, was for centuries virtually isolated. Although unity of a kind came with the Normans, it was a unity imposed by a foreign power, through a foreign language. Long after the early period of Norman settlement was over, many of the institutions of England remained saturated with French manners, ideals, and language.

Some of the changes which took place during this period in the structure of English — its sounds, its words, its grammar — will be mentioned in the following pages, and later in the book. But we shall predominantly be concerned here with changes of a different kind. The English of the Germanic tribespeople who first encountered the Celts of Britain was not the English of the Anglo-Saxon kingdoms at the time of the Viking invasions. By that time English had a written form, and was beginning to serve the functions of the developing institution of monarchy. The language had changed, that is to say, because it had been made to function in a different kind of society.

Language and social function

These considerations at once suggest the approach proposed in the Introduction: seeing language in terms of its functions, and relating language changes to changes of function. This is sometimes referred to as the *sociolinguistic profile* of a language. In the course of this chapter, we shall be attempting to sketch such profiles for the languages that came into contact with English until the end of the Middle Ages; also, of course, seeing how the profile of English itself changed, partly as a result of these contacts.

We have already referred to two of the most important factors: standardisation and literacy. These are so central to the sociolinguistic history and description of a language that in this book they are accorded a chapter to themselves. To recognise their importance, however, is not to say that a standardised, written language is in any way better or more important than its unwritten, unstandardised counterpart. Nor would it be true to say that languages of the latter type are inferior or handicapped. It means, rather, that the demands of speakers on their language are no more than those associated with the customary, local needs of small, technologically simple societies. A larger, more centralised society will make new demands on its language or languages, as specialised institutions — administrative, legal, religious, educational — are created. As we shall see in the next chapter, the adaptation of a language to such demands is closely bound up with the cultivation of standardised varieties and the written word.

We can see, then, that the range and kinds of functions that a language serves must be borne in mind when we describe its sociolinguistic profile. In general, languages that function in the *domains* of a centralised state can be described as *developed*, while we can use the term *oral vernacular* to denote languages with the alternative characteristics we have outlined. Both developed and vernacular languages can function in societies where they are the only languages their speakers need to know; and where this is the case, we can further describe them as *autonomous*. Thus, as a standardised, literate, national language of a modern state, English is autonomous today within England; but no less autonomous was the oral vernacular of the Germanic tribes who first settled here.

The notion of autonomy is important, since it enables us to describe the difference between a vernacular and a dialect. The term *dialect* is used in many different ways. Our description of a vernacular language may remind us of the characteristics usually associated with dialects, in that these are not normally written; neither are they used in the 'higher' domains of the centralised state. In fact, the term dialect has been used, confusingly, to refer to languages of this type: people have written of 'the myriad dialects of Africa'. In contemporary England, however, we think of dialects as regional variants of a language which also has a standardised, and therefore non-regional form. The use of dialect in this sense is limited to certain 'everyday' domains — for instance, it is spoken among family and peer-group — but the standard variety can, at will, be used for all purposes in all circumstances: it is fully developed, or omnifunctional. In general, then, the dialects in such a society are dominated by the existence of the more prestigious standard and are not, therefore, autonomous.

Dialects, then, can be described as undeveloped, oral varieties of a language that are *heteronomous* with respect to a standardised one. Unfortunately, different scholars at different times have used the term to denote different combinations of criteria, some social or functional, others more directly linguistic. In French usage, the term *dialecte* refers to a regional variety that has a written form, in opposition to a *patois*, which does not (we shall see the usefulness of this distinction throughout this book). Also, speech-varieties have been called dialects on the basis of purely linguistic similarities among them, such as shared words, similar sound-systems, grammatical patterns, and so on. Some scholars, therefore, have used the term to relate varieties that most of us would consider separate languages, and they have done this because they have drawn their lines on different parts of the linguistic continuum, as described in the Introduction. Thus, it has been said that the earliest speakers of English used a dialect of Germanic, similar in terms of linguistic structure to the other kinds of speech used by other, related, Germanic tribes. The term *Germanic* here denotes a kind of parent language. And in principle there is no knowing where to stop applying the term dialect, since it can be used, it seems, to relate any varieties that have some perceived linguistic feature in common. More often the line is drawn according to some notion of mutual intelligibility: when people stop understanding each other, they can be said to be speaking different languages. But this criterion is not nearly as useful as it seems. Unintelligibility can be total, or only partial; and it also depends very much on the motivation of speakers to understand each other. Indeed, some would argue that there are enough problems of intelligibility between different dialects in contemporary England to justify calling them separate languages.

Another crucial dimension in the sociolinguistic description of a language is the value placed on its different varieties by its speakers. Greater prestige tends to attach to standard varieties, since they can function in higher domains, and they have written forms. Developed languages, therefore, tend to be more prestigious than vernaculars. We shall see throughout this book that when developed languages come into contact with vernaculars, the latter tend to be influenced by the former. This is partly a reflection of power: developed languages tend to be used by societies that are more centralised politically, and these are usually better equipped to fight and survive. But it is also a reflection of attitudes to language. People who use a language with traditions of standardisation and literacy may develop a sense of *historicity*, a pride in their language's past, and its continuity with the present. They tend to be more keenly aware of their language's difference from other languages. They do not see their language as being under threat, and in danger of dying out: rather, they are aware of its *vitality*. These factors are extremely important in the modern world, when oppressed languages, such as the Celtic ones of Britain and France, and languages such as Pennsylvania German in the United States of America are being kept alive by their speakers. We shall bear all this in mind when we come to consider the status of Latin during the Roman Empire.

The prestige attached to standardised, written varieties of language is associated with the belief that they are the most correct forms of the language, and that they are perhaps the most 'beautiful'. Aesthetic judgments of this kind are even shared by people who may be illiterate, and who have little access to the prestige variety. This is most likely to happen where a *classical* variety, enshrining a literature either sacred or secular, develops in a language spoken over a very wide area, and where literacy is the preserve of an elite. In such conditions, the everyday spoken varieties of such a language may diverge quite sharply from the classical standard. The consequences of this divergence may be seen today in the case of Arabic. This language, to put it rather simply, has two forms: one based on an ancient, classical standard, the other on the colloquial usage of the present. But the situation is not the same as that found in, say, contemporary England, with its standard and its dialects. Whereas in England the standard can be used for all purposes, no contemporary speaker of Arabic uses the form deriving from the ancient literary standard as a medium of everyday conversation. In fact, the two varieties are functionally differentiated, just as they are evaluated differently by their users. The classical form, which is considered more correct and beautiful than the colloquial forms, is used in the prestigious domains like law, religion and education, and has therefore been called the *High* variety of the language. The *Low* variety – which uses many words, grammatical constructions, and sounds that are different from the High one – is subject to great regional variation (as distinct from the 'fixed' classical form codified in dictionaries and grammars) and is used in more informal contexts.

The situation just described is known as *diglossia* and it demonstrates the value of describing languages or linguistic varieties according to the ways in which they function in society. We shall return to diglossia later, in our consideration of Latin, which, like Arabic, was once the official language of a large empire.

Bilingualism

People will readily acquire a second language if they need one, and if they have access to its speakers. This is particularly common when speakers of different languages intermarry, and their children grow up bilingual. In some circumstances, a first, or native language, may not be as useful to an individual's daily needs as a second language: this often happens when people migrate to other countries to work. And in some conditions people learn a simplified version of another language when contact with its speakers is only intermittent; and they use it for very limited purposes, such as trade. These simplified languages are known as *pidgins.*

Bilingualism can be of various kinds. Where one person commands more than one language, we can speak of individual bilingualism. But this need not mean that both languages are actually spoken: scholars, for instance, can be fluent only in the written form of another language, and translation from one language to another can introduce linguistic changes that are far-reaching. Such cultural bilingualism, as we shall call it, is of great importance in the early history of English.

Where a society regularly uses two or more languages to carry out its affairs, we can speak of societal bilingualism. The restriction of each language to certain areas is referred to as geographical bilingualism. In parts of Belgium for instance, French is spoken as a first language, whereas Flemish is natively spoken elsewhere; and both languages have official status. Some people, of course, will be bilingual; and in most bilingual societies, one language-group is more bilingual, at the individual level, than the other. This is particularly so in the very common cases where one language is the official one, used in High domains, and the other is relegated to functions that can be described as unofficial, where it is merely tolerated (as in the case of immigrant languages in English cities) or actually proscribed (see chapter six). The speakers of the Low language are much more likely to be bilingual than those whose first language is the High one. In such situations one language is clearly the dominant one, and we can adapt the term diglossia to describe them, and speak of diglossic bilingualism.

Latin as the language of Empire

To anyone acquainted with the roles and status of English in the world today, a sociolinguistic profile of Latin at the time of the Roman Empire would make familiar reading. Latin was a developed, omnifunctional, autonomous, urbanised, standardised language. It had a classical variety which was codified by grammarians, and a writing system that could provide a model for other languages when it was their turn to require orthographies. This imperial language of a vast empire also became the language of an international religion, Christianity.

At first, the imposition of Roman rule over areas of ethnic, cultural, and linguistic heterogeneity would have led to the kind of bilingualism we have described as diglossic. Latin was the official language of High domains, while diverse local vernaculars served the everyday needs of many different subject populations. Thus, ordinary people would have been controlled in a language unfamiliar to them, as in so many parts of the world today. But it seems that this kind of societal bilingualism did not remain stable for long. The spread of Latin came to be not only geographical, but social as well. Subject peoples gradually, over the generations, acquired it as a second language, and subsequently as a first language. In short, the Roman Empire witnessed a process known to sociolinguists as *language shift*. The evidence for this is demonstrated by the fact that Latin formed the base of French, Spanish, Italian, Portuguese, and Romanian as they are spoken today.

There are a number of reasons why a process of language shift took place. The Romans conquered, but also administered; and their centralised rule lasted so long — several hundred years in many places — that Latin had the chance to take root. Since it was imposed over areas of great linguistic diversity, it could also function as a lingua franca for subject peoples. And finally, there were material advantages in learning it. The characteristic instrument of Roman rule was the town (supported by the agricultural economy of the villa), and to play any part in the life of the towns, it was necessary to learn Latin. Urbanisation, then, brought new influences, practices, and opportunities to people interested in exploiting them.

The successful spread of Latin over a vast area had much in common with the extension of other international languages in the ancient and early medieval worlds. The Hellenic Empire had spread Greek in the eastern Mediterranean, where Latin never displaced it. Later, over much of the Levant and parts of Africa, Islam extended the use of Arabic, religion being a powerful agency in its spread. And it has been argued that all three languages at different points in their history have exhibited the features associated with diglossia.

When today we speak of Latin we tend to think of the literary Latin used by writers like Cicero about two thousand years ago. This is because Classical Latin, as we usually call it, is the variety most often studied: it derives prestige from the great writers who used it, and it enjoys the air of regulation and fixity conferred upon it by the scholars who codified it in grammars. But we must not forget that Latin, like any language, had different varieties, just as many Classical writers themselves could not overlook the differences that were emerging between their metropolitan written usage (described as *urbanus*, which later came to denote refinement) and the local (*rusticus*) or popular (*vulgaris*) Latin which was to provide the basis for Christian writings in the following centuries. Classical Latin is certainly of great importance in the history of English, but it is on the spoken Latin, not of Rome, but of the Imperial provinces, that we must now concentrate.

We have already mentioned the significance of towns to the imposition of Roman rule. In the major Imperial cities, a small elite of Roman citizens used the Latin of Rome as the official language, teaching it in schools to the nobility of the conquered peoples. A major function of all towns was to raise enough cash to pay for the standing armies that were so essential to the maintenance of the Empire. It is in these armies that we can see the conditions for the genesis of new, local varieties of Latin. Drawing their complements from speakers of many different languages, the armies fostered Latin as a lingua franca: and it is likely that the spoken Latin of the soldiery bore the imprints of numerous mother-tongues, as a process of pidginisation occurred. Similar conditions existed among the trading sectors of the towns. As centres of commerce, the provincial towns attracted a mercantile element almost as multilingual in character as that of the army, and this would have assisted the spread of a local variety of Latin among the neighbouring population.

The spread of Latin was not as even, however, as the above account might suggest. In at least two parts of the Empire, its position was to prove tenuous. In the provinces of the east, Latin did not displace Greek, the prestigious language of an earlier Empire, as an official language; and in the west, it seems likely that the language was not learned at all among the agrarian population in the highland area of the province known as Britain.

The collapse of the Empire in the north

The subject populations of both Britain and Gaul were farming peoples known as Celts. Their society was a tribal one, and their language an undeveloped vernacular. The Celts were not literate (although they had an alphabet which they used for inscriptions) and it is probable that the British variety of the language could be understood in Gaul, and vice versa; hence, they could be said to have spoken different dialects of Celtic, if we use dialect in the sense of 'related language', discussed above. Under the Romans, Celtic would have been the Low language, though the pattern of individual bilingualism may have varied widely. Thus, in the remoter, less urbanised areas, monoglot speakers of Celtic may have predominated, while in the towns Latin may have been the only language used. In the areas influenced by the towns bilingualism was probably quite common.

It is impossible to gauge the extent to which Latin displaced Celtic in either Gaul or Britain. But as one of its most enduring and valued possessions, Gaul is more likely to have been the more thoroughly Romanised. In Britain, however, bilingualism may have had a strongly geographical character. Throughout the more inaccessible northern and western regions, including much of what is now called England, Celtic customs, organisation, and language remained to threaten Roman rule; whereas in the south and east, it is conceivable that Latin had displaced Celtic. Unfortunately, we can do little more than speculate on these matters; and, as we shall see, the oblique and even contradictory nature of what evidence exists is very much bound up with the subsequent fortunes of these two outposts of Roman rule. By the fifth century AD, both had fallen to invading Germanic tribespeople; among them, the Angles and Saxons, the speakers of a language that was later to be called English.

Of these Germanic tribes little is known. Like the Celts, they had developed none of the social, political, and economic institutions which demand the cultivation of a standardised language. They were farming peoples, locally organised on the principle of personal loyalty to a chieftain; tribal kings were only elected in times of crisis. Unlike the Celts, however, they had managed to keep the Romans out of their homelands north of the Rhine and Danube. But in their sustained defence of these areas, many of the tribes came into contact with the Romans, siding with them in campaigns against other tribes, and enlisting in the Roman legions. Such contact had its linguistic consequences: the word *cheese* was probably adapted from Latin *caseus* at this time, its pronunciation changing to fit the sound-patterns of the Angles and Saxons.

During the period of the Roman Empire, it seems that the inclination of the Germanic tribes was to expand, generally towards the south and west; but the organisational superiority of Rome kept them bottled up. As Roman rule faltered, however, it came to depend on some of the more Romanised tribes for its survival, and these often had imperial ambitions of their own. The Visigoths of the lower Danube area, for instance, were originally employed to regain what is now Spain from other Germanic adventurers; but as the collapse of Roman rule became imminent, they created their own Empire there. But Roman ways lived on. The Visigoths were rapidly Christianised. Above all, they adopted Latin; at first for writing, later in speech. It is their version of spoken Latin that forms the basis of the Spanish language.

Even those tribes who had not been caught in the Imperial net seem to have been impressed by the apparatus of the Empire when they encountered it in their invasions of the fifth century. At least, this is true of mainland Europe. The spectacularly successful Franks, who overran Gaul from their homelands by the lower Rhine in less than half a century, seemed content to respect the institutions of Roman rule and leave them intact. Quickly united under one leader, the Franks had been baptised before the end of the fifth century. With Christianity came Latinisation. Latin remained the language of administration and religion, and soon became the language of law. In the end the Franks, like the Visigoths, discarded their Germanic speech and adopted the spoken Latin of Gaul, the language that was to become French. It is probable that these two cases of language shift were led from above, by each ruling group.

The Germanic invasion of Britain

The rapidity with which the Franks settled Gaul and embraced the trappings of Latin civilisation contrasts markedly with the slow, less coordinated progress of the Germanic invaders of Britain. The groups of Angles, Saxons, Frisians, and Jutes who left their north German homelands for Britain in the course of the fifth century were not united under one leader; neither did they so swiftly secure military success. While the Franks seemed content to allow the town-and-villa economy of Gaul to continue untouched, the Angles and Saxons found resistance from Celtic chieftains, to whom authority had now passed after the withdrawal of the standing army had left Roman institutions undefended. The Germanic invaders of Britain might well have been content to co-exist peaceably with the Celts, as appears to have happened in Gaul; but naturally enough, British resistance was met with force. This resistance is likely, however, to have been relatively uncentralised and sporadic, so the pattern of Anglo-Saxon invasion would have varied in different places. Some Celts would have been killed in battle; others fled west, and some perhaps into what is now Brittany; some may have been enslaved; many would probably have carried on much as before. But without the possibility of a military response, those Celts who remained would have been gradually absorbed through intermarriage into the Anglo-Saxon hegemony.

We know very little about the early relations between Anglo-Saxons and Celts. Although the Germanic tribes possessed a runic alphabet for purposes of inscription, they had no use for written history, and have bequeathed us no contemporary account of their invasion. But we are left with one striking fact. The Anglo-Saxons did not abandon their language. The Celtic language was displaced, and English developed not from a local variety of spoken Latin, but from the Germanic language of the invaders. Unfortunately, much of the speculation about Anglo-Celtic relations at this time is based on linguistic evidence, which, as we shall see, is of uncertain value when other crucial information is missing.

One problem concerns the extent to which Latin was spoken in the south and east of Britain. Since the Anglo-Saxons landed on the eastern shores, they would first have encountered Latin-speaking Celts, if that language had taken root. The fact that the Germanic invaders did not then learn Latin may have two possible explanations. First, the Celtic resistance may have been long and bloody enough to have embittered relations with the invaders. Alternatively, it may have been the case that the Anglo-Saxons were simply unimpressed by what remained of Latin civilisation in Britain. Either the economy of town and villa was less flourishing than in Gaul, or the Anglo-Saxons had no desire to ape or adopt the institutions and language of Imperial Rome. As we shall see, Christianity, which was a potent force for Latinisation, came only slowly and gradually, like the process of settlement itself.

It is more commonly assumed that the Anglo-Saxons encountered a Celtic-speaking population rather than one speaking Latin. If this is the case, it is difficult to know how to interpret the linguistic evidence that exists. When we examine the origins of place-names, we find that Celtic elements are not uncommon in the west of what we now call England, suggesting that Celtic communities co-existed alongside sparser Anglo-Saxon ones. River-names (such as Axe and Avon) are often of Celtic origin, but this evidence conflicts with the extremely low incidence of Celtic loan-words into Anglo-Saxon. The place-name evidence has been taken to show that Celts and Anglo-Saxons co-existed peaceably, at least in some areas, while the dearth of loan-words might suggest wholesale slaughter, expulsion, or enslavement of a dominated people. The only conclusion we may be justified in drawing here is that we do not know how to evaluate these different kinds of linguistic evidence in the absence of other kinds of data.

There are also difficulties involved in making predictions or projections about the language-habits of a particular community on the basis of comparisons with situations elsewhere. It would be wrong, for instance, to argue that because the Anglo-Saxons did not learn Latin, as the Franks did in Gaul, the British Celts *must* have remained Celtic-speaking. In trying to specify the vital factors which determine the adoption of new languages by conquering peoples and subjugated populations, we need to bear in mind the numerical strength of the invaders, the degree of centralisation of their political organisation, their intentions (the establishment of a ruling caste, for instance, or the settlement of land for farming), the extent to which intermarriage occurs, and so on. We might also need to know something about the degree of resistance put up by the defending inhabitants, and their own degree of centralisation and military strength, as well as the extent to which they, and the invaders, share an international written culture or religion. In the absence of detailed knowledge of this kind, it is impossible to predict which language will prevail in any given case. On the available evidence, it seems likely that any comparison between the linguistic histories of Britain and Gaul would need to bear in mind the differing degrees of Romanisation, and the different aims of the Germanic invaders. We shall see the relevance of this discussion again, later in this chapter.

Whatever languages the British Celts spoke, the Anglo-Saxons successfully imposed their own undeveloped, oral vernacular. But this case of language imposition is very different from that of Latin as the language of an empire. While Anglo-Saxon was almost certainly the dominant language, its relationship with either Celtic or Latin could not be described as diglossic: each Anglo-Saxon kingdom took generations to establish. At first, too, bilingualism would have been societal, in that language use was determined by ethnic background, and was to a large extent geographical, since Celtic would have been stronger in the west. This pattern is likely to have been replaced by individual bilingualism on the part of Celts; and in some areas Celtic survived, perhaps for several centuries. It has been claimed that a vestige of it may even have survived into the nineteenth century, particularly in the area of the northern Pennines, in the numeral systems associated with counting sheep, stitches in knitting, and perhaps children's games: a Cumbrian version has *pedera* (four) and *pump* (five); the equivalent numerals in modern Welsh are *pedwar* and *pump*. But while the Celtic language was preserved in Wales and Cornwall – only to experience a further attack from English in later centuries – it was eventually displaced from most of England altogether.

The Anglo-Saxon settlement

The fact that the Angles and Saxons had to cross the sea before reaching their chosen territory greatly influenced the process and pattern of their settlement. It is likely that their tribal organisation was disrupted by the voyages: a charismatic leader might attract a boatload of adventurers drawn from different tribal units. The boats would sail up the major rivers like the Thames and the Humber and establish the first settlements – probably strongly fortified – at places on the banks, and then wait for the next boatloads before advancing further. When each centre of settlement was consolidated, the process of land-clearing and cultivation could begin. Archeological and place-name evidence suggests that the settlers used Roman roads and sites when it suited them: but it seems that the Anglo-Saxons preferred to take over the kind of site called in Latin a *vicus*, where civilians had settled outside the walls of military centres (giving place-names ending in -*wich*, -*wicham*, etc.). This contrasts markedly with the pattern in Gaul, where Roman villa sites became villages, and where towns remained intact and flourishing.

It was the Anglo-Saxon settlers who established the structure of villages in the territory we now call England. An overwhelming proportion of these villages have Anglo-Saxon names, many incorporating the names of local leaders, others the vocabulary of wood-clearing, drainage, and cultivation (see chapter three). In many places, the relatively undisturbed character of village life, and a largely immobile population, created over the centuries the conditions for sharp divergences in local

speech. But in parts of the more strongly Celtic west, Anglo-Saxon settlement was often later, and less dense. The settlers did not venture into
Wales or Cornwall (although a heavy 'buffer' settlement occurred in
parts of Devon, where Anglo-Saxon boundaries are still a dominant
feature in the landscape), and it seems they found the Cumbrian hills
uninviting. Here, pockets of Celts remained, and in other parts of the
northwest their presence may be attested by the Celtic place-name
Eccles, an adoption from Latin *ecclesia*, which denotes a place of worship. In these areas the Celtic language may have influenced the local
Germanic speech in ways that are no longer recoverable, accounting,
perhaps, for characteristic pronunciations of words like *boot* and *soon*
in the local accent of both Devon and Lancashire; the vowel has a
fronted quality, rather like that in French *tu*, which is unusual elsewhere in England.

The small communities of Angles and Saxons, with their oral culture,
were gradually organised into larger political units under petty kings. At
one point there seem to have been at least seven kings in different parts
of England, often warring amongst themselves. The most important
were those of Northumbria (the land north of the River Humber),
Mercia (the land with a *march* or border with Wales), Wessex (the land
of the West Saxons, who lived to the south of the western part of the
Thames), and Kent; but there were also kingdoms of East Anglia, Essex,
and Sussex. We shall see the importance of these separate kingdoms in
establishing regional varieties of English in the following paragraphs.

With the institution of kingship came the gradual introduction of
Christianity. And with Christianity came literacy. But for the Anglo-
Saxon kings, unlike their Germanic counterparts on the European mainland, Christianity was not synonymous with the use of Latin in both
speech and writing. Conversion in early English society was often the
work of Irish missionaries, and Ireland, never part of the Roman Empire although influenced by it, had developed as well as its own style of
Christianity a tradition of writing in its own language. Rather than use
Latin, they had adapted its alphabet in Ireland for their own purposes,
and this knowledge they passed on to the Anglo-Saxons. Each kingdom
eventually developed its own traditions of writing, using the local variety
of English: the Irish predilection for literacy in the vernacular had not
gone unnoticed. Perhaps the finest examples of Germanic poetry, like
the epic *Beowulf* and the elegiac *Seafarer*, are recorded in Anglo-Saxon.
But it is significant that much early writing in English was prose, used
for laws, charters, chronicles, and also for sermons.

The development of any literary tradition at this time could not, however, escape the influence of Latin. Christianity and Latin were virtually inseparable over much of Europe, just as the Church was the stablest and most highly structured political institution. The traditions of philosophical, theological, legal, and administrative writing in Latin were so long, pervasive, and prestigious that for Anglo-Saxon scholars like Bede in the eighth century and Aelfric in the tenth, it would almost have been the instinctive choice. Thus, while Latin was a spoken medium at this time in the monasteries, its use is most directly associated with writing, and it is on this level that the language comes into contact with English. Anglo-Saxon scholars would have been bilingual in English and Latin, but it was a bilingualism that was cultural in character, the preserve of an educated elite. And contact with Latin meant exposure to ideas, practices, and concepts that were Christian. The pagan tradition in poetry, as it was written down, was re-interpreted in Christian terms, and loan-words from Latin in the period of early Anglo-Saxon literacy were often associated with religion (*abbot, apostle, choir, mass*).

The fact that Latin was a model and an inspiration for the first writers in Anglo-Saxon England does not mean that it was in any way superior to the language of the English. Any language, or dialect for that matter, has the potential for use in any domain, and for any purpose. But if the speakers of a vernacular come into contact with a developed language, they will often interpret traditions of use within certain domains as evidence of linguistic superiority. The Anglo-Saxon scholars may well have thought that Latin was the natural and most suitable vehicle for, say, philosophical writing (just as many people think, or used to think, that French is particularly suited to theoretical argument). What was happening in Anglo-Saxon England was a process of language development, under the influence of another language. Latin may have continued as a High language, but English ceased to be an oral vernacular, as it came to be cultivated in the other's shadow. As English was made to serve some of the functions of the developing monarchies, and as it came to be written down, we can describe its profile as that of a partially developed, literate language. As yet, however, it was unstandardised. What scanty records remain show that distinctive regional varieties of English were emerging in the different kingdoms. And in time these varieties were to diverge to a point where we should need to describe them as different languages if the criterion of mutual intelligibility were to be the only one applied. It is more usual, however, to refer to these varieties as dialects. If this term is to be used, it should be remembered that each dialect of English at this time was, from a socio-linguistic point of view, a partially developed *language*.

In that they established centres of influence in different parts of England, the Anglo-Saxon kingdoms are of great significance in the history of English. Recent research into English dialects shows that these ancient divisions continue to underpin the regional varieties of English, nine centuries or more after the demise of the monarchies themselves. Unfortunately, we do not know very much about the Anglo-Saxon dialects, since very few texts have survived from the period, and we do not know anything about the relationship of written Anglo-Saxon to the spoken usage of the ordinary families as they toiled in the fields. A great deal of writing has been lost over the last thousand years. But the indifference, or vandalism, of subsequent centuries is not the only reason for the dearth of records. More Germanic settlers, this time from Scandinavia, very nearly overturned the few institutions of centralised monarchy that existed in the different kingdoms. Hostile to the developing Christian culture of monasteries and books, it was the Vikings who, ironically enough, succeeded in pushing the Anglo-Saxons into taking the first steps towards centralisation under *one* monarch.

The Vikings

The pattern of Germanic expansion which we have described above was continued into the eighth and following centuries by the Scandinavian tribes of the north. For nearly two centuries and a half, Anglo-Saxons and Vikings came into contact of one kind or another. A period of piracy was followed by military campaigns. One after another the Anglo-Saxon kingdoms were overturned, until Wessex was the only source of English resistance. Extensive settlement in much of northern and eastern England was followed by a further round of armed incursions, culminating in the accession to the English throne of the kings of Denmark themselves.

It is the period of settlement that chiefly concerns us here. As great traders, the Scandinavians were interested in securing footholds in the urban centres of Europe; and as farmers, they wanted new land, like the Anglo-Saxons before them. While Norwegians colonised Ireland, the Scottish Islands, the Isle of Man, and parts of England's north-west, Danes settled thickly in the north and east. The place-name evidence for Yorkshire, Lincolnshire, and Leicestershire suggests that Danes here outnumbered the earlier settlers: the Danish form *Ingleby*, 'settlement of the English', in north Yorkshire, indicates that Anglo-Saxons were scattered enough to have a settlement named after them. Wherever they settled, the Scandinavians brought with them their leaders, laws, and their own language.

Very little is known about the relations between the English and the newcomers. While at times these must have been bitter, it appears from recent research into place-names and settlement sites that on many occasions the Scandinavians did not displace the Anglo-Saxons from their own settlements, but grouped themselves near them, often in less fertile places. And although a third of England was occupied by speakers of Danish and Norse, the newcomers did not, and could not, impose an alien set of customs and institutions; nor could they impose their language. The independence of the area of Danish settlement, known as Danelaw, was undermined by the baptising of the Danish leaders, who knew that Christianity was a useful form of control over their subjects. And it was further undermined by the resurgent dynasty of Wessex. Alfred checked the Danes militarily and defined the limits of the Danelaw, while his progeny, Edward and Athelstan, carried the authority of Wessex throughout England during the tenth century. Finally, the period of Danish kingship under Svein and Cnut in the early eleventh century was short-lived. Danish could not, therefore, become the official language of England − unlike Norn, which persisted in Orkney and Shetland for nearly a thousand years, during a period of unbroken Norwegian hegemony.

The language that the Scandinavians spoke was an undeveloped, oral vernacular. Similar in sociolinguistic profile to the language of the Anglo-Saxons four centuries earlier, it was also similar in its linguistic structure. It is not improbable that the Anglo-Saxon small-holders were able to follow the speech of their Scandinavian neighbours. The records suggest that differences between the languages might have been akin to those characterising, say, the dialect of Devon compared to that of Aberdeenshire today. There would have been some predictable variations: the word for 'bone' in Anglo-Saxon might have sounded like *ban*, but with a longer vowel sound; in Scandinavian, like *bane*. But there may have been as many differences among the dialects of English as there were between English and Scandinavian (as in the relationship between British English and American English today). At any rate, similarity in language, as in custom and social organisation, facilitated the absorption of the newcomers in many parts of England.

Contact between the languages occurred at the oral level, in those areas where ordinary English people encountered, in face-to-face interaction, their Danish counterparts. In situations such as this, where the communication of basic information is at a premium, we are likely to find a process similar to pidginisation. Language is reduced to bare essentials, as it is when we send a telegram; and one of the clearest means of achieving this is to delete, or simplify, some of the patterns in our grammar. It is probable that grammatical re-structuring, a process described more fully in chapter four, took place wherever contacts were made, and the new forms gradually spread, at the spoken level, beyond the area of Scandinavian influence. As in the case of Anglo-Celtic contact, such innovations will have taken place in conditions where exact evidence is almost entirely lacking.

More obvious evidence of linguistic contact is the massive borrowing into English of loan-words. Not only have numerous words like *angry*, *awkward*, *get*, and *take* been borrowed into the core of our everyday usage, but indispensable pronoun forms such as *they* and *she* derive either directly or indirectly from Scandinavian. These words are now part of the standard variety; but in much of northern England, local dialect is still heavily 'Scandinavianised'. Forms such as *kirk* (church), *steg* (gander), *laik* (play), as well as pronunciations and grammatical forms (see chapters four and five) are still part of traditional usage, or were until very recently.

We do not know how long an 'unmixed' Scandinavian language survived in England. But the presence in Cumbria of Norse runic inscriptions from the eleventh century confirms the impression given by recent dialect research, that it was the area associated with part of the ancient kingdom of Northumbria that best preserved the Scandinavian culture. With York an important centre of Viking trade, Northumbria stood aloof from the rest of England. The strongly regional character of Scandinavian influence means that if we are to speak of Anglo/Scandinavian bilingualism, we should describe it as geographical in nature. The Anglo-Saxons could not dominate the new-comers as they dominated the Celts. Perhaps the linguistic relations between the two languages can best be described as a continuum, ranging from a relatively unmixed Scandinavian at one end of the scale to a relatively uninfluenced English speech at the other. In between, the languages co-existed, and then merged, with English forms and structures competing at first with the Scandinavian ones, then gradually spreading northwards.

At the other end of the country from Northumbria, the concept of

Figure 1.1   Linguistic map of the British Isles c. AD 1000

G–CELTIC — Goidelic branch of Celtic
B–CELTIC — Britannic branch of Celtic

Shaded portions indicate areas of
Viking settlement

'Englishness' was kept alive by the kings of Wessex. Alfred doggedly maintained the tradition of writing in Anglo-Saxon, particularly in prose; and his desire to translate works from Latin into English makes him one of the first vernacularisers in education (see chapters six and seven). Winchester became the important centre for English writing, and the West Saxon dialect became a kind of literary standard. Works written in different dialects at earlier times were copied into it, giving us a somewhat indirect insight into the output of the other Anglo-Saxon kingdoms. As we shall see in the next chapter, the influence of the Winchester scriptoria long outlived the period of West Saxon power.

Later kings of Wessex introduced political changes that also had far-reaching linguistic consequences. Athelstan instituted the system of shires, new political boundaries that by establishing new centres of power could influence the usage of surrounding areas. But the West Saxon dynasty itself was fragile. After further Scandinavian invasions and depredations had brought a Danish king, Cnut, to the English throne, another foreign dynasty was to be imposed on England; Scandinavian in origin, but speaking another language.

The Normans

The Viking adventurers who settled in Normandy in northern France during the early tenth century were also baptised and ceded territory like their counterparts in England. Again, they did not impose their oral vernacular, but were gradually assimilated to the customs and language of the more centralised lands they colonised. In France, however, they had to learn a language that was structurally very different from their own. That they did this, within about four or five generations, is evidenced by the fact that it was a variety of French that they imposed on England when, as Normans, they added this territory to their possessions by the military Conquest of 1066. For the next three centuries or so, French was to be a living force in England.

The Norman invaders were few in number, but well-organised. Their intentions were not those of their colonising ancestors, nor of the Anglo-Saxons before them. The Normans were interested in territorial annexation, and they overcame the English by means of efficient military campaigns. The superstructure of political and economic power — based on the ownership of land — was then almost exclusively wrested from English hands and given to Norman friends of William the Conqueror. The positions of power, in respect to both king and church, were thus in the hands of French speakers, who spent the next 150 years 'commuting' between their possessions on both sides of the Channel. It was only when this ruling class lost its possessions in Normandy at the beginning of the thirteenth century that it could begin to think of itself as English. By that time, French had become firmly established in England as the High language of law, government, administration, and also, to some extent, courtly literature and religion. It was not until the fourteenth century that English was re-developed within these domains.

We need to distinguish, therefore, two phases of contact with French. The first involves the Scandinavianised French of the Norman elite. This language would not have been more developed or more prestigious than that of the English; neither was Norman culture more international or more literate in character: probably the only technical advantage the Normans enjoyed over the English was their superior ability to build castles and cathedrals in stone. Norman-French was imposed by a ruling caste; but since Latin continued in its spoken form in the church, and as the written language of scholarship, the linguistic situation after 1066 may be described as *triglossic*.

There has been some controversy about the extent to which this state of societal bilingualism was realised at the individual level. Some have argued that French was very widely learned throughout English society; others, that its use was very limited. One thing that we can be sure about is that French did not displace English. Unlike Latin in the age of Empire, Norman-French did not offer linguistic unity or a prestigious, literate language to linguistically diverse, uncentralised tribespeople. Neither is it apparent that the Normans took much trouble to encourage English people to learn their language, still less to offer them material advantages. Norman-French was exclusive, the property of the major, and often absent, landowner.

While no wholesale language shift took place, it is probable that individual bilingualism came to exist among certain social groups. The motivation for learning a second language, however, may have been different in each case. Some groups would need to be bilingual, whereas for others opportunities for contact with the other language would have been minimal. Certain domains of usage would make different demands on people's linguistic repertoire. Moreover, we should not assume that language-learning was always in one direction.

About the social extremes there is some agreement. We know that the *first* language of the English monarchs was French until the end of the fourteenth century – long after the Norman dynasty. It is also probable that the upper aristocracy were monolingual French-speakers for a considerable time after the Conquest. At the other end of the social scale, there is no reason to believe that the ordinary people who worked the land spoke any language other than their local variety of English. In a society overwhelmingly agrarian, this class would constitute the vast majority of the population. During the period of French dominance, then, the regional variation of the Anglo-Saxon era was intensified.

Not all the Normans were aristocrats, however. They brought with them people who could administer their feudal estates; and these would have needed to be bilingual in their role as mediators between overlord and land-labourers. There were also adventurers who became lesser landowners: these were thinly spread in the countryside, and it is likely they would have adapted to local ways and language, just as many of those who went on to settle in Ireland eventually learned Gaelic (see chapter six). Norman craftsmen, merchants, and artisans settled in English towns in greater numbers, but they were never more than a small minority of the urban population. It is questionable whether they ever dominated trade, or even particular crafts, and it is not certain whether French was ever institutionalised as the language of commerce. The garrisons of Norman soldiers may have retained their language, as a marker of the male peer-group (so that bread-and-butter transactions with local people took place in a kind of Anglo-French pidgin), but in general it may well have been the Normans in the towns who learned a second language, rather than the English. If at this time bilingualism was at all common, it was perhaps quite unremarkable, as it is in so many parts of the world today. We do know that many Normans married English women, so it is likely that children in the towns grew up as bilinguals.

French was also less strongly institutionalised in the domain of religion. Writings in English emanated from the monasteries throughout the period of French dominance: the Anglo-Saxon Chronicle was continued for nearly a century after the Conquest, and in following centuries didactic religious texts circulated from mainly west midland sources. Sermons continued to be delivered in English, although there is some evidence for French. It has been argued that most of the lesser clergy were monoglot speakers of English, and that even in the monasteries newly founded by the Normans, bilingualism, rather than French, was expected. As an institution of learning, then, the church tended to promote fluency in more than one language, as it had done in Anglo-Saxon times.

At the top of the social pyramid, however, Norman-French was secure, as the language of official transactions and decrees, and of diversions for the powerful: a great deal of Norman-French literature was produced in England. About one hundred years after the Conquest, the first loan-words into English show how the language was associated with the instruments and offices of power: *prison* and *castle*, *cardinal* and *prior*. But the full weight of loan-words comes later, during the second phase of contact with French, this time with another variety of the language.

Cultural contact with the French of Paris

In 1204, the dukedom of Normandy was won by the king of France. While the kings of England still retained possessions in more southerly parts of France, the descendants of the Norman conquerors lost the sense of their ancestry. The ruling class of England became increasingly Anglicised, but it maintained its contacts with the French of the kings of France, a monarchy which by the end of the thirteenth century had become the strongest and most centralised in Europe.

From a sociolinguistic point of view, this second phase of contact with French is probably more interesting than the first. We see language come to be regarded as a social symbol, as it is identified with social groups of declared interests. The old Norman-French is seen as provincial and unfashionable, while the language of the French court is seen as the emblem of the most sophisticated and prestigious culture in the contemporary world. To use this French, then, is to impress. In the eyes of many, English had perhaps the aura of a peasant language, much like that of Gaelic in nineteenth-century Ireland. But among others, it became a marker of ethnicity, of national identity.

Individual bilingualism would have been extensive during this phase. While the court retained its devotion to French language and culture, the ruling class gradually acquired English. By the fourteenth century, we begin to see the linguistic consequence of this process. English is saturated with French loan-words, some of which have become such common currency that we tend to forget their ancestry — words like *pass*, *join*, *butcher*, *large*. Some, like *chase* and *guarantee*, had even been borrowed earlier, in the forms *catch* and *warranty*, from Norman-French. The taste of the Francophile court was reflected in much of the English poetry of this phase, which borrows French themes, techniques, and language; and in so far as the English poet was brought up in this atmosphere, we can best describe this period of contact as one of cultural bilingualism. It is also the case that many English people learned French. The prestige of French as a marker of high social status meant that some people learned it for its snob value. Since the Conquest, French had been the medium of education, and schools were a means of acquiring the language. A fourteenth-century writer, Higden, records that even people from the country busied themselves 'to speke Freynsh', so they could sound like 'gentil men'. If there was a demand for the language, people who could teach it had a vested interest in its continuance. Thus, we see in the same century edicts enforcing French in the domains of education and religion. That a similar entrenchment existed in the domain of law can be seen by the fact that 'Law French' was still in use, for some purposes, in the seventeenth century. For a lawyer, the possession of a special language is a powerful weapon, as can be seen in many multilingual societies today. The 'professionalisation' of law in the course of the twelfth and thirteenth centuries meant that its practitioners could exploit the advantages of knowing a special language: they could become parasitic on the people they were meant to serve.

If for some the French language meant social advancement, for others it aroused antagonisms. Cultural contacts with France were an increasing source of tension in English life. The monarchy of France came to be seen as a foreign power, whose interests often clashed with those of the people of England. Moreover, while some kings of England waged long, costly, and fruitless wars against France, others lavished the wealth of England on French favourites. Either was likely to upset baron, lesser landowner, and merchant alike. Frenchmen, and the French language, were increasingly disparaged. From its position as a tolerated language under the Normans, English became a *promoted* language, a mark of Englishness.

The promotion of English was associated with gradual changes that had been taking place in English society. The old feudal structure so successfully sustained by the Norman kings, the system of obligations between king and aristocracy, was giving way to an economy based, not on land, but on money. We see the emergence of new bases of power, new feelings of group loyalty. Alliances were made between lesser landowners, who were making money out of raising sheep for wool, and the rising merchant class in the towns, a pact institutionalised in the thirteenth century by the assembly that came to be called Parliament. The founding of universities stimulated mobility, both geographical and social, among certain sections of the population; and by the fourteenth century mobility had even spread to the land-labourers, who could bargain for wages now that labour was scarce. By that time, the balance of forces was beginning to favour an increasingly articulate, English-speaking merchant class. It was this class, with London as its base, that spoke what was to become standard English.

Chapter two
Standardisation and writing

In the last chapter we outlined the conditions for the emergence of a standard variety. During the last 600 years that variety of English has been established as the superordinate one. Today, at least within Britain, the process is probably as complete as it will ever be. In this chapter we shall trace this long and complex process, by first examining one of its key components, the writing system. We shall need to know about the nature of English spelling, and the sort of writing system inherited by the first printers, who played such a vital role in the determination and dissemination of the standard. We shall then see how standardisation proceeded in four inter-linked and often overlapping stages. First, we see the *selection* of the east midland dialect as the dominant variety; then we discuss the conditions of its *acceptance* by the powerful and educated classes, and the implications this has for speakers of other dialects. Third, we chart the *elaboration* of the functions of the standard, as it developed in the domains previously associated with French and Latin. Fourth, we describe the stage of *codification*, the attempts to 'fix' the standard variety in dictionaries and grammars, a process most clearly associated with the eighteenth century. Finally, we shall see how codification can be regarded as the expression of class attitudes to language.

The stages we have outlined above are applicable to the growth of standard varieties everywhere. Throughout the world, moreover, the process can be characterised by an important feature: it involves somewhere along the line an element of engineering, a conscious attempt to cultivate a variety that can be used for all purposes. A standard variety is therefore a fully developed one, to use the terminology of the last chapter. Coupled with this trend is the desire to have it recorded and regularised, to eliminate variations and, if possible, change. While the latter may be unattainable, the aims of standardisation remain inviolate. They have been described as maximal variation in function, and minimal variation in form.

The consequences of the process are far-reaching. We have already seen in chapter one how a standardised language gives its speakers a sense of historicity. Indeed, identification with the prestigious aura of the standard may be so strong that for many people the standard variety is the language itself. And an unfortunate corollary of this is that many have been convinced that they themselves do not speak their own language, or at least do not speak it 'properly', because they do not speak the standard. Yet while we defer to the notion of the standard, there is evidence that many have only an imperfect knowledge of its forms and structures. As we shall see, one of the effects of the codification process is that we have a much better knowledge of what to avoid saying than what we are taught it is correct to say. Despite exposure to print, and spoken manifestations of the standard in the mass media, knowledge of it is often more passive than active. This is a fact too often overlooked by educationalists, and indeed linguists. The process of standardisation cannot be seen as merely a matter of communal choice, an innocent attempt on the part of society as a whole to choose a variety that can be used for official purposes and, in addition, as a lingua franca among speakers of divergent dialects. It involves from the first the cultivation, by an elite, of a variety that can be regarded as exclusive. The embryonic standard is not seen as the most useful, or the most widely-used variety, but as the best. Moreover, all sorts of arbitrary and at times spurious arguments are found to justify its forms and structures. In short, the process means the creation of a class dialect, that is imposed on an often resentful, and sometimes bewildered, populace.

It is not surprising, therefore, that there should be some widespread misunderstandings about standard English. One of these is that it is restricted only to formal kinds of utterance. This idea has gained acceptance, presumably, from its association in people's minds with contexts and situations where power is exercised — the classroom, the courtroom, the institutions of government. But like any linguistic variety, the standard has its dimensions of variation, including that of informality-formality, since for many people it must function as the medium of everyday conversation. Unlike other varieties, though, it is peculiarly subject to debate and analysis — about what usage is permissible and what is held to be correct. As we shall see, this preoccupation with fixity has often acted as a kind of brake on the natural tendency towards variation and change.

The standard is less fixed and monolithic than many suppose, partly because today it has a widely used spoken form (used, moreover, by many people without their realising it!). Since speech, by its very nature, is less amenable to being fixed than writing, the concept of standard English makes most sense when we are referring to the written word. When we are taught to write, it is standard English that we are taught. Moreover, this is largely true wherever English is learned in school; and the written standard is much the same in every part of the world where English is known and used.

Writing, then, is an indispensable component of standardisation. Indeed, it is difficult to conceive of a standard variety without a written form. At the same time, the existence of a writing system does not presuppose the existence of a standard. As we saw in the last chapter, West Saxon was used as a written standard when no spoken one existed. But once a standard variety has been selected, writing is a powerful agent for its dissemination especially as literacy spreads and printing makes written materials more readily available. As the written forms acquire prestige, and are considered to be 'correct', they increasingly exert a pressure on speech. The written standard acts as a norm, a yardstick, and a guide.

The nature of the writing system

The spellings we use today were largely fixed in the eighteenth century. Such was the prestige of Johnson's *Dictionary* of 1755 that it was Dr Johnson's decisions about the spelling of words that have influenced modern practice. Since that time, the idea that words should have only one spelling has become so deeply rooted that it takes considerable effort to accept the fact that until quite recently in the history of English, invariant spelling was not even regarded as a desideratum.

A degree of fixity was conferred before the eighteenth century, however, by the introduction of printing in the 1470s. It is too expensive for compositors to keep changing spellings, either through personal whim or social custom, so that since the fifteenth century certain spellings owe their continued existence to the convenience of the printers. But in personal correspondence, and hand-written documents of many kinds, spelling continued to vary enormously long after the time of Caxton. While it is essential to bear in mind this distinction between printed and hand-written traditions – the relevance of which we shall see again below – we should note the crucial fact that the use of print is nearly as old as the standard variety. Very loosely, then, the period of printing corresponds with the period of standardisation.

Although spelling may be fixed, pronunciation continues to vary and change, so that the relationship between sounds and spelling is likely to be somewhat indirect, to say the least. If we remember that the spellings of many words represent their pronunciation, in a particular region, of centuries ago, it is not surprising that we find what seem to be disparities between how we pronounce and what we write. But there are a number of misunderstandings about the nature of this relationship. It is not uncommon to find many people, including some historians of English, describe our spelling as arbitrary, illogical, and even chaotic. Yet it can only be described thus if we perversely expect it to do what it no longer can. In order to understand this we must look more closely at the nature of writing systems in general.

Different languages have developed writing systems which represent different levels of linguistic structure. In simplified terms, some languages, such as Chinese, symbolise whole words, or syllabic components, by using a very large set of characters. This kind of *logographic* system represents language at its most expansible level, since in principle there is no limit to the number of new words or concepts a language can acquire. Other languages, such as those of Europe, make use of an alphabet, a series of letters which encode the most restricted and limited level of linguistic structure, that of sounds. In so far as users of the first kind of system must master an enormous number of symbols when learning to read, they may be considered to be at a disadvantage in comparison with those who have access to alphabetic writing.

The potential for mass literacy, therefore, is greater when the second kind of system is available, and the reason for this is that alphabets encode the sounds of language in a very specific way. While in the course of speech we make a vast number of different sounds, all of those sounds are related, and relateable, to a finite number of sound-units, called *phonemes*. It is ultimately to these units that the letters of the alphabet relate. For no alphabet can represent the wealth of phonetic variation that exists in any variety of speech. For instance, we pronounce the initial sound of *pit* in a slightly different way from the 'same' sound in *spit*: the *p* is aspirated in the first example only. But while that distinction might be important in some languages, such as Urdu, it is not so in any variety of English, so there is no reason why it should be signalled in spelling. At best, then, a spelling system might be *phonemic*, in that there is one spelling for each phoneme – about 44 in most varieties of our language. But as any modern reader knows, the writing system we have inherited is decidedly not of this kind. There are at least seven ways of representing what is for most people the same vowel sound, for instance, in *tree, these, leaf, field, seize, key,* and *machine.* The reasons for this lack of fit are very complex. But before we try to discuss them, it is essential to point out that there are insuperable problems involved in establishing a standard, consistent spelling system. Quite simply, this is because sounds vary enormously, as we have already said. We pronounce differently according to whether we are speaking formally or casually (as we shall see in chapter five). And sometimes the same word has different phonemes associated with the amount of stress placed upon it. *Must* and *from*, for instance, are differentiated when stressed, but in unstressed positions they have the same 'neutral' vowel /ə/. Finally there is the problem associated with regional pronunciation, or accent. Our sounds relate us to different localities and social backgrounds, and to some extent accents have different sound-systems, with varying numbers of phonemes. A phonemic spelling system can only hope to represent one accent, but the problem is, whose? The selection of one discriminates, in principle, against speakers with other accents.

By encoding the sounds of speech in an inconsistent and often arbitrary way, our spelling system at least manages to favour nobody. Contrary to what some people think, it is not a representation of the accent spoken by a small minority of the wealthy and privileged. We are all equally disadvantaged by it, and that is one of its strengths. Moreover, there is often more pattern in it than is at first apparent, particularly if we abandon the expectation that at all points spellings must represent different sounds. The plural ending in *cats, dogs,* and *horses* is pronounced in three different ways, but little would be gained by replacing a useful grammatical marker with an unnecessary amount of phonemic information. Secondly, our spelling signals lexical relationships: connections among related words, such as *nation* (the first syllable of which has the vowel of *name*) and *national* — with the sound of *nag.* Finally, our spelling often usefully separates homophones, different words which, in some accents at least, sound alike, like *meat* and *meet.* This example shows us the value of knowing about other kinds of writing systems than our own, for here we see something of the logographic principle: we have learned to read *meat* and *meet* not as sequences of sound, but   as individual words with different *meanings.*

The scribal tradition

The devising of a phonemic writing system has posed problems since the earliest times. The first scribes in Anglo-Saxon England did not invent their own letters, which could unambiguously represent the sounds they needed to symbolise. As we have seen, they were taught to write by monks from Ireland, who had themselves adapted the alphabet of Latin. The Romans, in their turn, had borrowed their letters from the Greeks, to whom the principle of alphabetic writing had spread from the Middle East. Largely the same stock of letters, therefore, came to be used to represent the myriad sounds of many languages. The Anglo-Saxons had to try and match up the symbols to the sounds of English, in so far as the Latin sound-values of those symbols were reminiscent of English sounds. Where there was no symbol available for particular sounds, as in the *th* sound, the scribes had to use their ingenuity. Sometimes they adapted signs from the runic alphabet: the sound just mentioned was represented by þ. In sum, alphabetic writing has always been characterised by a process of adaptation.

The spelling traditions of the Anglo-Saxon scribes were further complicated by the superposition of French spelling habits after the Norman Conquest. Words of French origin were spelt in the French way, so that the /s/ in *grace* is written *ce*, while the Anglo-Saxon *grass* retains the native *s* graph; but French spellings were also used to 're-form' the representation of Anglo-Saxon words. *Cwic* has adopted the French *qu* spelling, and become *quick*. Thus we have at least two different traditions in our spelling – a Germanic one, and a Romance one – and there was, as can be appreciated, an arbitrariness as to which tradition was resorted to in different cases.

Other features of scribal practice led to further heterogeneity in the writing system. Before the printing press, spelling habits were characterised by spectacular diversity. When we look up a word in the *Oxford English Dictionary*, we are immediately confronted by a bewildering range of spellings. There are two main reasons for this. First, scribes wrote in their own dialects, so there were different spelling systems in different parts of the country. Second, scribes were more often guided by their own speech-habits than by written precedent, which meant that changes in pronunciation were often mirrored in spelling. 'Bone' in Anglo-Saxon was spelt *ban*, but by the fourteenth century it was *boon*. It is impossible to know the extent of this sensitivity to sound-change, but we can gauge some of the sociolinguistic implications of these practices. In particular, scribes would not have developed a responsiveness to the individual word. We know, for instance, that when they copied manuscripts written in dialects other than their own, they showed little concern for the original spellings, but changed them to accord with their own traditions and preferences. Moreover, if they failed to understand a word in the passage they were copying, they would change it to one they did know. We shall explore this matter further in the next chapter.

We may summarise the scribal writing system by saying that in general, spellings were less consistent, more individual, more subject to variation in space and time, then they were to become in the subsequent period of print and standardisation. But before we go on to discuss the latter, we need to mention two developments in the scribal era which tended towards fixity rather than diversity. The first of these was the establishing of a written standard based on the West Saxon dialect of the tenth and eleventh centuries. Spellings associated with the Winchester 'house style' persisted well into the early days of printing, as we shall see. The second concerns the growth, by the end of the fourteenth century, of a class of scribes who were professional. Up to that time, the copying of texts had been undertaken in ecclesiastical institutions; but from then on a young man could be trained in the writing conventions of a particular secular scriptorium, and get paid for it. And by then, of course, it was the written dialect of the east midlands that could be disseminated from these institutions.

Selection of the standard variety

The origins of the standard variety of English lie with the merchant class based in London. The dialect they spoke was the east midland one — associated at first with Norfolk, later with Northamptonshire, Leicestershire, Bedfordshire — and already by the fourteenth century this was a class dialect within London. The lower class spoke another dialect, a south-eastern one, the antecedent of Cockney. The dialects were similar in many respects but there were some regular differences; for instance, the merchant would say *mill*, with the short *i* of *pin*, but the tradesman said *mell*, with the *e* of *pen*. Vestiges of this pattern have been found in Cockney speech today. It is important to stress this linguistic stratification in London, since the subsequent history of the standard variety has much to do with its relationship to the speech of the Londoner in the street.

By the end of the fourteenth century, East Midland was an embry-onic written standard. Within the dialect, however, there were variations, often associated with the birthplaces of bourgeois immigrants into London; so at first we see in use a number of different written standards. After about 1430, however, one of these variants became increasingly dominant, its use in government and official documents aided by the newly-established secular scriptoria mentioned above. By the end of that century, the fixing of the selected variety was greatly strengthened, and accelerated, by the printing press.

We cannot yet assume the existence of a standard that is spoken. It is one thing for a minority of literate people to adopt a different written form; quite another for them to change their speech-habits overnight. As we shall see, it took some time for the east midland speech of the London merchants to acquire prestige. But there is another reason why East Midland, or variants of it, may have been quite widely adopted during the later Middle Ages. Students from all over England mixed in the two universities of Oxford and Cambridge, both only about sixty miles from London. In the triangle formed by these three centres, a great deal of east midland speech would have been heard, and possibly used as a kind of lingua franca among a mobile social group. If such a popular standard existed, it would have helped to spread East Midland, not because of its prestige value, or because it was imposed by the most powerful group, but because of its usefulness in communicating with people who spoke another dialect. One of these uses, among lower-class people, was as a medium for popular culture: in particular, the tradition of folk-song, which flourished in the age of standardisation. From the broadsheets of the sixteenth century to the song-collections of contemporary singers, the linguistic medium for folk-song is one that does not, on the whole, reflect regional differences. We do not know whether this is to be attributed to the people themselves, or to the commercial presses: but it seems clear that while ordinary people spoke in their local dialect, they did not sing in it.

So far, we have identified both regional and socio-economic factors in the selection of the standard variety. There is a political dimension as well. A standard tends to emerge when ideas about nationhood and political autonomy are gaining currency: and we find that in other European kingdoms where a degree of centralisation had occurred early, standard varieties were emerging at this time. But they were not always associated with the same power base in society. In both France and Spain, it was the usage of Court and monasteries in the areas of

political power — the regions of Paris and Castile respectively — that
determined the selection of the standard. In countries where political
autonomy was achieved relatively recently, standardisation took a different course. Thus, while Tuscan developed as a literary standard
during the later Middle Ages in Italy, it did not have a political dimension until the unification of the country in the 1860s. By that time, the
municipal standards of Italian in the old, independent city-states had
become regional standards; and not only do these persist today, but
they are tolerated to an extent unknown in France and England. Nor-
way today has two competing standards: one a Danish-influenced
legacy of Danish rule, the other a standard consciously engineered after
independence from Denmark in 1814, and based on the Norwegian dialects of the west. These examples show the inextricability of language
standardisation and social, political, and economic processes; and we
shall be seeing this again in Part 3.

Acceptance of the standard

By about the middle of the fifteenth century, the east midland dialect
had been accepted as a written standard by those who wrote official
documents. But its acceptance was tacit rather than explicit, a matter
of convention rather than *diktat*. For when Caxton — who had spent
much of his life on the continent — came to set up his press, he did not
realise that the variety he was printing was a written standard. Instead,
he complained about the difficulty of choosing a dialect that all could
understand, and also — like a good many people since — about how
English had changed since he was young.

By the sixteenth century, the standard variety was well-established
in the domain of literature. If we contrast the literary output of the
Elizabethans with the great flowering of literature in the fourteenth
century, we find a striking difference in language. For the dialect of
Chaucer was not the dialect of Langland, who wrote *Piers Plowman*;
and different again was the dialect of the unknown poet who wrote *Sir
Gawain and the Green Knight*. The student of fourteenth-century English literature must come to terms with a range of regional vocabularies,
grammars, and spelling-systems that seem bewildering in their diversity.
Thus, while Chaucer wrote in the east midland dialect as it was spoken
in London, he was not yet writing in a *national* literary standard, since
his contemporaries had their own, local standards. By Shakespeare's

time this regional variation in the language of printed literature had all but disappeared.

The establishment of a national literary standard had crucial repercussions, not only for literature, but for fixing the sense of a linguistic norm. In medieval England, there could be no sense of a norm for English usage, for reasons already explained above. Once a norm has been established, at least in the written language, it becomes possible to break it for stylistic purposes – in particular, for representing the speech of people from regions far away or belonging to social groups whose language is supposed to have certain clearly identifiable characteristics. In the later Middle Ages, regional differences in speech were as familiar to some people as they were to Caxton in the fifteenth century – and, in the writing of the Cornishman Trevisa, subject for some caustic descriptions – but it was hardly possible for a medieval writer to try to represent dialects other than his own, if the scribes copying the manuscript in other parts of the country were going to change it into their own dialect. A famous example of this in fourteenth-century literature is Chaucer's depiction of northern speech in *The Reeve's Tale*. When the manuscript was copied in the north midlands, the language was changed to such an extent that the linguistic differences between the speech of the north country students and the rest of the poem were ironed out. Chaucer's norm was not the norm elsewhere, so his copyists could not appreciate his attempt at deviation.

In the course of the sixteenth century, the growing sense of a literary norm can be seen by the numerous attempts to represent the speech of foreigners, the linguistic characteristics of Welsh, Scottish, and Irish people, and the speakers of other dialects of English. It is now that we begin to see the social stereotyping of such speakers. Increasingly, they play the role of buffoon or boor. Non-standard speech is equated with simplicity or roughness; and in order to depict those qualities in literature, some form of *marking* for non-standard features is adopted. A tradition is established which has lasted until the present day, and which has been translated into cinema and television soap-opera: deviation from the norm implies social comment in the minds of author and audience alike.

Acceptance of the standard, therefore, occasions a rejection of kinds of English that are felt to be outside the norm. While in the fourteenth century Chaucer could depict the speech of people whose dialect was not his own, and Trevisa could rail at the 'scharp, slyttyng and unschape' speech of the York area – the words are so expressive of the writer's attitude that they barely need a modern translation — differences in dialect were only differences, even if regrettable: dialects spoken in areas outside London were not automatically the emblems of stupid, quaint, or base-born people. But in the earliest years of the sixteenth century, one dialect had already been singled out by playwrights and others as the butt for a cheap laugh. That dialect was Kentish. A county that had long been densely populated, and often visited, Kent was close enough to London for its dialect to be well-known. At this time, Kentish shared features with dialects to the west — those which had developed from the old dialect of Wessex — and these features were sufficiently different from the dominant east midland forms to be easily exploited as a marker of comedy, boorishness, or rusticity. The latter quality is exemplified in *King Lear*. The high-born Edgar, forced to disguise himself throughout the play as various lowly-born characters, switches to the dialect when defending his blind father from their enemy, Oswald. Responding to Oswald's challenge of 'base peasant', Edgar is shown, in a striking piece of textual deviation, to pronounce *sir* and *so* as *zir* and *zo*, *folk* and *fortnight* as *volk* and *vortnight* (along with other dialectalisms). What is interesting here is that by Shakespeare's time the dialect seems to have been conventionalised, in that the selection of dialect features is rather a random one. This stage Kentish, moreover, was known and appreciated by the playwright's London audience, who must have seen the point of the stereotype.

Such literary practices reflect the growing awareness of a standard variety in the course of the sixteenth century. By then, attempts were being made to *define* the standard: it had reached the stage of explicit acceptance. But we must not forget that it was only a small minority of educated, courtly people who were in the business of defining it. We do not really know how far their comments are descriptions of current usage, or merely desiderata; how far they were reflecting opinion, or leading it. On balance, the latter seems more likely. As we shall see, the 'market' for scholarly ideas about usage does not really open up until the latter half of the eighteenth century.

For the first time, it was the issue of a spoken standard that was raised. And while the comments of the sixteenth century scholars are sometimes difficult to interpret — we often do not know, for instance, whether they are talking about sounds, grammar, vocabulary, or even style — it is clear that many of these writers were concerned about matters of pronunciation as much as anything else. In the course of the century a number of references are made to a 'natural' and 'true' pronunciation. As we shall see, early phoneticians were already noticing discrepancies between sound and spellings, which were prompting them to comment; but the interest in pronunciation may reflect uncertainties about usage, itself suggestive of extensive variation.

In the absence of other guides or models, a spoken standard has to be anchored to a particular social group. It was a phonetician, Hart, who did this most clearly. In three works (1551, 1569, 1570) he mentions the 'learned' and 'literate' elements, and this theme is renewed during the following century by Price (1665) and Coles (1674). What these people were ultimately doing was describing their own usage – a tendency not uncommon among linguists of the twentieth century. Other observers are more specific about locale. The standard is set in London, particularly at Court; and a famous observer, Puttenham, writing in 1589, may be referring to the London-Oxford-Cambridge triangle mentioned earlier when he states that the best speech can also be heard within a radius of sixty miles round London.

It is highly significant that early attempts to define a spoken standard involve an element of evaluation. From the first, the issue of standardisation is bound up with notions about what constitutes the 'best', or 'truest', or 'most courtly' speech. The educated speech of the Court in London was now prestigious, and people like Hart and Puttenham were concerned with the speech-habits of aristocratic and wealthy people living in other regions. For now that urban speech in London was also *urbane*, speech in the countryside was 'barbarous', as Edmund Coote described it in 1597. It was incumbent on the provincial gentry to adapt to the standards cultivated in the capital.

A crucial question to be asked about this stage of the standardisation process is, acceptance by whom? Acceptance by government functionaries and small groups of literati is not the same as acceptance by the aristocracy of the shires; still less is it acceptance by the vast majority of ordinary people who worked in the fields. But by the end of the sixteenth century, we have an accepted written standard, and some prestigious speech forms, that were being promoted consciously and unconsciously by a tiny elite. We do not know, however, the extent to which we can speak of a standard of pronunciation at this time, or how widespread that pronunciation was among the aristocracy in general. What we can be sure of is that the prestige of one dialect triggers the disparagement of the others. Kentish is only the first to be stigmatised. In the course of the following centuries, the dialects of other parts of England are labelled variously as 'offensive', 'disgusting', 'barbarous', and 'cant',

And by the beginning of the twentieth century, the mud-slinging has come back to its source. Disparagement is directed this time towards an urban dialect, that of London itself; but it is the working class dialect, Cockney, that is singled out in a School Board report as speech unworthy of citizens living in the capital city of an Empire. By then, of course, standard English is a subject taught in schools: and 'acceptance' is backed up with the teacher's rod.

Elaboration of function

The dialects lost status for another reason. As we have seen, they lost their writing systems as the standard was developed; and so they were no longer used for either literary or devotional writing. In short, their range of functions was restricted as those of the standard were elaborated. They became *patois*, unwritten vehicles for informal, everyday conversation among equals. The process of standardisation may be said, therefore, to have involved an accompanying process of patoisation.

The new standard had to function in those domains previously associated, either fully or in part, with the use of Latin and French: law, government, literature, religion, scholarship, and education. Progress for English against the incumbent languages in these domains was often rather uneven, slow, and at times controversial, and the circumstances of its adoption were often different in each case. Inertia, the jealous guarding of ancient privileges, or feelings about the inadequacy of English delayed the advance of the standard. Occasionally even Acts of Parliament were required to support its implementation.

The stage we are describing points towards one of the two major goals of standardisation: maximal variation in function. And since the standard has to be omnifunctional, it will develop new structures and new meanings, appropriate to its use in different domains. Each group of specialists — lawyers, the writers of religious texts, administrators, and later, journalists and advertisers — cultivate their own varieties within the standard; and each new recruit to these professions must learn to write it, and often to speak it too. Thus the standard cannot be as monolithic as people like to imagine: it has to develop variations to suit its wide range of functions.

The linguistic consequences of this process were profound. The major source of variation was no longer regional, as different styles (some linguists call them *fields of discourse*) developed their own particularities. Often these were influenced by Latin and French usage, as though the early practitioners were trying to match the dignity of those languages by distancing their use of English from the everyday. Extreme cases of this are the English of religion and the English of law, whose special qualities today derive from the fact that they were in process of formulation during the sixteenth and seventeenth centuries. In all styles, words developed additional technical meanings as they came to be used in certain contexts, and these technical meanings often influenced casual spoken usage, as we shall see in chapter three. In sum, English vocabulary became differentiated to an extent previously unknown, in that words can be identified as 'literary', or 'legal', or 'technical' in one sphere or another.

We have already seen the importance of the fourteenth century in the development of the standard. In 1362, for example, English was used for the first time in the domains of both government and law. But in the first of these, the use of French in written documents persisted for about a century after this date; and in law, it was used in some circumstances until the eighteenth century. An Act was passed in 1731 to limit its use in this domain once and for all, along with Latin (which was also occasionally used for keeping records). Today, legal English still employs Law French and Law Latin phraseology, such as *fee simple* and *habeas corpus*.

That English could function as a literary medium was apparent to all by the end of the sixteenth century; but acceptance of its potential in this respect was won only after a great deal of controversy. For many writers and scholars had a crisis of confidence about the suitability of English for great works of literature; they felt it could never match the heights achieved by the writers of ancient Rome and Greece. What is important here is not that English was in any way actually impoverished as a language, but that some people felt that it was. At one extreme, English was felt to be so 'dull', 'cankered', and 'barbarous' that it was irredeemable. At the other, some thought that there was nothing worth saying that could not be said in English. A compromise view held that English could attain the *eloquence* of the classical languages if two courses of action were taken. The first was to produce handbooks of composition, based on the classical manuals of rhetoric, to guide writers of English. The second was to inject thousands of Latin loan-words into the language. Some advocates of this second course — contemptuously known as *inkhorns* — went overboard in larding their speech with Latinisms, and became figures of fun in Elizabethan drama.

In *Love's Labour's Lost*, the pedantic Holofernes spends a great deal of time exercising his ability to translate backwards and forwards between Latin and English.

By about the 1580s, the air had cleared. The middle view had prevailed, and English was declared to have achieved a state of eloquence. A balance had been achieved between native usage and foreign importation, and the patterns of rhetoric had been successfully applied to literature in English. Moreover, some poets like Spenser and Sydney had written works that many felt were a match for any literature. And with this new-found self-confidence came a self-*conscious* delight in the flamboyant manipulation of stylistic levels. We can see this in the way Shakespeare sets off the native English idiom against the polysyllabic Latin one, by associating them with different kinds of character, or different moods. Also, he dramatises such differences of vocabulary, either by juxtaposing them within the same speech, or by intensifying a dramatic moment with the most simple language. In *Measure for Measure*, the returning Duke pretends to honour his self-righteous but corrupt deputy, Angelo, by saying his record in office deserves 'A forted residence 'gainst the tooth of time/And razure of oblivion' (V. i. 12-13). 'Tooth of time' is native; 'razure of oblivion', latinate. But when it is Mariana's turn to plead for Angelo's life, a key moment in the play, every word is from the Anglo-Saxon: 'O my dear lord,/I crave no other, nor no better man' (V. i. 428-9).

The power of the Anglo-Saxon tradition can also be felt in another domain, that of religion. Protestantism gave the English monarchy a further chance to assert political autonomy and nationhood, by appropriating the Church; and the national character of the church was expressed in what was now the national language. The sixteenth century witnessed a flurry of Biblical translation, and the preparation of prayer books and other Christian texts. While people had been used to hearing sermons spoken in English, these printed texts seemed to bring to them the word of God itself, in their own language. This process of vernacularisation culminated in the publication of the Authorised Version of the Bible in 1611, a text often regarded as a landmark in the history of English. By responding to the desire of many to hear a dignified and elevated language in church, it furnished English with what might be called a classical variety of its own. In addition, it gave many households the possibility of owning a text that greatly enhanced the status of their language: increasingly, it came to be seen as a monument, a reference-point, and a stimulus towards a sense of historicity. These sentiments were very important when English people came to settle overseas, as we shall see; and they can also be vital in the maintenance of minority or suppressed languages. For the possession of a Bible in a vernacular language has been seen as one way of generating feelings of language-loyalty, a matter to be discussed in Part 3.

The air of dignity associated with the language of the Bible derives from the fact that it is distanced from ordinary spoken usage. This distancing is achieved, however, not by the use of either French or Latin models of prose, nor by the adoption of a polysyllabic vocabulary derived from those languages. Rather is it achieved by archaism, by setting the text in the tradition of native religious discourse, particularly the sermons of the Middle Ages. It is noteworthy that already in the early seventeenth century the Authorised Version reflected the usage of a couple of generations before. We shall see in chapter four how it is the Anglo-Saxon mode of clause- and sentence-linking that is exploited in this text, rather than the mode associated with Latin.

It has been suggested that the crucial stage in functional elaboration is the development of a medium for serious, expository prose. Inspired by the example of the Authorised Version, writers began to cultivate prose to such an extent that the seventeenth century has been called the century of prose: and a significant aspect of that trend was the increased use of English in writing of a scientific and scholarly nature. Although, as we have seen, the tradition of prose in English stretches back as far as King Alfred, and persisted during the Middle Ages for religious texts of a didactic or devotional nature — written, it has been suggested, for women, who were not allowed to learn Latin — that tradition had been weakened in contact with French and Latin. This was particularly so where scholarship is concerned. The tradition of scholarly writing in Latin was so long, its audience so wide, that as late as 1687 Newton chose to write his *Principia* in that language. But this choice of Newton's stands at the end of a tradition. Fed by a developing interest in science and philosophy, people wrote political pamphlets, journals, essays, and the first newspapers, in English. By the end of the seventeenth century, the range of possibilities for expression in prose had expanded to cover imaginative, fictional writing. Such a wide functional range engendered further self-consciousness among writers of English, and enhanced the status of the language.

The displacement of Latin as the automatic language of scholarship was part of a wider process, the extension of English in education. In considering the roles of language in education, we need to distinguish between languages that are taught, and those that function as media of learning. In the Middle Ages, Latin had been both a taught language and the medium of instruction in the universities. But in schools the latter role had been filled by French. Both languages were being challenged in the education system by English as far back as the fourteenth century. A contemporary observer, Trevisa, records that in grammar schools throughout England French was being abandoned as the medium of instruction; and in the University of Oxford an edict of 1340 forbidding the use of English among students suggests that the latter had made their preferences clear. Two trends underlie these changes: the general reaction against French, and the gradual loosening of the Church's hold on institutions of learning and literacy.

Formal education was extended throughout the fifteenth and sixteenth centuries. Grammar schools were founded, often for the children of merchants; and some of these deliberately excluded clergy from teaching positions. The growth of secular education increased the demand for learning in English: and this was met after the introduction of printing. Books in English sold more widely than those in Latin. And when the Protestant Reformation had promoted the English language as a medium for religious instruction, the identification of Latin with learning was undermined still further.

A major goal of education still remained, however: the learning of Latin, and the cultivation of a good written style in that language. During the literary and cultural Renaissance of the sixteenth century, Greek was added to the syllabus; and Latin, ironically enough, was the object of renewed interest and enthusiasm. But it was the classical Latin of writers like Cicero, rather than the medieval variety of the Church, that was studied and analysed. Latin had received a fresh boost, but as a taught language rather than as a medium of learning. Paradoxically, enthusiasm for Latin ultimately furthered the cause of English. It promoted the debate about the suitability of English discussed earlier, and it led to massive translation into English, which in turn directed people's minds to the forms and structures of the vernacular. One outcome of this was the beginnings of interest in the history of English itself.

During the Renaissance, education seems to have lost some of its exclusiveness. We must remember, moreover, that in this period, like any other, education was not synonymous with schooling. There is evidence of extensive elementary literacy during the Tudor and early Stuart periods: in Shakespeare's London, perhaps half the population could read. The broadside presses printed ballads in their hundreds of thousands; and by familiarising people with written English, the Authorised Version provided the basis for the teaching of reading and writing in the many different kinds of schools that were established for ordinary people until education was made compulsory after 1870. Latin remained important to the education of elites: it was still a requirement for certain university courses, and hence for certain occupations until well into the present century. But education for most people, if, when, and where it was available, had been vernacularised; and it was the standard variety that had become the medium of teaching. In time, however, it was also to become the form of English taught not only to foreign and second-language learners, but to the English themselves.

Codification

We said above that a standard variety is one that can be taught. A taught language inevitably becomes increasingly subject to attention and scrutiny, aimed at describing its forms and structures. But as we have seen, one of the two goals of standardisation is the attainment of minimal variation of form. In practice, this means trying to eliminate variation within the standard, and stemming the process of linguistic change. Both these interrelated aims — which run counter to the natural development of language — constitute the stage in the standardisation process that has been called codification.

Codification is undertaken by a small elite of scholars. Its method has less to do with description of linguistic forms, however, than with *prescription*: the evaluation of variants as 'correct', and the stigmatisation of variants which, for one reason or another, are felt to be undesirable. As we shall see, the arguments for justifying one variant in preference to another are often arbitrary, irrational, and inconsistent. This is because variants are associated, inevitably, with particular social groups; and certain social groups are felt to be more worthy of emulation than others. Unfortunately for the codifiers, the speech of London in the early years of standardisation was extremely mixed. There was still considerable variation in the usage of upper-class society, particularly in pronunciation; what is more, such usage was constantly being pulled hither and thither by aristocratic fashion, educated pedantry, and the unmonitored speech of ordinary Londoners. But by the early nineteenth century, the recommendations of the codifiers could be embraced by those social classes who felt the need to mark their speech off from that of the class below.

In the codification of English, the example set by other languages is of paramount importance. The codifiers looked back at Classical Latin, and envied the illusion of fixity and order lent by the Latin grammarians, and the matching usage of the great writers like Cicero. But they also had other models to go on. Both Italy (in 1582) and France (in 1635) had developed Academies — bodies of learned men, who could make pronouncements on particular variants and changes. For a time, the idea of an English Academy was mooted. But by the middle of the eighteenth century, support for such an institution had fallen away' The Académie française, it seemed, had failed to fix the unfixable, just as it is failing today. Perhaps also, the English codifiers wanted to retain the freedom to make, and break, the rules as they chose. Thus codification in France has always been a more centralised and formalised affair than in England, where it has tended to be more *ad hoc*. Either way, the effects are much the same. It seems the higher the premium on codification is set, the less tolerant and the more rigid is the attitude to linguistic variation and change.

Recommended usage in England, therefore, is identified not with the decisions of a committee, but with particular books, written or compiled by established scholars and literary men. The most famous of these is undoubtedly the *Dictionary* of Dr Samuel Johnson. We have already mentioned this in connection with spelling; but it is even more important for the codification of words and meanings. When we think of dictionaries today, we have in mind what Johnson achieved — an alphabetical list of all the words in the standard language, with their meanings. Before Johnson, what dictionaries were available were not of this type. They were either dictionaries of hard words, or bilingual ones. The first was a list of those words which were felt to be difficult to understand because they were largely unassimilated into the mainstream of usage: they were often polysyllabic, Latinate words. The time for such dictionaries, not surprisingly, was the early seventeenth century; the 'inkhorn controversy' might have been resolved, but people needed to know about those foreign loan-words which made English 'eloquent' (see page 45 above). The second type of dictionary corresponded largely with our idea of a 'French-English' one — an aid to translation, rather than a statement of the vocabulary of the standard variety. What Johnson did was altogether different. He listed the *range* of meanings for each word, including the commonest; and he illustrated each strand of meaning with quotations from writers. But in addition to this, Johnson saw lexicography as a contribution to the study of a language. Not only does he catalogue words and meanings, but he also has something to say about the nature of language, its history, and also its grammar. The prestige enjoyed by the *Dictionary* during the late eighteenth and early nineteenth centuries was enormous. This was partly because it answered a need frequently felt by educated and literary people, and voiced as early as two centuries before by the scholar Mulcaster. But it was also because Johnson was regarded as a great man, with an established literary reputation. A dominant element in our cultural tradition has been the cultivation of the idea of the great mind, whether literary, philosophical, or whatever; and just as Classical scholars needed their Cicero, so the English literati of the late eighteenth century saw Johnson as the source of knowledge and wisdom about the English language. His *Dictionary* could even be viewed as constituting the language itself.

The individuality of Johnson can be seen on almost every page of his *Dictionary*. He can be as frivolous, prejudiced, and wrong, as he can be erudite: but one thing we never lose sight of is his personality. Since Johnson, unfortunately, we have tended to forget the fact that dictionaries are compiled by people. Instead, we tend to revere them as the products of some mysterious, superhuman omniscience. The effects of this legacy, especially regarding our perception of words and meanings, will be discussed in the next chapter.

The second half of the eighteenth century was also the high water mark for the codification of grammar. It is with regard to this aspect of linguistic structure that the prescriptive nature of codification can be seen most clearly. Certain grammatical forms and structures were judged as 'correct', while others were stigmatised as 'vulgar'. The legacy of these pronouncements is still strong today: many people are extremely nervous about being incorrect in speaking and writing. And certain of the stigmatised usages have become embedded in our present-day consciousness, as pitfalls to avoid. In general, people have a much clearer idea about what they are supposed to *avoid* saying, than what the codifiers recommend for them.

The grammarians sought to justify one usage at the expense of another by applying certain principles. The most important of these is probably the example of Latin. Grammars of Latin had been available for centuries, and all scholars knew and used them; hence, the grammatical categories established by the Latin scholars were applied, ready-made, to the grammar of English. The fact that by the eighteenth century Latin was usually encountered only in its written form gave rise to the idea that it was a fixed, regulated, and invariant language. English, by comparison, seemed untidy: it was therefore felt to be appropriate to promote grammatical variants which corresponded, in one way or another, to equivalents in Latin. Thus, the English pattern *it's me*, which had been common for centuries and still is, was deemed incorrect since the Latin construction *ego sum* made use of the subject form of the pronoun, *ego*, rather than the object form *me*: English people should therefore say *it's I*. The pervasiveness of such reasoning can be judged by the fact that people still write about this shibboleth in letters to the press.

Knowledge of Latin presupposed a knowledge of etymology, the origins of words. As well as disliking variation, the grammarians also hated change: hence, correctness was associated with what used to be the case, and the further back you could go, the better. Such arguments were very common where the meanings of words are concerned, but the 'etymological fallacy' was also applied to justify certain constructions. *Different from* was preferable to *different to*, or *different than*, because the *di* part of the word originally indicated 'division' or 'separateness'; and therefore *from* suits the etymological argument better. Similarly, the constructions *averse to* and *under the circumstances* were considered incorrect, since the meanings of the *a* in *averse* and the *circum* in *circumstance* are respectively 'from' and 'around', and these meanings were not felt to be congruent with those of *to* and *under*. The grammarians failed to see that the use of such prepositions as *to* and *from* is in any language highly idiomatic.

A final principle involved the application of a kind of algebraic logic to stigmatise some constructions and promote others. Perhaps the most notorious example concerns the pattern of negation in English. In common with many languages today, English had since Anglo-Saxon times signalled negation by the cumulative use of negative particles. Hence, *I don't know nothing* was a traditional English pattern. By the end of the eighteenth century this had been condemned as illogical, by applying the principle that 'two negatives make a positive'. That great writers like Shakespeare used the traditional construction was a source of some embarrassment to the grammarians.

As in the case of dictionaries, we tend to forget today that grammars are written by people, who are not only individuals, but who also may reflect the interests of certain social groups. Grammar also has its great mind, to some extent, in that many people today look to Fowler and his *Modern English Usage* as an arbiter of usage. In Fowler, too, we find a personality, who is able moreover to temper the tradition of prescriptivism with a liberalism that acknowledges linguistic variation and change. But the strength of that tradition should not be underestimated today, and we shall see how our perceptions of grammar are dominated by it in the course of chapter four.

Pronunciation is the most difficult aspect of language to codify. As we have seen, our spelling is a most imperfect and inappropriate model for the sounds we make; yet people have felt bound by it for more than 400 years. Already in the sixteenth century some scholars interested in the codification of pronunciation had begun to consider the relationship between sounds and spellings: their arguments in effect are a rehearsal of those discussed above. Hart, a phonetician, argued that spelling should be reformed so as to draw it into line with pronunciation. Mulcaster, a headmaster, rejected this plea for a phonemic model, arguing that people pronounced differently. But others were already proposing the inversion of this priority. Sir Thomas Elyot, author of the immensely influential *Governor* of 1531, wrote that noblemen's sons should omit no letter in their pronunciation, a view echoed by the pronouncing dictionaries of 300 years later, and heard ever since.

Attempts to base pronunciation on spelling were not helped by developments in the writing system in the early phase of standardisation. The early printers introduced spellings that had nothing to do with sounds, like the *ue* of *tongue*. Other spellings were remodelled by scholars themselves, to show their origins: the nativised spelling *dette* had a *b* inserted to show that it came from Latin *debitum*. In cases like *debt* and *island* (where the scholars got the etymology wrong: they put an *s* into *iland*, thinking it to be from Latin *insula*) pronunciation has remained unaffected, and we are left with a spelling difficulty; but in other cases, as in *perfect*, the etymological spelling gives us the basis for modern pronunciation, displacing *parfit*. Such pedantry was not the only complicating factor. As we said before, the early standard was a very mixed variety, mingling not only the pronunciations of different areas, but also to some extent their traditional spelling systems. The spelling of *busy*, for instance, may reflect the old Winchester standard, whereas its pronunciation is an east midland one. Some pronunciations themselves appear to have a south-western origin. The glide consonant /w/ in *one* can be heard at the onset of other words, such as *oak* (*wuk*), in that area today. (Other dialects, for example those in Northumberland, have a different glide, the initial sound of *yet*; hence, *one* is *yan*.) Finally, some pronunciations seem to have had an East Anglian source. The famous example of spelling irregularity in *bough, though, rough, cough*, and *tough* shows how spelling can create the illusion of relationship among words that are either of different origin (the vowels of some of these words are historically unrelated) or whose pronunciations have diverged. We find that in the first two words, the final consonant, represented by *gh*, is no longer sounded, but the last three have the eastern /f/.

We do not know the circumstances governing the adoption of some pronunciations rather than others. It has been suggested that in some cases choice was motivated by a desire to maintain or even establish distinctions among pronunciations that were either not made in other dialects, or were being lost in them. Thus, the adoption of a south-western pronunciation of *one* could create a useful distinction between that word and *own*. Though this may be true in some instances, it is wrong in any event to conclude that 'standard' pronunciation (or grammar and vocabulary for that matter) is richer in distinctions than other dialects or varieties, as we shall see in the next three chapters. Traditional distinctions may be preserved by teaching them as correct, but adherence to tradition may deprive us of a variety of useful innovations.

In the early years of standardisation, the precepts of the codifiers had to compete with the push and pull of fashion. Some pronunciations were undoubtedly adopted because, for one reason or another, they were considered prestigious. But by the end of the eighteenth century, codification of the other levels of structure led to the production of the pronouncing dictionary, a book in which the pronunciation of words in the standard variety could be looked up. In these works, there is both an appeal to spelling as a guide, but also an appeal to tradition.

Johnson's *Dictionary* had codified not only words but their spellings also; and now that spelling was virtually fixed, it was a good deal easier to recommend pronunciations based on them. Moreover, Johnson himself had written that the best pronunciations were those that accorded with the spelling. This precept was put into effect by John Walker, the writer of *A Critical Pronouncing Dictionary* (1791). If there was an *h* in the spelling, then *h* should be sounded. The verbal ending *-ing*, as in *going*, should not be pronounced *-in'*, for the same reason. The pronunciation of whole words, like *forehead*, *often*, and *waistcoat*, should moreover be reformed in accordance with spelling, to replace *forrid*, *offen*, and *weskit*. Certain pronunciations, however, were too firmly entrenched in upper-class society to be changed. Admitting that the new pronunciation of *cucumber* suited the spelling better than the old *cowcumber*, Walker felt reluctant to recommend it. But the spelling-pronunciation won out in the standard variety, and *cowcumber* is now only heard in dialect.

There is another crucial dimension to Walker's approach. Notions of correct pronunciation are formulated against a background of what to avoid; and it becomes increasingly clear that it is lower-class pronunciations that must be avoided. And the most barbarous kind of pronunciation was that associated with the Cockney speech of London. Cockneys, said Walker, should know better, since they did not have the excuse of living miles away from the centre of power, culture, and fashion. Thus, the differences that existed between their speech and that of so-called polite society were 'a thousand times more offensive and disgusting' than differences which occurred elsewhere.

By the early nineteenth century, then, correct pronunciation was an issue of class. And the identification of the 'best' pronunciation with a particular social class is given institutional expression by the development of the fee-paying public school system. In these schools, a pronunciation that may be described as codified grew up, or was cultivated and taught. The desiderata of the scholars could at last be put into practice in controlled conditions. But the recipients of this privilege have always been only a tiny minority, a minority drawn primarily from the wealthy and powerful groups in English society. In no other country in the world are pronunciation and social class so closely and clearly linked.

In the public schools, the predominantly east midland basis of the upper-class London pronunciation gradually lost its regional colour. It became a purely class accent, and was accordingly evaluated in ways which reflect the attitudes of the most powerful social group. Known today to linguists as Received Pronunciation − a term in which the adjective 'received' has the now obsolete sense of 'socially acceptable in the best circles' − this accent is still widely claimed to be the best form of pronunciation (although linguists themselves usually attest their neutrality on this matter). Received Pronunciation (RP) is often described, not in terms of the class that uses it, but as the most beautiful and euphonious of accents. Most strikingly, its status as an accent has even been denied: if you speak RP, you speak English 'without an accent'.

It need hardly be said that this view was often accepted and even fostered by ordinary people wherever English was spoken. Persuaded that their own regional accents were ugly or slovenly, people have often accepted the view that RP offers a prestigious norm. Many of our popular designations of RP − 'Queen's English', 'Oxford English', 'BBC

English' — reflect its association with power, learning, and influence. And as we shall see in chapter five, RP has been a powerful agent in the re-structuring of regional pronunciations which originally had quite different sound-systems. Yet while RP exerts prestige at the overt level, there has been no widespread, wholesale adoption of the accent. For the vast majority of the population, RP may be all the things we have listed above, but it is also the speech of a social class that they have no ambition to emulate.

Codification and social class

We have seen that from the first the standard variety is associated with power in society. Throughout the period of standardisation, an increasingly dominant source of power has been the ownership of capital. By the nineteenth century, the factory system was producing enough wealth for its owners to acquire positions in society. But ownership of a fortune does not guarantee refined behaviour or courtly manners. The new entrepreneurs needed to be 'socially acceptable in the best circles'. What more accessible way of doing this than to embrace the standards of correctness in speech, now that these had been codified and made widely available?

Recent research in both England and the USA shows that the class most anxious about linguistic usage is the lower middle class. Insecurity about social status is reflected in nervousness about being incorrect in linguistic behaviour. In the early nineteenth century, it was the industrialists who felt insecure about status, and who therefore provided the need for a 'superior' kind of English. The adoption of the codified standard would mean that your speech could be sharply different from that of the working class, who, as a consequence of the process of industrialisation, were flooding into the cities in their hundreds of thousands. It was in *their* speech, appropriately enough, that the stigmatised pronunciations and grammatical items could be found.

Codification could be said to have become a weapon of class. What the codifiers had done, ultimately, was to propose and cultivate a code of linguistic forms which were in some degree different from those in use among the vast majority of the population. By analysing 'correct' usage in terms that only a tiny minority of educated people could command, the codifiers ensured that correctness remained the preserve of an elite. The usage of most people was wrong, precisely because it was the usage of the majority. The worst aspects of the codification process were institutionalised in the compulsory state education system introduced after 1870. The doctrine of correctness was preached with mechanical inflexibility: attention to linguistic form overrode considerations of linguistic function. Not surprisingly, millions of people left school convinced that not only were they ignorant of their own language, but they were stupid as well.

It would, however, be mistaken to suggest that the codifiers were a tightly-knit group of conspirators extending across several generations, intent on laying traps for the unwary. In fact, they did not by any means represent a homogeneous body of opinion; they often argued amongst themselves, and some laid the foundations for the serious study of language and of linguistic history. But the codifiers did pave the way, however unwittingly, for the mystification that has often characterised discussion about language. Many people today, when they examine the work of the eighteenth-century grammarians, are struck by the triviality of the examples cited, and by the tortuousness of the arguments. And if the judgments are arbitrary, and the result of special pleading, it may well be because the codifiers themselves were not unaffected by allegiances of class and background.

Codification of the standard was not based on an informed and systematic analysis of language. It is not surprising, therefore, that there is little consensus today about what items upset us or gladden our hearts. A recent survey among employers, examiners, and teachers shows that while some people make a fuss about *it's me*, others like to wax haughty on *different to/than/from*. We all have a linguistic *bête noir*. But one of the most depressing results of codification is that as well as encouraging this prescriptive stance, it has tended to elevate personal taste into a norm, a characteristic particularly apparent in the pages of Johnson, Walker, and Fowler. In view of the social history of the past two centuries, this was perhaps unavoidable: but we should remember today that individual preference and informed understanding are not necessarily the same thing.

Part 2

Changing patterns of usage

Chapter three
Words and meanings

Contact with other languages, as we saw in chapter one, has greatly influenced the word-stock of English. New words are more easily added to a language than grammatical forms or structures, or sounds, and so the word-stock of a language, or its lexicon, can be considered to be more open-ended than its grammar or sound-system. Social and cultural changes are accordingly clearly reflected in changes in vocabulary: and this is one aspect of the history of English about which it is possible to make some simple, clear, and fairly safe observations. We know, for instance, that the vocabulary of English has vastly increased in size during the last 1500 years, as an accompaniment to the process of functional elaboration discussed in chapter two. In the present chapter we shall examine the process of word-borrowing, and some sociolinguistic issues raised by it, such as how it might reflect social needs; and this in turn will lead us to further issues, such as the ways in which our notion of the word as an isolable unit has been shaped by literacy and the dictionary. We shall need to look at the complexity involved in the study of meaning (and again, the way in which our perceptions are influenced by the dictionary), and consider how many traditional accounts of semantic change tend to underplay the importance of different groups of users in changing meanings, or in adding new meanings to particular words. We shall try to illustrate the role of these factors by considering in detail three recent examples of semantic change. Finally, we shall explore parts of our vocabulary which can be shown to have been socially sensitive, by discussing the notion of 'key-words', the vocabulary of power and status, terms of address, and words which refer to women.

From a social point of view, more interesting than the mere addition of new words to our vocabulary is the change in the character of our word-stock, from one which can be called Germanic to one that is also partly Romance. Exposure to Latin, and its offspring French, has been sustained throughout much of the recorded history of English, and it is this that helps give the language its European flavour, in that many of our words are quickly recognisable to speakers of French, Italian, and

Spanish. This exposure has been pervasive enough to give rise to some popular notions and stereotypes about parts of the English lexicon. Speaking 'in words of one syllable' appeals to the Anglo-Saxon element (the reason for this monosyllabic quality, the loss of inflexions, is discussed in the next chapter); 'talking like a book', to the more learned, polysyllabic lexical material derived from the Romance languages. Like most popular ideas about language, these associations are only partly justified: 'four-letter words', for instance, are not generally recorded in Anglo-Saxon texts, and there are plenty of words from French that have entered dialectal English rather than the standard variety. But these associations do square with an important *stylistic* trait in the language. Romance loan-words are common in domains associated with power and prestige, and it is a matter of everyday experience that formal business letters tend to favour the French *request* rather than the Anglo-Saxon *ask*, and that military medals are awarded for *gallantry* or *courage*, rather than for *guts* (deriving from an Anglo-Saxon word denoting bowels and entrails).

There have also been fundamental developments in the principles of word *formation*. In Anglo-Saxon times, new words could be coined from established ones, a process generally known as compounding. There were some productive prefixes, such as *for-*, *under-*, *mis-*, and suffixes like *-some*, *-craft*, *-dom*, and *-ness*, and these could be combined in various ways with other words: thus, poetry was *wordcraeft*, medicine *laececraeft*. The technique is similar to that often found in modern German, which might have *Ausgang* ('way out') where we are likely to use the Latinate *Exit*. While we have not abandoned this technique altogether, it is generally true to say that English has been particularly receptive to the possibility of absorbing foreign words; instead of making up new words, we borrow them; and not only, of course, from the languages mentioned. In fact, the borrowing process has been so dynamic that we have taken up prefixes and suffixes as well as words: the French *-able*, for instance, can be tacked on to words of Anglo-Saxon origin, for instance, as in *likeable*.

This tendency to borrow rather than create has its social consequences. It has been argued that the Anglo-Saxon habit of word-formation kept the meaning of a word transparent and was therefore democratic: you can work out what a new word means, because you know the meanings of the parts. It is certainly true that foreign vocabulary has often been used, and is still used, to dominate or mystify; and it is easy to laugh at people who, unfamiliar with the sound- and syllable-patterns of the Latinate vocabulary of, say, medicine, mispronounce words or use them inappropriately. On the other hand, can words in themselves exemplify either a democratic or an undemocratic trend in a language's development? The desire to be either of these things must be in reality a matter for the users of a language. Indeed, when it comes to demagogy, it is just as possible to manipulate people by using words drawn from a less heterogeneous vocabulary. The meanings of Anglo-Saxon words like *hearth*, *home*, *kith*, *kin*, *child*, *father*, *mother*, can easily be exploited in persuasive language, since they are words to which strong emotions are often attached; often learned early in life, some resonate with associations of familiarity and intimacy.

The motivation for borrowing

A number of sociolinguistic issues are raised by the question of why words are borrowed in the first place. It is a common misconception that some languages are inferior, or more handicapped than others, because they lack not only words but concepts that can be seen to find expression in other languages. These misconceptions falsely assume that certain topics, and some modes of discourse, depend on particular vocabulary ranges. Therefore, the argument goes, English borrowed words because it needed them. There are several objections that can be made to these notions. First, as we have seen, words are often borrowed into particular varieties of a language, and become part of the technical or specialised usage of certain groups of users only. Writers used to reading, say, philosophy, in another language, will grow accustomed to a certain range of vocabulary and a particular kind of expression; and they may well conclude that their own language is deficient by comparison. But the association of a vocabulary with such subjects is largely traditional. Though we might expect to hear in a discussion of economics words like *profit*, *demand*, and *recession*, there is no reason why these terms could not be glossed by others, or that notions akin to them should not be expressed differently. Second, as we have already noted, words borrowed from other languages often develop a particular resonance that is stylistic: we expect to encounter them in certain contexts, either written or spoken, formal or informal, official or literary. Thus, they can be said to parallel already existing usages rather than fill in the gaps of an impoverished language. Third, borrowed vocabulary is very often used as a means of marking social distance.

Since ordinary people might be impressed by a high-sounding utterance, there is a demand among elites for foreign vocabulary: thus, the motivation for borrowing may be as much to do with social snobbery or social differentiation as anything else. Finally, it can be shown that thousands of borrowed words introduced nothing that was conceptually new; English was already adequately served. One consequence of this, as we shall see, is that the meanings of older words tend to be changed by the admission of the new.

Linguists usually argue against the notion of handicapped languages by asserting that all languages develop vocabularies that fully serve the needs of their users. In general, vocabulary is more finely differentiated in fields or subject areas which are culturally valued and significant; so that if a language has more words than another in relation to, say, rice, it will reflect the interests of its speakers. The fact that English has borrowed so many words in its history is not, however, so much a reflection of need as of the enduring cultural dominance of languages like French and Latin. Unfortunately, global statements about the needs of different speech-communities mask an important fact about language and its relation to society. Different groups of speakers may have different needs. Within one language like English, for instance, it will be necessary for a group such as farmers to classify cows and bulls with a more specific vocabulary – more sensitive to age – than most of us have need of. Similarly, I have a richer vocabulary of address to a loved one – ranging from Christian name, nickname, pet-name, terms of jocular abuse – than to a colleague of only slight acquaintance. In culturally diverse, literate, technologically complex societies such as our own it is more difficult to identify areas of general social need than in more homogeneous societies (such as the commonly noted example of Eskimos and their many words for different kinds of snow). At the same time, it is fair to assume that the more homogeneous Anglo-Saxon tribes had a clearer need for a vocabulary denoting natural topographical features than we do today. For the Anglo-Saxons, the process of settlement was of crucial importance, and it is reflected in a great many English place-names whose meaning is obscured for us. Unless we are foresters, we no longer need single words to refer to such features as 'wood on a slope' (*hangra*, preserved in Oakhanger, Hants), 'sacred grove' (*hearg*, as in Harrow, Middx), 'land covered with brush or small trees' (*hese*, as in Hayes, Herts), or 'wet land liable to be overgrown with alders' (*sceage*, as in Shaugh, Devon).

Despite what has been said in the paragraph above, it is still possible to point to certain areas of human life in which all the groups of users of English have a common interest. There is a general sensitivity about subjects like sex, defecation, drunkenness, and death, and there are clear social norms about ways of referring to them. Vocabulary tends to proliferate around such taboos, as we might expect of subjects that are culturally salient. When we examine the relevant vocabulary, however, two clearly different modes of reference can be distinguished. One, associated with the more 'polite' social groups is towards euphemism. New words are selected, or coined, to replace existing ones which are thought to have picked up the unpleasant or undesirable associations characteristic of the referent. Thus, in some contexts *die* is felt to be abrupt, and phrases such as *passed away*, *departed this life* are used to soften the fact of death. Other social contexts, however, permit a more jocular periphrasis, such as *snuffed it*, *kicked the bucket*, etc. What both tendencies have in common is the need for novelty: with euphemism, the need to find new ways of avoiding unpleasantness, and with slang, new ways of sensationalising, humourising, or actually cultivating offensiveness. The desire for newness, then, provides another motivation for borrowing.

Unfortunately for the historian of English, detailed information about words and meanings in these socially sensitive spheres is often lacking for past centuries. This is partly because ways of referring to them are covert, and partly because many such terms were until very recently rarely written down. If they ever reached print, they may have changed their meaning, and so do not provide evidence of ways of verbalising taboo subjects. The further back in history we go, the narrower the range of texts available. On the basis of the texts we possess, it is very difficult to know what subjects, if any, were taboo for the Anglo-Saxons. It might be argued, however, that the Anglo-Saxons had already devised euphemisms for death and dying. Our word *die* is not firmly evidenced in Anglo-Saxon (although related forms *deaþ* and *dead* exist) and it is possible that the concept was referred to by means of words which were historically euphemisms: *sweltan* (compare modern *swelter*), which originally meant 'burn slowly'; and *steorfan* (cf. modern *starve*), originally meaning 'become stiff'. The modern form *die* is probably a borrowing from Scandinavian *deyja*, and the reason for its borrowing may well have been that the other words had become too closely identified with their sensitive referent. The other words develop modified meanings: *swelt* does not become part of the standard language, but it survives in dialect to mean 'faint with heat'; in *starve* the meaning is specialised, with the cause of death specified: hunger in standard English, cold in dialect.

A further meaning of *starve* in contemporary English brings us to one more 'universal' in our discussion of users' needs — this time of a more abstract nature. It is quite common to hear people say *I'm starving* when they are only more than a little hungry. In other words, they achieve emphasis by choosing a word whose dictionary meaning, as it were, is too strong for the context. The desire for emphasis has weakened the meanings of a great many words, such as *awfully*, *terribly*, *frightfully*, *marvellous*, *glorious*, *stupendous*, because they have been used where what is of paramount importance are the attitudes of the speaker. In such *affective* uses of language, the desire for emphasis creates the need for new terms, in that the affective content of words rapidly becomes diluted: we therefore find a motivation for borrowing similar to that discussed in the last paragraph. Furthermore, an important dimension of attitude is the desire to register approval or disapproval of certain objects, practices, ideas, and so on. A great part of our everyday vocabulary tells other people about our likes and dislikes: we often want to place things on a scale of evaluation, and our vocabulary is often correspondingly vague, as in the ubiquitous *nice*. At the extreme ends of the favourable-unfavourable continuum, new words are constantly being introduced — like *fabulous*, and more recently *magic*, with its handy antonym, *tragic*.

Codification of words and meanings

Having discussed some of the general changes in our vocabulary, and some of our ways with words, it is now time to consider how the process of codification, outlined in the last chapter, has influenced our perception of words and meanings. We need to do this not only because a number of intrinsically interesting issues are involved, but because we cannot begin to understand the process of semantic change unless we try to free ourselves from the notions of fixity and correctness associated with standardisation. We can do this if we remember that standard varieties of language are by no means universal, that many of them are relatively new, and that their influence is not uniformly felt throughout society. Since these observations can also be made about literacy, we shall also need to bear in mind the importance of the written word in our cultural experience.

A significant effect of the codification process is that we tend to think that the primary unit of linguistic structure is the word. This is partly because the most accessible handbook of English is the dictionary, a list of words; and our perception of words as isolable, fixed forms is reinforced by our writing tradition, which accustoms us to the spaces between words on the page. Above all, we perceive the word as something that is spelt, in an invariant form. When we consider the importance of the word in the school system, as a means of assessing linguistic competence (by estimating vocabulary size), or in such things as spelling tests, it is not surprising that it is this component of linguistic structure that tends to be uppermost in our minds when we think or talk about language.

In unmonitored, informal conversation, however, our perception of words is quite different. We treat them almost as abstractions: changing their pronunciation in different environments, altering their function in different kinds of sentences and making them mean many different — and sometimes apparently contradictory — things. No one, moreover, keeps words separated when they are talking off-the-cuff. Despite what many of us think, it is not only speakers of non-standard English who run words into each other. In our everyday use of language, words are not treated as isolable entities, but as parts of bigger units, the utterances of speech; these, in turn, form part of larger units, which may be called discourses or texts. It is in this way that we first encounter words as children; and such pre-literate perceptions underlie our unselfconscious speech, however much we may prefer to think that it accords with the precepts of a fixed, codified, literate norm. It is only when we learn to read and write that our natural tendency to think of words as parts of larger units is broken down, and the history of the form *alright* shows how the failure to analyse a familiar phrase into its constituent parts brings into being a new, single word. In similar fashion, schoolchildren often write *a lot* as one word.

A great deal of what we have said about our informal treatment of words is relevant when we consider how words are perceived in non-literate societies. We need to remember that if words are only encountered in face-to-face, oral interaction, their *meanings* will be more immediately tied to specific contexts. Literacy, by contrast, diversifies culture, introducing new traditions; hence words come to be experienced in a wider range of contexts, and consequently a more generalised, less concrete, and less immediate perception of their meanings arises. And as the functions of language are elaborated, words take on meanings associated with particular domains of usage. So we can begin here to see a process of contact between specialised usage and the language of the everyday: just as languages can borrow words from each other, so borrowing can occur among varieties of the same language. A word consequently accrues layers of meanings as it is used in a widening range of contexts, the more so if it is used in many different kinds of writing. Thus, consciousness of the individual word is reflected much more strongly in the poetry of a literate culture than in an oral one. While the former cultivates ambiguity and word-play, oral poetry makes use of the formula, usually a string of words, habitually co-occurring, to express common ideas, actions, and processes; it chooses words for their overall sound-effect rather than for their subtleties of meaning. Even within a literate culture oral poetry can survive, as in the case of the sung ballad; and we can find some of its characteristics in the literature of the Anglo-Saxons, and to a lesser extent in the poetry of the Middle Ages. The absence of a standardised codified variety, and of a universal spelling system, meant that the medieval poets could not expect their works to remain unchanged if they were written down by scribes in other parts of the country. Not only words, but even whole phrases might be changed in the course of transmission.

The way in which literacy affects our perception of words is subtler than the more dramatic and overt influence of the dictionary. Unfortunately, many people tend to treat dictionaries with reverence: rather than being seen as a record of usage, they are often regarded as the arbiter of it, a source of enlightenment for the ignorant non-specialist. In fact, the traditional arrangement of words in dictionaries gives people a strange idea about language. The alphabetic arrangement disassociates a word from the company it keeps, presenting it as a unit isolated from context and words of similar meaning. More important, many dictionaries give the impression that words have only one meaning, to be found on the right-hand side of the page. Even the fullest dictionary, the *Oxford English Dictionary* (*OED*), which shows the whole range of meanings by citing examples of a word *in use* at different periods of its history, puts the meanings first, then lists the examples, thereby obscuring the process involved in deriving the meanings; for we learn the meanings of new words most efficiently by hearing them in a wide range of contexts. Most dictionaries, for economic reasons, cannot run to several volumes like the *OED*, so tend even more to give the idea that meaning is clear-cut and straightforward. It is not surprising, therefore, that people often misunderstand them.

The dictionary is the one reference book about language that is widely used. People writing to newspapers, for example, often preface their comments with something like 'I see from my dictionary . . .'. Unfortunately, a great deal of public debate about words and their meanings is conducted in an atmosphere of prescriptivism. It is assumed that the meaning listed in the dictionary is the true or real one, to which usage should conform. Identifying 'true meanings' is a favourite game in media discussions about language, and newspaper letter columns regularly print letters which highlight alleged errors or imprecisions in the use of *infer* or *sophisticated*, and so on. An assumption that underlies correspondence of this kind is that the etymology, or origin, of a word is a guide to its true meaning; in other words, the first recorded meaning is the correct one. The consequence of applying this logic through the entire English lexicon would produce strange results indeed. *Deer* would then mean any kind of animal (like the German *Tier*) and a *glamour* contest would be a test of brains, not beauty. But many people have a sincere desire to preserve distinctions that they feel are valuable, such as that existing between *infer* and *imply*. A careless use of the two words blurs a useful line between different processes; the original meanings therefore need defending. Though the concern for precision is laudable, it is rather an apocalyptic view of language that focuses its attention solely on 'lost distinctions'. The same so-called careless usage which is blurring *disinterested* and *uninterested* also failed to distinguish between *r* and *l* in *grammar*: we now have two words, with separate meanings, for the price of one – the other is *glamour*. A contrast lost, a contrast gained; such is linguistic change. The temperature needs to be lowered when meanings and changes in meaning are being discussed.

A final point to be made about dictionaries reminds us that it is not only the non-specialist who adopts a reverent attitude to dictionary authority. Many linguists and other scholars tend to regard the *OED* as definitive, even oracular, as if it had not been compiled by a group of people with certain presuppositions and even prejudices. Certain social and political values lie behind its apparent impersonality. The aura of objectivity associated with the *OED* is dangerous, since it expresses such values in a covert and anonymous way, unlike the dictionary of Dr Johnson, which is full of overt expression of the compiler's personality. In any case, the particular tradition of scholarship which gave rise to the *OED* was more concerned with the origins of words and their variations of form and meaning, than with the ways in which words of similar or related meaning have influenced each other. An inquiry into certain parts of our vocabulary, such as the words associated with political discourse, shows the problems involved in establishing definitive meanings. Different groups in society use words like *class, democracy*, or *radical* to mean very different things, and the editors of the *OED* may have displayed, however unconsciously, the 'consensus' values of university academics whose work began in the 1870s and was completed in the 1920s. (Subsequent changes recorded in the Supplements to the *Dictionary* have involved additions rather than revisions.) We cannot write a social history of English without exploring the social position of those who study, or comment on, the language.

The complexity of meaning

The dictionary is of limited usefulness in the study of meaning and semantic change because the notion of meaning itself is so complex. We shall confine our discussion here to that part of our vocabulary that comprises so-called lexical words: nouns, like *horse, kettle, army*; verbs, like *walk, start, ride*; adjectives like *hard, brave, refreshed*; adverbs like *slowly, fast, noisily*. Lexical words such as these can be discussed in terms of their 'meaning content', in contrast to grammatical words, such as articles, prepositions, conjunctions, and pronouns.

We shall distinguish six types of meaning. The first, and most important kind, we shall call *conceptual* meaning. The meaning of many lexical words may be discussed in terms of what they denote; or, to put it another way, what their reference is. This type of meaning is sometimes called denotative or referential meaning. Many words 'stand for' objects, events, or processes that exist, or are felt to exist, in the real world; and such objects, and so on, are called referents. If we take the two words *woman* and *lady*, we can see that despite differences in meaning between them (which we shall discuss below) both words refer to an entity that is human, adult and female. Thus the conceptual meaning of both words may be related to this irreducible core of meaning.

This notion of reference is often misunderstood. It should be emphasised that the relationship between the form *woman*, and the thing it refers to, is a purely conventional one: there is nothing inherently feminine about the word itself, and in principle any other word would do to signify a woman, as long as we all agreed on the matter!

But many arguments about the real meanings of words are based on an assumption of identity between word and referent. Such 'magical thinking' has often played an important part in so-called primitive societies, but it will not get us far in trying to understand the problem of meaning and semantic change.

The relationship between words and referents, then, is a fluid one; and this comes about because as human beings we must *conceptualise* the objects, events, and processes that we find around us. These conceptualisations, being products of the human mind, are themselves inclined to change. There are of course different kinds of conceptualisation, according to the criteria used for relating words to referents. We use the word *mountain* to apply to a range of objects which conform to certain criteria, such as height, size, shape, substance, and so on; in sum, we apply the word to referents whose form satisfies the criteria listed. *Formal* criteria of this kind are less important, however, in applying the term *boat* to a range of objects. If we want to cross water, we need something that will carry our weight and stay afloat; size, shape, substance are of less concern, and a raft might do as well as an ocean liner. The word *boat* can refer to all shapes and sizes of things, as long as they *function* in a particular way (thus, we need to exclude model boats from this discussion). So far, then, we can distinguish very broadly between formal and functional criteria in our exploration of conceptual meaning, and we can test their validity by assessing the role of formal criteria in the applications of *boat*, and functional ones in the case of *mountain*. While we may think of a certain range of shapes when we use the term *boat*, it would not be true to say that the word is applicable to anything that happens to be boat-shaped, unless we are speaking metaphorically. Similarly, a mountain is something that can be climbed; but this aspect is not criterial, since we are not justified in applying the word *mountain* to, say, a ladder, simply because we can climb it. A third kind of conceptualisation involves criteria that are *evaluative*. When we use the term *hovel*, we specify a residence that seems to us to be dirty, tumble-down, or squalid. What is uppermost in our minds is our attitude to the referent: we have placed it on a scale of evaluation, of approval or disapproval. The importance of this dimension of meaning cannot be over-emphasised: the impetus towards evaluation, as we saw earlier, is very strong, and we shall see this again as we examine the history of some English words.

So far, we have discussed what is perhaps the most important dimension of meaning, but we have yet to account for other, incidental perceptions, that may not form part of the central core of meaning, but that are highly relevant when we consider how language functions in society. They are also instrumental in the process of semantic change. Another type of meaning, for instance, can be termed *connotative*. We saw above that *woman* and *lady* have roughly the same conceptual meaning, but a moment's reflection will remind us that we use the two words very differently. *Woman*, for instance, connotes a relatively open-ended set of properties, including the ability to bear children, the tendency to be warm and sensitive, the ability to satisfy men's sexual needs, and so on. The connotations of *lady*, on the other hand, tend to be associated with social status and graces. It is important to remember that though a word's connotations may vary from one individual to another, they are not purely personal or subjective; they often reflect the values of a particular social group at a particular time, and in the case of *woman*, the word will probably connote different things to men than to women.

The next type of meaning can be called *stylistic* meaning. Certain words advertise themselves as belonging to particular contexts of use. Thus, while we may agree that, say, *horse* and *steed* have the same conceptual meaning, we are unlikely to take a steed for a Saturday morning's ride (neither would we take our *gee-gee*, unless we were talking to very young children). We recognise *steed* as a word appropriate to certain contexts of use, such as poetry, or prose romance: it belongs to a particular 'style'. From a historical point of view, stylistic meanings develop as the language is functionally elaborated, and certain words are specialised in particular fields of usage. Thus, *steed*, from an Anglo-Saxon word meaning stallion, has been associated with poetic language since the sixteenth century.

Our fourth type is *affective* meaning. We have already noted the importance of attitude and evaluation in shaping our use of language. The words we use to address, or refer to, other people are often highly partisan, particularly where differences of social class, race, sex, region of origin, or political persuasion are concerned. Certain words become so emblematic of a point of view that their conceptual content is pushed into the background. *Nigger*, originally a word denoting a racial type, has virtually become a term of abuse; and a similar development has occurred with parts of the political vocabulary, such as *fascist*.

The fifth and sixth types of meaning are respectively *reflected* and *collocative* meaning. Certain words over the centuries have developed more than one conceptual meaning, and sometimes more than one meaning is perceived by the user. The Anglo-Saxon word *deore* originally denoted things of great value, and was later applied to people in the sense of 'esteemed', from which the sense 'dear' subsequently arose. It is possible for poets to exploit both meanings, 'costly' and 'beloved', so that such words in certain contexts may be said to *reflect* both. Finally, collocative meaning concerns the somewhat idiosyncratic properties of certain words like *pretty* and *handsome*. While both words share a similar conceptual meaning, they habitually co-occur with different sets of nouns, from which they contract associations. Thus, *pretty* collocates with *girl* rather than *boy*, *village* rather than *typewriter*. While both *pretty* and *handsome* mean much the same thing, they are not normally interchangeable, for part of their associative meaning is derived from the collocational company they keep.

Collocational meaning reminds us of a vital point about words made earlier in this chapter. We are accustomed to hearing them strung together with other words: and the rules which specify which words can collocate with a particular word constitute an important part of that word's meaning. Thus, we can extend the notion of collocational meaning, and speak of collocational *range*. Some words, like *big*, can qualify almost any noun, referring to a wide range of referents, human and non-human, animate and inanimate, abstract and concrete, and so on; whereas *rancid* can collocate with very few, and *flaxen* with only one. As we shall see, extension or contraction in the collocational range often promotes a change in meaning; and a change in meaning of one word usually brings about a change in another. For words enter also into another series of relationships with other words, forming little systems of meaning: *big* patterns with *large* on one scale, with *gigantic* on another, with *small* on yet another, and so on. Thus, it is unwise to pluck a single word from its network, and discuss it in isolation, as is so often done; we should keep an eye on the fortunes of its peers.

Types of semantic change

We have already encountered the difficulty of explaining the notion of meaning without referring to the past. For the rest of this chapter, we shall be seeing the relevance of our six types of meaning in discussing the processes of semantic change. This again is an issue of great complexity, and many histories of English present it in rather a forbidding way. For example, they often present us with instances of spectacular change, isolated from contexts of users and use, and with no attempt to show how these instances pattern with words of related meaning. Thus, to read that *treacle* once meant 'pertaining to wild animals' may afford a shock of pleasure or puzzlement, but if we are denied discussion of the intermediate links in the chain we can easily get the impression that words change their meanings by themselves, while the user stands helpless on the sidelines.

To give some idea of the *process* of semantic change, let us look at three words which have developed new meanings within living memory. All three are borrowings from either French or Latin. Each has a meaning that is not accepted by everybody in contemporary English society; though this need not surprise us, since speech-communities are never truly homogeneous, and there is no reason to believe they ever were. What is more, each has been cause for overt comment from people who object to certain meanings; and this shows that changes of meaning are in general more consciously felt than changes in grammar or pronunciation.

Our first example is the well-known case of *sophisticated*. A borrowing from Latin, the word is first recorded in English in the form of the verb *sophisticate* during the fifteenth century. Letters to the press, especially in the 1960s, often complained that the word had come to be used to describe technologically advanced weapons or other devices, with the sense 'elaborate' or 'highly refined'. This use of the word, associated sometimes with certain groups, such as broadcasters, or scientific and military commentators, was at variance with the so-called definitions of the word's meaning in the *OED*, which lists 'adulterated', 'artificial', or 'falsified'. Such complaints show how misleading a dictionary can be: the meanings it lists do not seem to square with the ways in which the word is most commonly used. (The most recent meanings are actually recorded in the *OED* Supplement.) When we inspect the kinds of words with which *sophisticated* collocates, and the kinds of people who use the new meanings, we can begin to see how changes in meaning are brought about. We shall find above all that these depend on whether *sophisticated* collocates with words having inanimate referents (where the meanings already discussed are appropriate) or human ones (where it has the contemporary meanings 'urbane', 'worldly-wise', or 'refined'). In this respect, it is rather like *dear*, as we saw from our discussion of reflected meaning. In its earliest usage, *sophisticated* clearly had an evaluative meaning, implying disapproval, and its use seems to have been limited to the description of inanimate things: if you sophisticated wine, you adulterated it, and if Art, or pleasures, were sophisticated, all primitive simplicity and naturalness were taken out of them. In all probability it was a word more appropriate to written than spoken discourse. Gradually, the connotations of the word changed, as it was used in a widening range of contexts by different groups of users. What is natural and pure to some, is to others naive and ingenuous, and such new connotations affected the word's conceptual meaning by the time it was applied, at the end of the nineteenth century, to people. The word has now lost its disapproving sense, and is used in popular speech to mean 'refined'; and when the word is re-applied to objects, it denotes those things that appeal to people of taste and experience. It is thus only a short step to the sense of 'technically advanced' in the usage of certain groups of specialists. And today, taking our cue from this latest application of the word, we speak of sophisticated cameras, tape recorders, stereo equipment, and so on.

In many histories of English, *sophisticated* is cited as an example of the process of *amelioration*, a type of semantic change in which a word originally denoting disapproval is given either a neutral or even a favourable meaning by its users. The use of terms such as this, though they may highlight dramatic shifts in meaning, not only obscures the complex and subtle pattern of interaction among varieties of the language, written versus spoken, technical versus everyday, but also the variations in connotation at a given time. For today, many educated speakers of English may try to monitor their use of *sophisticated* by restricting its use to descriptions of people; and even then many groups of people may acknowledge the meaning 'urbane' without necessarily upholding the values associated with this meaning. In other words, it can be used in a rather tongue-in-cheek way.

One word with which *sophisticated* patterned, in its early sense, was *vulgar*. Here, the relationship was one of contrast: *sophisticated* meant 'artificial', *vulgar* 'ordinary', 'everyday'. Deriving from the Latin *vulgus* (the common people: hence Vulgar Latin), *vulgar*, like *sophisticated*, originally collocated with words denoting inanimate referents; but by the sixteenth century it was being applied to people. By the mid-seventeenth century, it had developed its modern meaning, 'coarse', by a process known as *pejoration*, in which a word acquires a negative evaluation − the reverse of amelioration. If what was ordinary had become coarse, then what was adulterated could be refined; so that the development of new meanings in both words could have been mutually influential. We shall see later how words similar in meaning to *vulgar* have followed a similar semantic development.

Educated speakers today may also balk at using our second example, *chronic* in its recent sense of 'bad' or 'awful'. The word was borrowed in the course of the seventeenth century from Latin *chronicus* (reinforced by the French form of the same word) in the sense 'relating to time'; but the most usual meaning was that associated with the field of medicine in late Latin, where the word meant 'persistent', in contrast to 'acute'. By the nineteenth century this technical application of the word had loosened, and we find wars and doubts defined as chronic. The shift to its present meaning, however, probably comes from popular use. People were most likely to hear the word in medical contexts, as in 'he's got chronic bronchitis', and gradually the word acquired evaluative connotations: persistent bronchitis is unpleasant. What starts as a connotation becomes, in time, criterial; and now, in the sense of 'bad', it can collocate with a wide range of words — teachers, holidays, cars, can be chronic. In this meaning, it is used affectively: it conveys first and foremost information about the speaker's attitude, and has thus become a handy word to fill the evaluative slots discussed above. Also, an important part of the word's meaning is, as we have said, also stylistic; this now belongs to informal spoken usage. The *OED* Supplement records the new meaning from the very end of the last century, describing it as 'vulgar', not, it should be added, in the sense of 'coarse', but in the older meaning — though it is difficult for the modern reader not to feel the disapproving sense *reflected* in this use of the word!

Our third example is a word whose recent semantic development is of a less organic, and more consciously manipulative kind than those of the two cases already discussed. With *gay*, in the recent sense of 'homosexual', we are dealing with a word where a specific group-consciousness is involved, and where a very deliberate concern with language is manifested. A fourteenth-century borrowing from French, the word has retained the meaning 'merry', 'jolly', 'light-hearted' from that time, but by the seventeenth century an additional meaning had developed. Light-heartedness could also be interpreted as frivolity, lack of seriousness, or even hedonism. The meaning 'addicted to social pleasures' developed, and the word came to be used euphemistically, of people who lived immoral and dissipated lives. Its downward path continued into the nineteenth century: in slang usage, a gay woman was a whore. And by the first third of the present century, a gay man, in slang, was 'homosexual'. The last few decades have seen the attempt by homosexuals to get the word accepted as a standard term of reference, now that the earlier associations with immorality and prostitution have been forgotten.

Groups who occupy a subordinate or oppressed position in society invariably suffer from linguistic disparagement. Homosexuality is regarded as deviant behaviour, and is often referred to in abusive terms (like *bent* and *queer*), just as women and Black people find themselves at the receiving end of a rich vocabulary range, at best patronising, at worst offensive. Sometimes these words are wielded innocently, in that some people are genuinely unaware of their pejorative meaning; but more often than not they are used as conscious symbols of an attitude. And, just as politically-conscious Black people have struggled to promote words like *Black* at the expense of *nigger* or *coon*, so *gay* has become instrumental in the cause of homosexual equality; moreover, people who support such causes are expected to use these terms, since the use of the traditional terms is an index of a social stance. Thus, on a range of sensitive social and political issues we have to choose our vocabulary with care, and cultivate a conscious, highly self-critical attitude to the issue of words and meanings.

The heightened awareness of language exhibited by such groups as gays and feminists is the intelligent response of the exploited or the powerless. It stems above all from the recognition that language has a vital part to play in the exercise and consolidation of power. Not unnaturally, the powerful in society have long recognised this. It is a matter of everyday experience that in political discourse meanings are manipulated and words chosen to load the dice in favour of one point of view. Evaluative connotations of words like *democratic* are cultivated at the expense of their conceptual meaning, so that a word denoting particular kinds of political organisation becomes what we might call a 'purr' word, used merely to win approval for a particular position. The word *moderate*, connotatively favourable but referentially vague when applied to politics, has been widely used to enlist support for people whose political views are often fundamentally conservative.

Key-words

If certain words are emblematic of particular social stances, other words act as keys to whole systems of belief. Students of medieval English literature need to learn that the thirteenth-century French borrowing *cortaysye* cannot be translated by its modern form *courtesy*; more than just politeness and respect are involved, since for poets and audience the word was a central element in the conceptual edifice of chivalry. Similarly, we need to recognise the theological assumptions underlying the use of *grace*, *mercy*, and *nature* – again, all medieval borrowings from French – in the plays of Shakespeare. These words reflect critical social, political, and ethical concerns, but we must beware of assuming that particular systems of belief were always accepted by all groups in society. There can be little question that at all times a *dominant* set of beliefs existed; but at times certain groups articulate different values, and evolve their own vocabulary, or their set of meanings for common words, to express them. The meaning of *nature*, for instance, has been adapted in the course of over 500 years to suit various ideologies. Its fourteenth-century meaning, 'inherent force directing the world, or the human race, or both' was fluid enough to permit significant variations of focus. By the early eighteenth century, the word referred to the material world, and part of that included the world of people: their way of doing things. Thus, a set of social relations could be legitimised by appealing to the notion that it was 'natural'. By the late eighteenth century, however, nature had become the state of original innocence before human beings had created imperfection. These essentially static conceptions of nature were challenged in the nineteenth century by the post-Darwinian focus on the competitive and destructive aspects of nature as an inherent force; and again, certain types of human behaviour and organisation could be justified by citing what happens 'in nature'. As contemporary arguments about 'human nature' show, you can almost make the word mean whatever you like.

It is clear that in the past words were manipulated by their users just as they are today. And in so far as words emblematic of certain values are handed down through the generations, it is arguable that the vocabulary we learn conditions or even determines our thoughts on various subjects. Earlier in this chapter we noted how some languages, or some varieties within a language, had richer vocabularies with respect to certain fields of thought or activity, and it is often claimed that differences of this kind lead to differences of perception: where the gardener sees weeds, the botanist, or American Indian, sees a variety of interesting or potentially useful plants. A bolder articulation of this idea was that advanced by the American anthropological-linguist Benjamin Lee Whorf, who, influenced by his teacher Edward Sapir, suggested that different languages structured the perceptions and thoughts of their users in very different ways. By comparing languages like English with some of those spoken by American Indians, Whorf concluded that there existed very different notions of time in the different speech-communities, notions based on differences of grammatical structure. English, for instance, could 'objectify' time by permitting such constructions as *they stayed ten days*, in which a day is treated as a discrete entity, like a man or a chair; whereas Hopi, an Indian language, handled time as a continuum. Language, then, as viewed by Whorf is a kind of perceptual strait-jacket: we are at the mercy of the inherited vocabulary and grammar of our mother tongue.

The Sapir-Whorf Hypothesis seems to ignore the fact that languages are not homogeneous, and that they are subject to change. It seems more fruitful, therefore, to concentrate on how our thoughts and responses are shaped by particular users of our language, since we know that various kinds of propaganda will not work unless they can exploit the fact that much of our thinking is habitual and unreflecting. In this way, we may be able to see more clearly how some words change their meanings.

The vocabulary of power, rank, and status

The proposition that different social groups may use words differently extends to the words used for the social groups themselves. As we have said, such words are particularly sensitive to the development of pejorative or affective meanings. It is therefore instructive to explore some aspects of the vocabulary of rank and status: how reference is made to the social hierarchy, and how people of different status address each other. We shall suggest three major trends in the history of the words chosen. First, terms originally denotative of rank often become evaluative; second, those denoting the more powerful groups are most likely to retain their status as rank-terms; and third, there are interesting changes in the possibilities of using these words in direct address.

While the relationship among these status and rank terms, being based on a hierarchy of power in society, are clear, they are more fluid than those of more highly structured hierarchies, such as the army. The army has evolved a *set* of mutually exclusive terms, the individual meaning of which depends entirely on an understanding of the meaning of the others: thus, we can only know what *captain* means if we understand its relation to *major*, *lieutenant*, and *corporal*, and so on. Social relations are in general, however, less static, so the meanings of their terminology are more susceptible to change; but we must beware of assuming that any change in meaning automatically accompanies, or signals, a change in social structure. The relationships between the words and the things they signify are more complex than that, as we shall see. The Anglo-Saxon system of rank-terms was largely re-structured after the Norman Conquest. *Cyning* and *cwen* (king and queen), *hlafweard* and *hlaefdige* (lord and lady – the former being a warden of loaves, the latter a kneader of them) survive, in senses known to the Anglo-Saxons; but other terms were pushed into new meanings by the introduction from French of *duke, prince, squire, villain*, etc. The Anglo-Saxons used *aldormann* to denote a man responsible to the king for administrating a large territory, *þegn* (modern 'thane' or 'thegn'), a lesser landowner, and *ceorl* (churl) to denote the lowest rank of freeman. Another word was *eorl*, which denoted high status in general, and which, like *þegn*, was used in poetic texts in the sense of 'warrior'. In the period of Viking power, the meaning of *eorl* was influenced by the related Scandinavian word *jarl*, which had a similar meaning to *aldormann*; and the word has survived the Norman Conquest in this later sense. *Aldormann* has become specialised, in terms of municipal power and status, while *þegn* has been superseded by the French *baron*, and interestingly enough by the Anglo-Saxon term *cniht*. Originally *cniht* was not a rank term, but denoted a boy or lad; inferiority in age gave way to inferiority of status, and the word came to mean a servant. But there are different kinds of servant: a king's servant had to be of noble blood, and the word was specialised to the kinds of meaning hitherto represented by *þegn*.

The meanings of words denoting low social status seem to have been affected by further borrowings from French. One of these, *gentle*, had already acquired an evaluation of approval by the time it was borrowed into English in the thirteenth century. Originally it had meant 'highborn', but its meaning widened to include those characteristics felt by the high-born to be appropriate to their social position. If *gentle* – something of a key-word in the history of English – denoted good breeding and gracious behaviour, then words like *churl* could be associated with coarseness. By about 1300, *churl* had lost its technical sense as a term of rank, and indicated low breeding in general; from that point, connotations of 'rudeness' gradually became criterial. Interestingly enough, the French borrowing *villein* dropped even further. By 1300 again, its primary meaning was 'base'; from there it is only a short step to the present wholly pejorative meaning of 'villain'. While both these words have become pejorised, a later borrowing, *peasant*, has retained its early meaning, 'one who works the land', as well as a later pejorative one. By the end of the sixteenth century we find it used affectively — almost as a 'snarl' word — in Elizabethan drama, notably in Marlowe's *Edward II*.

In the examples cited, the criteria relating word to referent have shifted from the functional to the evaluative. It is difficult not to interpret this development as the projection of attitudes that are upper-class on to the words. To put it another way, the connotations that become criterial originate with the socially powerful: the dominant class imposes the dominant connotations. We see this process at work among words that were not associated with rank, like *vulgar, common, illiterate*, and *lewd*. The last two examples show the high social value that has come to be placed on literacy and learning. *Illiterate* is now a rough synonym for 'stupid', and the meaning of *lewd* has changed dramatically over the last thousand years. Originally meaning 'lay' at a time when learning and the Church were virtually synonymous, it could also mean 'unlearned'. By the seventeenth century it was applied to those of low social status, implying that by that time learning was associated with class. By about 1700 it meant 'worthless' of objects, 'unprincipled' of people; and from the latter meaning, a special kind of unprincipledness became criterial, that relating to sexual conduct. Hence the meaning 'lecherous'.

A more complex pattern of class attitudes has affected the history of *bourgeois*. As a word that has not been thoroughly assimilated into English from French, *bourgeois* is an excellent example of a word whose meaning depends on the loyalties of its users. This is partly because, like *exploitation*, and so on, it forms part of the technical vocabulary of Marxist thought, and has therefore acquired a certain stylistic meaning. For this reason many people avoid using it. On the other hand, it is used today, in a more affective sense, by groups such as students, who see it as a term exemplifying certain tastes and types of behaviour which are 'respectable'. The fortunes of the word have depended on the attitudes of the classes in the social hierarchy above and below the bourgeoisie. Its thirteenth-century Anglicised form *burgess* (town-dweller, enjoying full municipal rights) points to its association with the mercantile town, and this meaning remains in the background, as it were, of the re-borrowed form *bourgeois*, which retains more of the phonetic characteristics of its source. Originally *bourgeois* in French was rather like a rank term: it denoted, for instance, residence of long standing. Associated by the eighteenth century with the commercial class, especially those able to live off invested income, the term came to be used contemptuously by the class above, the landed aristocracy. The evaluative meaning arose because the characteristics of the mercantile class — solidity, stability, sobriety — were perceived as being small-minded, narrow, and complacent by the upper class. The same attitude came to be shared by artists, writers, and some intellectuals who derided the 'respectability' and 'safe' views of the bourgeoisie. But the *technical* sense of the word, as used by Marx, arose from a recognition of the dominance of the bourgeoisie in society: they were the employing class, the group who controlled capital, in whose factories things were manufactured. These roles and functions gave them definite ideas about society and their place within it, and, according to Marx, it is they who have been able to present their own values and ideology as given, universal, immutable, and necessary.

Elizabethan terms of address

If we follow the fortunes of *gentle* into the sixteenth century, we find that it acquires, in the compound *gentleman*, a considerable social significance. It has been considered the most important rank term in use at this time, since it differentiated the privileged and unprivileged. By the sixteenth century, however, the sources of privilege were changing. Power and status could increasingly be achieved through education or entrepreneurialism: hence *gentle* could in principle be extended to people whose status no longer derived from its traditional source, the ownership of land. By the 1580s a *gentleman* could be someone who was able to live comfortably without having to 'engage in trade'. And since then, of course, it has lost its function as a term of rank and become a polite word for any kind of man.

It seems that the Elizabethans were particularly sensitive to the issue of rank and status. If a social hierarchy is *felt* to be changing, people will become uncertain about who is entitled to be called a *gentleman*. The same can be said for the word *master*, another class-defining term, which was widening its range of application at the same time. It may be this uncertainty that underlay the Elizabethan fondness for using terms of address. It has been concluded from a survey of such usage in Shakespeare's Falstaff plays that in about 1600 people liked to 'place' each other in the social hierarchy when they were conversing in the more formal contexts. Thus, titles, occupational terms like *parson* or *cook*, generic terms like *man*, *woman*, and *gentleman*, even terms of relationship like *husband* and *wife* (used freely between spouses on good terms) were frequently used in direct address; and if none of these was appropriate or available, a vague word like *neighbour* was even used. Condescension, even open insult, could be indicated by the deliberate use of terms inappropriate to the status of an addressee. The Germanic word *fellow* used to mean, literally, one who lays down money (*fee*), thus a partner in business; by the fourteenth century, as a term of address it implied polite condescension; and in Shakespearean address its use is an insult to anyone not greatly inferior in social status. Similarly, *goodman* denoted in its early sense the master of an establishment: as *gentleman* expanded down the social scale, it pushed *goodman* with it, so that by the seventeenth century it could be a term of abuse. In *Measure for Measure*, Lucio addresses the Duke, in his disguise as a Friar, as 'goodman baldpate'. So that we can see that new meanings may develop as words are used, in face-to-face interaction, as terms of address.

This aspect of Elizabethan speech-behaviour contrasts in certain ways with usage today. Many people now limit their terms of address to the Title + Last Name pattern (indicating a respectful, neutral distance), and reserve *sir* or *madam* to mark greater politeness, Christian names or terms of endearment like *darling* or *sweetheart* to mark intimacy, nicknames or generic terms like *mate* to mark solidarity. While our usage depends to a certain extent on social class and group loyalties, it is possible to make some generalisations: for the Elizabethans, greater intimacy was required before 'first-naming' was possible. There was greater fluctuation between the use of first names and surnames, and men could be freely addressed with both.

There is another way in which our language of address contrasts with that of four centuries ago. The Elizabethan habit of referring to social status in their mode of address is similar to that of some modern Europeans. Power relationships in the sixteenth century could be marked by a choice in the grammar, involving the pronouns *thou* and *you*: you could say *thou* to a subordinate, and expect a polite *you* in return, a choice still found in many European languages which have retained the two second person pronouns. As we shall see in the next chapter, this system has given way to one based on mutual respect where one pronoun, *you*, is used reciprocally. What is interesting is that it is the pronoun of neutral distance that becomes generalised, like the Title +

Last Name pattern among the terms of address. More interesting, however, is the fact that at the same time as the Elizabethans were showing
such concern about naming in direct address they were beginning to dis-
card the traditional use of second person pronouns. We shall explore
this matter in the next chapter.

The semantic disparagement of women

Power relationships do not of course necessarily involve social stratification. Adults have generally exercised power over minors, and women
have been controlled by men, in ways that cut across class boundaries.
Male power, and male attitudes, therefore, are reflected in the ways in
which women are talked about. Men have developed a rich vocabulary
of affective words which denigrate women who do not conform to a
male ideal; and there has been a constant tendency to develop new
meanings denoting the availability of women as sex objects. It has been
estimated that there are over 1000 words which in their history have
denoted women and have also meant 'whore'.

   Words which classify women by age tend to reflect the male predilection for the younger, sexually attractive female. Unfortunately,
many of these words are not recorded in early varieties of English, so
that it is often difficult to trace their history. *Hag* is rare before the sixteenth century, but is probably related to an Anglo-Saxon word for
witch; from the fourteenth century, it meant a repulsive old woman,
and this pejorative sense survives. *Crone* may derive from a Norman-
French word for a cantankerous woman (from the fourteenth century
it has meant 'withered old woman', and suchlike), but it could also
come from a Germanic word for an old ewe — a sense in which it is
used between the sixteenth and nineteenth centuries. Either way,
women are hardly flattered. If old age is unforgivable in a woman, ugli-
ness or slovenliness invites further ridicule. *Drab*, a possible loan from
Irish Gaelic, is recorded in the sense 'ugly woman' in 1515, and *slut*,
deriving perhaps from Scandinavian, means a dirty one from the fifteenth century. Some words denoting young women had at first no
sexual connotations, but they were not slow to develop them. *Doll*,
originally a pet name for Dorothy, was used in the sixteenth century as
a generic pet name for a mistress; and *mynx*, deriving perhaps from
minickin, a word for a pet, came to mean a young girl, and later a
wanton one.

A great many of these words developed the meaning of 'whore' at some stage in their history. The same is true of many other endearment terms, such as *sweetmeat* and *Kitty*, occupational terms like *nun*, *spinster*, even *laundress*; and kinship terms, such as *aunt* and *cousin*. But this process of semantic 'disparagement' does not necessarily mean that men have always regarded women of all kinds as little more than objects to be bought for self-gratification. Sexual relations among men and women have often depended on the brothel. Although even the most powerful in the land might indulge in it, whoring was socially taboo; and like all taboo subjects it generated a proliferation of terms, many of them euphemistic. In the covert patronage of prostitutes, it was necessary to keep the flow of terms going; hence even words like *nun* and *laundress* found themselves used in this sense.

We shall end this chapter by considering a word which may show the influence of male attitudes in a more complex and subtle way. The meanings of *buxom* have changed dramatically over the last 800 years. Today its meaning unites two separate properties; one associated with physical appearance, of 'plump comeliness', even voluptuousness; the other involving mental attributes, 'jolliness', 'openness', perhaps 'sexual uninhibitedness'. Today, the word is used only to refer to women, and even then it collocates with a very restricted range of words – like *barmaid*, *wench*, *lass* – which lend it a stylistic flavour that is mock-poetic or even archaic. When we look back at how the word has been used in the past, however, we find that there were far fewer restrictions on the kinds of word it could modify: men, and also inanimate objects like air, can be buxom. Like *sophisticated*, then, the change in meaning is closely linked to changes in the kinds of words with which it could co-occur. In its earliest recorded uses the word meant obedient, in the moral sense, and this meaning remained fairly constant from the twelfth century until the nineteenth. (Originally it may have meant something like 'ready to bow', as its elements were *bow* + *some*, as in *handsome*, *winsome*, etc.) Out of this core meaning other related senses developed: 'submissive' by about 1300, then in the course of the fourteenth century 'gracious' or 'kindly'. Until about the middle of the sixteenth century, then, to be buxom meant to be generally well-disposed and tractable; and we find by the end of that century a new set of connotations developing, related to the old, but gradually replacing them. Throughout the seventeenth century the word could be used in the sense of 'physically obedient', or 'pliant', and we begin to see the origins of the modern sense of the word as it is used in relation to women. At the same time as 'physically pliant', the old sense of 'kindly' was extended, so that from the sixteenth to the nineteenth centuries it also meant 'blithe', 'lively'; and this gives us the second dimension in the meaning of the word at present. The sense 'blithe' was re-applied, as it were, in the physical dimension: the physical counterpart of 'jolliness' was 'comeliness', 'healthy well-favouredness', and we find the word used in this sense from the end of the sixteenth century until the present day, with the use of *buxom* gradually limiting itself only to women from the nineteenth century (influenced, perhaps, by *bust*). It is difficult not to see the projection of masculine attitudes towards women embodied in this example of semantic change. Men, it seems, have wanted women who are sexually submissive, and if possible comely and well-favoured too.

Chapter four
Grammar

There are probably more misconceptions about the term 'grammar' than any other term in the popular vocabulary of linguistics. Disseminated in classrooms, and therefore widely believed throughout society, these misconceptions tend to identify grammar with a certain kind of book which has been written about a language; more specifically, about the *standard* variety of a language, in its written manifestation. In this chapter, we shall examine the nature and the source of some of these notions, and show how inadequate they are to describe either the variation in a language at any given time, or the process of grammatical change. We shall need to look at some basic categories of grammatical description, and subject to scrutiny some common misunderstandings about the nature of rules in grammar. Aspects of the grammar of the Anglo-Saxons will be discussed, in particular its reliance on a system of endings known as inflexions; and we shall see how these inflexions can be said to have been simplified in the course of centuries. This process of grammatical simplification will be examined in the light of sociolinguistic variables, such as pidginisation. The agency of social factors will be clearly seen as we describe changes in the system of pronouns, and we shall see the importance of linguistic variation for describing the trend towards syntactic elaboration. Finally, we shall ask how the grammar of written English has acquired not only great prestige, but also a reputation for cognitive superiority.

Grammatical change is often less consciously felt than the adoption of new words or the creation of new meanings. Thus, it is difficult to isolate and describe changes that have been recently introduced into English. Yet when we stand back and view the changes that have occurred during the last 1500 years, we see developments of a particularly striking kind. The grammar that the Anglo-Saxons used seems to have been a radically different kind of grammar from the one we use today (subject to the qualifications we shall note below). It has been suggested that this difference entitles us to classify Anglo-Saxon English and the English of today as languages of quite distinct types. In making sweeping comparisons of this kind, however, it is as well to remember that Anglo-Saxon English was no more monolithic than the language we use today. Though the dimensions of variability may have been fewer, Anglo-Saxon grammar had its own variations, associated with region, the difference between speech and writing, emphatic and unemphatic language, and formal and informal usage. We shall see the importance of these variations in the course of this chapter, and in particular, the process by which new variants come to be associated with certain social groups, and hence acquire either prestige or stigma.

In recent years the emphasis of linguistics has been less on the social aspects of grammar and more on its psychological implications. Grammar has been seen as the crucial level of linguistic structure. Many linguists have been absorbed by the process of language acquisition, the apparently effortless and highly efficient way in which people learn their first language from a very early age. While we cannot do justice here to this recent and important tradition of inquiry, we can abstract one of its most important precepts. By about the age of five, we have mentally internalised an immensely complex system of grammatical rules. The essential feature of these rules is that they are creative: they enable us to make up new sentences. From a social point of view, our attitude to these rules is revealing. We do not regard them as rules, since we have been educated to think that grammatical rules are something formulated by people who know better than we do, who incorporate them in grammar books, rather than part of our birthright. Thus, our treatment of our grammatical knowledge is much like our attitude to words discussed in the last chapter. We apply our internalised system of grammatical rules unreflectingly and unconsciously; and just as words change shape and meaning in new environments and contexts, so we constantly adapt and extend our grammatical patterns as similarities with other patterns and forms are perceived. In many traditional histories of English, grammatical change is very often explained by reference to such a process of analogy: a vague term, but one which reminds us that human language is creative, in that we are constantly re-structuring and expanding our grammatical knowledge by the ceaseless process of making connections.

Some misconceptions about grammar

We can find at least five ways in which the word *grammar* is used to give a misleading idea of the nature of this part of language structure.

One of these is the notion mentioned above, that some people are supposed to 'know' the grammar of the language, while others do not. A
second is that grammar is something which belongs to the written language, but not to the spoken. Third, there is the somewhat archaic use
of the term to refer to a book, a written account of a language's grammar; so that someone might say 'lend me your grammar'. Fourth,
grammar is something that can be either 'good' or 'bad'. And finally,
grammar is something which some languages have more of than others;
people say that language x has more grammar than language y.

These misconceptions stem from the view of language held by the
people who began to codify English grammar during the eighteenth century. To a large extent, our whole perception of grammar has been dis-
torted by their work. Many people have been left with the impression
that the grammar of the language they speak is the preserve, even the
invention, of a small group of scholars. From this, the whole idea of
what constitutes a grammatical rule has been perverted: for many
people, such rules consist of do's and don't's, such as the prescription
that 'whom did you see' is more correct than 'who did you see'. In
other words, the notion of a grammatical rule has been taken in its prescriptive sense — it tells you what you should or should not say. But as
we have already seen in chapter two, such prescriptive rules were formulated, unsystematically and often arbitrarily, with respect to the
structure of Latin, to the written mode, in its formal tenor. The rules,
then, apply to only a small part of our linguistic repertoire, and not
even the most important part. And many of us do not obey the rules
even in formal written style: they are too redolent of pedantry, and
irrelevant fussiness.

It seems hardly worth saying that the rules of prescriptive grammar
are repeatedly broken in casual, informal speech. What we need to do is
redefine the notion of grammatical rules, to cover the patterns that in a
variety of contexts we actually produce. Such rules must be descriptive
ones, capable of explaining, for instance, why 'book the your liked
father' is not an acceptable sequence in any variety of modern English.
The explanation here would involve principles of word-order; but because as speakers of English we apply rules of this kind so efficiently
and unconsciously, we are not aware of them as rules. The irrelevance
of prescriptive rules in accounting for basic structural patterns in English can be readily seen when we examine the kinds of mistakes that are
made by foreign learners of the language. How do we explain, for instance, that *are you hearing*? is in general a less acceptable structure in

contemporary English than *do you hear?* or *can you hear?* And what about the order of the words in *his nice new leather jacket?* Is any other word-order possible? If not, how do we formulate the rule? From the above discussion, then, it should be clear that we are using the term rule in the sense of a 'pattern', of a structuring principle that we conventionally use without being aware of it. The rules will vary (at least with respect to surface patterning) according to the tenor of the situation, the dialect of the speaker, and the field of discourse; the rules for newspaper-reporting will differ from those of recipe-writing. And in general, the rules for spoken English will often be different from those of writing. Unfortunately, the association of grammar with the written mode has meant that we often judge speech against writing, and not surprisingly we find the former wanting. Our impressions of the matter are confirmed when we confront transcripts of tape-recorded speech. The following is an extract from an informal conversation between university graduates:

> We – I wanted to – er – you know – go on a bit further but well the – there were six – seven of us I – wait a minute – no – I – well anyway when – my chain broke a bit later – we were going down this hill this really steep hill. . . .

On paper this looks garbled and formless, but it would not necessarily appear so if we were to hear it. This is because we organise our spoken utterances in association with a battery of devices that have no matching counterparts in writing. We use, most importantly, a system of *intonation*; this is the set of 'tunes' into which we embed our every utterance, to distinguish some kinds of questions from statements, and to signal uncertainty, sarcasm, anger, disbelief, and many other kinds of meaning. Intonation, stress, pitch, and tempo are all integrated into the spoken mode, as are the many paralinguistic and extralinguistic features that accompany our speech; we use our eyes and heads, we gesture with our hands, change our voice-quality. In short, conversation involves the whole of our bodies, and is a form of physical behaviour, and thus totally distinct from writing.

In describing the grammar of speech, then, we must take account of the features outlined above, just as in the description of writing we must consider punctuation and the special grammatical devices for achieving emphasis, like inversions of normal word-order. We have said above that we are more used to thinking of grammar in connection with written texts: but the more we examine the wide range of texts that we are quite capable of reading and understanding in the course of everyday life, the less useful the prescriptive rules seem to be. For instance, a recent advertisement has the following structure:

The crisp new look of glistening aluminium frames around big bright windows!

This is not school-English: it contains no verb, and for many it would therefore be incorrect. Such verbless sentences are very common in advertising English, however, so that school-grammar is perhaps not the best tool with which to analyse it. If we continue to view specimens of contemporary English through prescriptive spectacles we often miss the most interesting and innovatory features of particular varieties. While advertising English tries to capture the spirit of informal conversation in its use of verbless sentences, it also innovates by casting words in new roles: as in *the NOW cigarette*, where 'now' is used as an adjective. At the other extreme, the respected, even revered, language of prayer has a different kind of grammar. In this opening, written to be spoken aloud:

Almighty God, our Heavenly Father, who of thy tender mercy didst give thine only Son Jesus Christ . . .

we find not only the preservation of a pattern common in the early seventeenth century in *didst give*, but the only use in English of a *who* clause directly after a noun in direct address, *God*.

So far, we have tried to expose the first two fallacies about grammar on our list, by referring to their origins. We can deal with the next two in a similar way, by remembering that it was the standard variety to which the Latinising, logic-orientated rules of the codifiers were applied. Thus, for many people today the notion of grammatical rules only exists in relation to the standard. Rules of grammar are to be found in books about standard English; therefore it is this variety that possesses grammar. From this point it is only a short step to the notion of grammar as a book, to be kept in your desk at school. Whatever is not in the book, moreover, must be ungrammatical: and this will include all varieties of non-standard English. Since grammar came to be evaluated, what was ungrammatical must be incorrect, or bad; so that if you spoke a dialect, you spoke ungrammatically, therefore badly, and deserved to be corrected. Once again, we see that the full range of variation in English is not taken into account in popular notions about grammatical rules, in that regional speech is felt to be synonymous with bad grammar.

What was said earlier in this chapter about different varieties of English having their own grammars must apply, of course, to the regional dialects. Unfortunately, the notion that dialects have their own grammars, which their speakers unconsciously apply when they talk to each other, has been the preserve of only a small group of language scholars, the philologists and dialectologists, and only for little more than a century. Rather than formulate rules such as '*I am* is standard: *I be* is south-western dialect', the eighteenth-century codifiers either ignored regionalisms, or listed them as traps to avoid. But while their prescriptions are widely acknowledged, many people persist in using the stigmatised forms and patterns. Some of these, like the cumulative negative construction *I don't know nothing*, are probably used at times by a majority of people in England. Also very common are the use of *them* as a demonstrative (as in *them books*), differences in present and past tense forms of verbs (*he do, he done it*), the pattern in reflexive pronouns (*he's washing hisself*), the form of certain adverbs (*he ran slow*), and the plurals of nouns after numerals (*three mile*). All these examples, many of which will be discussed in the course of this chapter, either preserve patterns which were once more common than they are now, as in the case of the prayer discussed above, or are representative of tendencies towards grammatical change that are very common in the history of English.

Some categories of grammatical description

The word *grammar* is also used, of course, by linguists, in their attempts to analyse the structures we hear and see around us. To put it simply, grammar for linguists is the level of their analysis of linguistic structure which concerns the organisation of words into sentences. If we are to understand how language works, and how it changes, we must devise some basic categories for grammatical description.

The advertisement for aluminium window frames from which the extract above was taken, contains elsewhere the simple structure *our own experts handle the installation*. Using this sequence as a pattern for our description, we find a group of words in subject position, *our own experts*, consisting of a noun, *experts*, in head-position, preceded by a possessive pronoun, *our*, and adjective *own*. The rest of the sentence is the predicate, and this part must contain the verb, *handle*. The remainder of the predicate, *the installation*, consists of a group of words like that in the subject-position, where *installation* is the noun in head-position, and *the* is an article; here, though, the noun-group is called the object of the verb, so we have the familiar subject-verb-object sequence. We can summarise the structure as shown in Figure 4.1.

Figure 4.1   Structure of subject-verb-object sequence

Subject			Predicate		
noun-group			verb	noun-group	
our	*own*	*experts*	*handle*	*the*	*installation*
(possessive)	(adjective)	(noun)	(verb)	(article)	(noun)

The first point we need to make in connection with this structure concerns the order of the words: can they be re-arranged, without adding or subtracting anything, to form an equally acceptable sentence in English? If not, then we must conclude that word-order in this sentence is rigid; and, as we shall see, it is a feature of the history of English grammar that the constraints in the system on the ordering of words have become less flexible over the centuries. This aspect of our grammatical system, that of the sequencing of elements, is known as syntax.

We have also just said that two words in our sentence, *experts* and *installation*, are nouns; and the grammarian will be interested in the fact that the form of the two nouns is different, in that the former has the -*s* plural marker. This is the commonest way of marking the plural in English, although as we shall see, there were many other patterns available when the language was first spoken in these islands. Grammarians refer to this aspect of grammar — the altering of a word's 'shape' to signal its function — as morphology. Although it is essential to make this distinction between syntax and morphology, we shall find in practice that it is not always easy to discuss one without referring to the other.

It is often convenient, however, to deal separately with those structures associated with the noun — in other words, the noun-groups — and those associated with the verb. How, for instance, do the other words pattern with the head of the noun-group? Is it that the head is premodified by words such as articles and adjectives, as in our example, or can we describe it as being post-modified, by the use of structures beginning with prepositions like *in*, *with*, or relative pronouns like *who*, etc.? Immediately we investigate this area of grammar we see the importance of linguistic variation, particularly the differences between the grammar of speech and writing. A characteristic of many types of written English, for instance, is the so-called heavy pre-modification. Examples from scientific and technical writing abound, such as *Boeing 747 leading edge flap failure alarm mechanism*, where the last word is the head-noun. But we also find that newspaper headlines and written advertisements have developed their own characteristic patterns of pre-modification. Such compact language, however, is far less common in casual conversation: for one thing, it is too dense for the ear to process. When it does occur, adjectives are often unremarkable and sequences stereotyped, as in *all those nice little primary schoolchildren*. But in certain types of spoken English, such as the sports commentary, audience familiarity with basic technical terms can lead to structures that are almost as weightily pre-modified as post-modified. The reader can try to find the head-noun in subject position in *that running forehand topspin passing shot at full stretch down the line over the high part of the net gives him match point*.

We can make one further point about the subject head in our model sentence. As a noun, *experts* could be substituted by another word if it had already been established that experts were being discussed. We could say *they handle*, where *they* is called a pronoun. Pronouns, like articles and prepositions, are sometimes referred to as grammatical words; they constitute a relatively fixed part of our vocabulary that is less amenable to the kind of semantic description undertaken in the last chapter. Such words, especially pronouns, will accordingly be dealt with here as the occasion arises.

When we analyse verb-groups, the interdependence of morphology and syntax becomes clear. Of great interest are the forms and structures associated with tense. With regard to morphology, an immediate point to be made is that if we were to substitute in our model sentence a singular form of the noun in subject-position (i.e. *expert*), the form of the verb itself would change to *handles*. This addition of -*s* to the verb form marks the agreement of subject and verb: both the *handle* and *handles* forms of the verb mark it as present tense. The system of tense in contemporary English is very complex, and we can only do it scant justice here, but the following paragraphs will make some of the important points.

It is often said that our tense-system comprises two parts, present and past. The most common way of marking a past tense lies in the addition of an -ed ending, or inflexion, so that the past tense form of the verb in our sentence would be *handled*. Some verbs, however, form their past tense by changing the vowel in the stem. If the verb had been *break*, the past tense form would have been *broke*. Verbs of this kind, few in number but frequently occurring in most varieties of English, are known as strong verbs. Speakers of English have treated more and more of these verbs over the centuries as weak ones, which means that the ending -ed has been added to the base form of the verb, rather than changing the vowel. In other words, -ed has been interpreted as the ending that is productive, just as -s has become the common marker of plurality, and we can notice how young children, when they are first picking up English as their first language, produce forms like *goed* instead of *went* because they have made a generalisation about -ed as the invariant past-tense marker.

This brief account provides us with a broad base on which more complex verbal structures can be built. For English has a variety of means with which to refer to time, past, present, or future. We do this most typically by sequences of verbs which form complex verb-groups. However, as soon as we begin to analyse such groups, we must acknowledge the existence of another system, called aspect, which intersects the system of tense. In general, aspect concerns the ways in which actions in time are viewed — are they habitual, ongoing, or completed? A few examples will make this clear. If our sentence had been *our own experts are handling the installation*, it would have been marked for continuous aspect; that sentence differs from our model in that the action of handling is now seen as something that is going on at the present time, whereas the simple present form *handle* refers to actions which might take place in the future, or which might have taken place in the past. There is a similar distinction to be made between *handled*, and *were handling*, where the action is related to past time; the latter form is also continuous. But aspect can also be perfective; that is, an action can be presented as completed in the past, as in *our experts have handled the installation*, and by combining the elements already cited in these examples in different ways, we can build up verbal groups of greater complexity with regard to tense and aspect like *have been handling*.

Such complex verbal groups consist of a main verb, in this case *handle*, and one or more auxiliary verbs. The auxiliaries mentioned so far are *have* and *be*, and a significant, perhaps even revolutionary part of the history of grammar in English consists of the gradual extension of these auxiliaries into more and more patterns. Today, the complexity of this part of our grammar can be seen by the fact that it is the system of tense and aspect that is commonly re-structured by speakers of some overseas varieties of English, and which continues to cause problems for foreign learners of English.

Have and *be*, then, can act as auxiliaries, and another well-known example, *do*, is so important that it will be afforded considerable space below. There is another group of auxiliaries, however, that are distinguished from these three, partly on morphological grounds (they do not have an -*s* ending after *he, she,* or *it*), and partly in terms of the kinds of notion (obligation, necessity, possibility, etc.) that they signify. These verbs, such as *can, shall, will, must, may, could, should,* etc., are called modal auxiliaries. The range of meanings associated with their use can readily be seen if they are inserted before the verb *handle* in our model sentence. The importance of two of these verbs — *shall* and *will* — for the present discussion owes to the fact that they are used to refer to actions or states related to future time. Otherwise, the use of the modal auxiliaries can be related to the grammatical category of mood, a category which necessarily overlaps that of futurity, since the future inevitably involves an element of 'possibility'.

We have so far isolated tense, aspect, and mood, with respect to the verb-group. There is one last category to be dealt with in this section, that of voice. The information encoded in our model sentence could have been put in a different way, with the addition of auxiliary *be*, and the preposition *by*, changing the form of the main verb and altering the word-order. Thus: *the installation is handled by our own experts.* The changed form of the verb (it usually ends in -*ed* or -*en*) is known as the past participle, and this kind of construction is called passive. Our original sentence was active. We shall be commenting on some sociolinguistic observations that have been made about voice towards the end of this chapter.

We alluded above to the significance of *do* as an auxiliary, and this part of the chapter will be concluded by referring to two basic syntactic functions which depend, in contemporary English, on the use of *do*. These are negation and the question form. To make our model sentence negative, we insert *do not* between subject and verb: *our own experts do not handle the installation;* and to make it into a question, we start the whole construction with *do*, as in *do our own experts handle the installation?* Both these uses of *do* are relatively new in the history of English. Originally, negation was expressed by distributing negative particles on either side of the verb, so that our sentence might have looked like this:

Our own experts ne handle not the installation.

In other words, the cumulative negative, so often condemned today as illogical, was the usual means of expressing negation. The question form was achieved by inversion of word-order, thus:

Handle our own experts the installation?

We still see this pattern operating when auxiliary verbs are involved: we say *can he run fast?* rather than *does he can run fast?*, but in most cases, *do* is used. We shall be returning to this below.

The 'synthetic' grammar of the Anglo-Saxons

From the point of view of morphology, there are some striking differences between contemporary English and the language as it was spoken by the Anglo-Saxons. The student of early English is confronted by tables, lists, and paradigms presenting the rich morphology of nouns, verbs, adjectives, and pronouns. Superficially, Anglo-Saxon appears to have more grammar than modern English, and this brings us to the last misconception on our list. Many people think of grammar as morphology, rather than seeing that the latter is included in the former; and since studying Anglo-Saxon requires us to learn a great deal of morphology, we think it must therefore have more grammar. What it does have, of course, is a different *kind* of grammar, and it is for this reason that we can classify Anglo-Saxon as a different type of language.

For the linguist, the significance of the difference between the grammars lies in the fact that in Anglo-Saxon the relationships among words in the sentence are often signalled by inflexions that are put on the ends of words. The shape of a word changes according to whether it is the subject or the object. Thus, it is not so much the order of words in the sentence that determines, say, the subject, as is the case with contemporary English: in theory, words in Anglo-Saxon can be put in any order, because it is the endings that specify their function. Anglo-

Saxon, then, is like Classical Latin, in that syntactic relationships are achieved by what is called synthesis, the building up of the word by adding inflexions to the stem.

A very simple example can show us how a synthetic grammar works. We have seen how there are no possibilities for changing the word-order in *our own experts handle the installation*. In some other sentences in contemporary English, however, word-order can be changed to achieve radically different meanings. In the subject-verb-object structure *the boy killed the bear* the noun-group in final position *can* function as the subject, producing *the bear killed the boy*. Both boys and bears can kill, and we need word-order to tell us who did what. But in classical Latin, word-endings will tell us who did the killing, irrespective of the word-order. Thus, in Latin, the sequence can be *puer interfecit ursum, ursum puer interfecit*, or *interfecit ursum puer*: but in all these examples, we know what the object is, because it has the distinctive *-um* ending. In principle, the same is true in Anglo-Saxon. The order of the words in *se cnafa of-sloh þone beran* could be re-arranged in a similar number of ways. But we would always know which word functions as the subject because of the ending: *cnafa* (modern 'knave') ends in *-a*, which in this kind of noun is the inflexion associated with subject-position, as *-n* is with that of the object. We should also note how the definite article agrees in form with the noun it immediately precedes; *se* in subject position, *þone* in object position.

What we have been describing is the grammatical category of case, the signalling of relationships among words in a sentence by adding specific endings to the words in question. Above, we saw the association of *-n* with the object, or *accusative* case, with one class of noun, and we saw how the form of the definite article changed. Other kinds of function are also signalled by different case-endings. For instance, a relationship between nouns that might be loosely called possessive is specified by genitive case-endings, of which one, *-'s*, still survives today as in *John's book*. And an indirect object relationship, that of 'to the youth' in *I'll give a pound to the youth*, is often (depending again on the type of noun, etc.) specified by adding *-e*: this is the dative case. Thus, *cniht* (youth) becomes *cnihte*. In general, the Anglo-Saxon case-system is very similar to that of modern German; although the former also has another case, of minor importance and only affecting adjectives, called the instrumental.

The case-system in Anglo-Saxon is considerably more complex than our brief description makes it appear, partly because the cases discharge a wider range of functions than those listed, but also because there is no single range of case-endings that apply to every noun. The student of Anglo-Saxon has to learn to which class of nouns a word belongs before assigning it the correct endings. To some extent, the nouns are also classified according to gender — masculine, feminine, neuter — as in modern German (or as in French, except that it has no neuter).

We can see how a close knowledge of Anglo-Saxon inflexions is needed to understand the kind of language exemplified in this extract from the epic poem *Beowulf*:

> Oft Scyld Scefing sceaþena þreatum
> monegum mægþum meodo-setla ofteah

We must know, for instance, that the verb *of-teon* (of which *of-teah* is the past form that goes with *he*, *she*, or *it*), 'take away', demands particular case-endings on the words functionally dependent on it: the person deprived must be in the dative case, the object taken in the genitive, rather than the more usual accusative case. Only if we know the system of endings can we identify these parts of the sentence. The object is *meodo-setla*, the genitive plural of *meodo-setl* (mead-bench); the subject, *Scyld Scefing*, a Danish king, has deprived *þreatum*, the dative plural of a word meaning 'troop' (cf. 'threat'), of enemies (*sceaþena*) from many (*monegum*) tribes (*mægþum*). The whole sequence means 'Scyld Scefing often took away the mead-benches from troops of his enemies, from many tribes' — in other words, he brought many of his enemies to heel (the 'mead-bench' is a highly compressed way of expressing the power of the chieftain by referring to his custom of giving mead to his followers). This short extract is not untypical of the language of the longest, best-known, and possibly the best of the Anglo-Saxon poems.

The loss of inflexions

We need not conclude from our brief discussion of Anglo-Saxon grammar that our ancestors were splendid linguists, able to write and understand the complex language of the extract above: our own unconscious handling of the modern system of tense and aspect, as described earlier, is no less remarkable. Moreover, it is difficult to know how far such synthetic patterns were representative of ordinary Anglo-Saxon speech.

For it is quite possible that Anglo-Saxon poetry consciously preserved, as a form of poetic licence, a kind of syntax that was already archaic at the time the poems were set down in writing. Unfortunately, we have no evidence for the conversational usage of those times, but it would not be surprising if the grammar of written usage were more synthetic than that of the spoken. There is some evidence to suggest that while Classical Latin retained the full range of inflexions in writing, popular spoken Latin had begun to dispense with them.

Even within Anglo-Saxon writing we find that prose, for instance, is in general less synthetic than poetry. In prose sentences where verbs govern direct objects, as in our model, we find that word-order is more often than not the same as in modern English. Thus, the case-endings in *se cnafa of-sloh pone beran* are largely redundant if *se cnafa* is always likely to come first in the sentence: it has no need of distinctive endings to tell us it is the subject. We can conclude, then, that certain varieties in Anglo-Saxon, since the beginning of literacy, were already placing less reliance on the system of inflexions than others.

What we have seen since Anglo-Saxon times is the gradual erosion, in all dialects, of those inflexions. The term which is used to denote this process – *simplification* – does not imply that generations of lazy speakers have merely taken innumerable short cuts in the grammar. The loss of case-endings, for instance, meant that other means had to be found for signalling relations among words in the sentence, since such endings had a syntactic function. Prepositions, like *for*, *of*, *by*, etc., began to serve those functions; and word-order became less flexible. In this, therefore, we see the *quid pro quo* of much linguistic change: while something in the language may be abandoned by its speakers, something else will emerge as a counterbalance.

The dropping of one part of the system of noun-endings occasioned the same process in other parts of the system. The complex classification of nouns according to three genders was simplified, and with it the half dozen or so patterns of plurality which existed in Anglo-Saxon. In the case of plurals we see the selection of just one inflexion as a productive pattern, which is generalised for most nouns. In different dialects, however, different plural inflexions, associated with frequently occurring nouns, became dominant. In the north, -*s*, was selected, whereas in much of the south and south-west, it was -*n*. Today, the system of plurals is still not regularised in any dialect. The standard variety preserves fossilised instances of the older range: the -*en* in oxen, the vowel-change in *feet*, *geese*, etc., and the unmarked plural of nouns like *sheep*.

Other dialects retain more -*n* forms, as in *een* (eyes) in the north and west midlands, and have extended this pattern to nouns like *house* which originally had no plural inflexion (as in parts of East Anglia and the west midlands). And in non-standard speech generally, the Anglo-Saxon uninflected plural is common in nouns specifying measurement: *three ton of coal, three pound of potatoes, three mile away*. Thus, the selection of plural endings, and their allocation to particular words, seems to have proceeded in a way that strikes the modern speaker as arbitrary. And most arbitrary, in a sense, is the standard variety, which from the advent of printing has tended to fix its own idiosyncratic selection, while in dialectal speech the process of restructuring has continued.

We cannot say, therefore, that the selection of plural forms in the standard variety is more logical, or in any way better, than that of other varieties, just as we cannot attribute any kind of linguistic superiority to our different kinds of grammar, inflected or modern. Neither is it appropriate to apply the kind of Whorfian thinking discussed in the last chapter to the process of grammatical simplification, and conclude that such a profound change in grammar must have been accompanied by a shift in the way English people have perceived the universe. Perceptual differences associated with the different kinds of grammar can be discussed at a much more mundane level. The fact that the demonstrative *this*, for instance, was fully inflected in Anglo-Saxon times, meant that every time speakers said *þes* rather than *þis* or *þeos* they were restricting the number of nouns the listener might expect, since *þes* specified masculine nouns, *þis* neuter ones, and so on. Such expectations would have been exploited to the full in literature, so that the modern reader finds difficulty in appreciating all the nuances of meaning in *Beowulf*. But while we may have lost the communicative value of the inflected demonstrative, the loss of distinctive forms for, say, nouns and verbs, could offer enormous syntactic possibilities for a poet and dramatist like Shakespeare. *Lip* is traditionally a noun, but once it has lost its endings, it can be used as a verb, so that in *To lip a wanton in a secure couch* (*Othello*, 4.1.73) Shakespeare uses it to mean 'kiss lecherously'. Poetic licence for the Anglo-Saxons may have meant the preservation of inflexions; but the loss of them provided poetic licence of another kind for later poets. It is characteristic of contemporary English that many words can act as either nouns or verbs, a freedom exploited to the full in everyday speech, and extended by advertisers – as in the example cited earlier.

It is very difficult to know the why and the how of the process of morphological simplification. As we said at the beginning of this chapter, it is by no means easy to document grammatical change as it occurs in our own lifetime. Such study needs, above all, a detailed knowledge of linguistic variation: and we have little evidence for this in the early period of English. But one thing we do know about is the erosion of inflexions as spoken languages come into contact, especially in those conditions that produce pidgins or cause pidginisation. Pidgins are a type of language that may be said to have pushed the process of morphological simplification to its limit, by abandoning any inflexions that might be considered redundant. Thus even the plural ending, which most English people would probably consider indispensable, is eradicated in a sequence like *di tu big pepa*, 'the two big newspapers' in Cameroon pidgin. Since plurality is already specified by the numeral *tu*, it is not absolutely necessary to inflect the noun in this instance.

The notion of redundancy can be readily appreciated when we look at verbal inflexions, and see how they pattern with pronouns. Taking a verb like *go*, we can set out the contemporary standard English paradigm thus:

I	go	
you	go	
he		
she	goes	singular
it		
we	go	
you	go	plural
they	go	

We see here that apart from *you*, each pronoun has a different form, whereas there are only two verb-forms: the third person form agrees with the *he, she, it* pronouns by taking the − (*e*)s ending. The inflexion in the third person is a relic of the fully inflected verb in Anglo-Saxon, which in West Saxon took this form:

ic	ga	
þu	gaest	
he		
heo	gaeþ	
hit		

we   gaþ
ge   gaþ
hie   gaþ

Here we find four distinctive forms of the verb, including not only endings but vowel changes. And all the pronouns have distinct forms, including, significantly, the second person ones þu and ge (modern thou and ye). But when we compare this paradigm with the more highly inflected verb in Latin, we find that pronouns are unusual, and there is maximum differentiation in the forms of the verb:

eo
is
it
imus
itis
eunt

From this comparison of three different paradigms, we can say that languages, or varieties, that have a more fully differentiated system of pronouns which function in concord with distinctive verbal endings can be said to exhibit a greater degree of redundancy than those which have simplified either pronouns or inflexions. Thus, Classical Latin has less redundancy than West Saxon, since it makes do without pronouns in subject position (though pronouns were available for emphasis) and modern standard English points towards the elimination of redundancy by retaining only the -(e)s ending. Cameroon pidgin, however, has removed even this:

a   go
yu   go
i   go
wi   go
wuna   go
dem   go

The loss of the inflexion in the verb form is compensated for by the plural you form, wuna, in the pronominal system.

We cannot say for sure that a process like pidginisation caused the abandonment of the Anglo-Saxon system of inflexions. But it would

not be surprising if the process was at least hastened in the first instance
by contact between the English and their Scandinavian neighbours and
subsequently by contact with the Normans. We have already seen how
certain pronoun forms arose from such contact with Scandinavians,
suggesting a thorough and close mixing of the two speech-communities.
In these conditions, there would have been pressure to level inflexions
in the interests of spoken communication. New forms, originating in
various parts of the Danelaw and along its borders, could then gradually
spread at the level of popular speech. It is noteworthy that the two instances of inflexional change that we have noted – the -s plural and
third person verbal ending -(e)s – arose in areas well away from Wessex,
and were gradually adopted into the standard variety.

Today, morphological simplification is most clearly associated with
working-class speech. While the standard variety preserves some vestiges
of the older pattern, dialects get on with the elimination of irregularity
and redundancy. In Norfolk, for instance, we can hear the same verbal
paradigm as in Cameroon pidgin. And many dialects make a consistent
paradigm of the reflexive pronouns: I wash *myself*, you wash *yourself*,
he washes *hisself*, where they are possessive throughout. But as it is in
process of consolidating, the standard variety begins to freeze earlier
patterns in morphology, and even cultivate variety of form as a mark of
education. In short, we are back to the idea that grammar is a matter
of morphology.

Morphological simplification and social stigma

Two other ways in which the morphology of the verb has been simplified involve the conversion of strong verbs to the weak pattern (see
p. 95 above), and the simplification of the strong verb itself. The first
has resulted in about five-sixths of the 360-odd strong verbs recorded
in West Saxon being changed to the weak pattern. Thus, while some
verbs, like *drink, swim, break*, and *bear*, remain strong, and still signal
past tense by means of an internal vowel change, many others, like
glide, seethe, fret, and *fare*, have adopted the simple -ed past inflexion.

West Saxon has seven recorded strong verb patterns. An example,
fleogan (fly), had five distinct vowel changes in its various tense-forms.
As well as a past in *fleag*, and a past participle *flogen*, there were vowel
changes *within* each tense: in the present, the form was *fliehþ* after *he*,
she, or *it*, and in the past, *flugon* occurred after plural pronouns.

Today, we find that the number of vowel changes has been reduced to three, so we get *fly, flew, flown*. But in non-standard speech, we often find a reduction to two forms, so we hear *I flown it, I done it*, etc. Here the past participle form is used for marking past tense.

It is customary, among historians of English when describing the evolution of verb morphology, to attribute such changes to the principle of analogy. In using the different forms of a verb like *fleogan*, it is suggested that speakers will be reminded of other verbs which are similar in some parts of the pattern, but not others; thus, verbs originally belonging to different verb classes are blended in the mind of the speaker, and new forms for these verbs, based on parts of the pattern of vowel changes in other verbs, are created. Moreover, the different dialects of Anglo-Saxon may well have had differences in various parts of the strong verb patterns (if they had none at first, they were soon to develop them); and contact between speakers of different dialects would have produced re-structuring in the system. We find in recent dialect speech that variation in verb forms is apparently endless, as different strong verb patterns compete with the dominant weak ones. Finally, it is the presence of that two-part weak pattern, present versus past, that may account for the reduction to two forms in the strong verbs that remain.

It is not only in non-standard speech that the tendency to reduce strong verb forms to two has occurred. In my own speech, I have noted hesitations about the past tense of *drink*; is it *he drank*, or *he drunk*? The likelihood is that I will simplify the paradigm by using the past participle form *drunk* for the simple past *drank*. Sometimes, however, the process involves the reverse selection: in Jane Austen's narrative, we sometimes find the past tense form used for the past participle, as in *the tables were broke up*, and *much was ate*. Thus, the process of simplification used to be as true of so-called educated speech as it is today of non-standard. What has happened is that the tendency to reduce the forms of the verb to two has been stigmatised. There is some evidence to suggest that as early as the sixteenth century new past tense forms in verbs such as *steal* and *break*, possibly arising from the extension of the past participle forms *stolen* and *broken*, were labelled as 'vulgar', and avoided by people with social pretensions. Avoidance of the new *o*-forms as in *stolen*, etc., seems to have led to hypercorrection as well. In sixteenth-century literature, we find that verbs which had long had an *o* in the past tense, like *write*, were written as *wrate* – perhaps the reaction of educated people to a change originating in dialectal, or even merely informal, speech.

It was the eighteenth-century codifiers, however, who legitimised such sociolinguistic stratification by insisting that a tripartite pattern in the strong verb was proper and correct from the linguistic point of view. English, like Latin, they suggested, should distinguish between past tense and past participle. The richer the morphology, the better; and one grammarian, Lowth, thought it essential to restore inflexions, and vowel-alternations, wherever it was possible. English grammar, he declared, was getting too easy, and needed stiffening up.

The social meaning of pronouns

In discussing the verb, we have already noted two kinds of change associated with pronouns. One concerns the forms themselves. Many parts of the pronoun system preserve three distinctive case-forms: the nominative, accusative, and genitive, or possessive, *I/me/my*, *we/us/our*, *he/him/his*, *they/them/their*, although other parts have been reduced to two, as in *you/your*, *she/her*, *it/its*. As we have seen, some of these forms have arisen from contact with Scandinavians. Parts of the area formerly known as Wessex, well away from Scandinavian settlement, still use Anglo-Saxon forms. Thus, an earlier accusative or object form of 'he', *hine*, has recently been recorded as *en*, as in *I hit en* (I hit him); and the older form of 'I', *ic*, as *utch*.

The second change concerns the meaning and functions of the pronouns. In our discussion of *you*, we noted that some languages, or varieties, had a number distinction in the second person pronoun: one form for *you* singular, another for *you* plural. This was the case in Anglo-Saxon. Not only was there a singular *þu* (thou) and plural *ge* (ye: later replaced by its object form, *you*), but distinctions could be made between 'you many', and 'you two', 'we many', and 'we two': these are known as dual pronouns. These distinctions have been lost in the standard variety, although some dialects have the form *youse* for 'you many', and other dialects have evolved other patterns of contrast. In parts of the south-west, *us* is sometimes used in subject position as an unemphatic pronoun, while *we* marks emphasis. It is noteworthy that Classical Latin, which as we have seen could manage without pronouns, had a set of pronouns which could be used emphatically; these have subsequently become the pronoun forms in French.

In classifying vocabulary, pronouns are usually said to constitute a closed system, as we explained above. Clearly, there are not many possibilities for adding new pronouns to the system: but we still find that the system changes, because the use of pronouns is so closely bound up with the process of social interaction. Pronouns occur very frequently in speech — one reason, perhaps, for the continued use of the dialect forms — but more important is the fact that from time to time they arouse our social sensitivities. Recently, the lack of a neutral pronoun, unmarked for gender, to signify third person singular, has been an issue raised in the cause of sexual equality. Women understandably resent the airy use of *he* in reference to unspecified people of either sex. In earlier centuries, however, it is the second person pronoun, the pronoun of address, that is at issue; to such an extent that the Revolution in France in the eighteenth century and the Russian Revolution in the twentieth both stimulated legislation on the matter, so central did linguistic usage in this respect seem to be to the creation of equality.

We saw in the last chapter how Elizabethans could address each other with *thou* or *you*. These pronouns had different social meanings. Someone you did not know well, with whom you might want to establish a relationship of neutral, respectful distance, could be addressed with *you*. And you could expect *you* in return. For someone you felt especially close to, either emotionally or socially, a reciprocal *thou* might be appropriate. The equality of these relationships was underlined by reciprocal pronoun usage. But in unequal relationships, different pronouns would be given and returned. It was necessary to address a superior by the use of *you*, and *thou* would be expected in return. Moreover, you could be defiant, or insulting, by breaking this code: using *thou* to a superior, or to someone of equal standing who had no reason to expect it. And heightened feelings could be registered — sympathy, tenderness, anger, reverence — by switching from *you* to *thou* in the middle of a conversation.

This system of pronominal address, inherited by the Elizabethans, can be represented in a diagram as shown in Figure 4.2.

Figure 4.2

Anyone with a knowledge of modern European languages like French, German, and Italian will see similarities between this system and pronoun usage in those languages as it was almost until today. What we have to account for in English is the widespread loss of *thou*, and with it the means of 'power-coding' relationships by addressing someone as *thou*, and getting *you* in return. Of particular interest is the displacement of the original second person singular pronoun by the *you*-form, which originally indicated plurality.

The use of the plural pronoun *you* as a respectful marker of address was a change led by the most powerful social groups. Originating in the Latin of the later Roman Empire (there were two Emperors, so to address one was to address the other as well) the custom of using, and demanding, the polite plural pronoun spread into many European languages during the Middle Ages. Once established in French, it was adopted by the Francophile English aristocracy. At first, *you*, as a marker of special esteem, was rare, an emblem of courtly custom; but gradually, relationships such as parent/child, lord/servant, husband/wife were power-coded, in that the former in each pair demanded *you*, and returned *thou*. By about 1500 it seems that this practice had been copied by the middle class, and *thou* was becoming the 'marked' form. It could be used for special effects; moreover, it was the reciprocal pronoun of the lower class.

In that *you* was emblematic of upper-class manners, as *thou* was of working people, the widespread adoption of *you* in the course of the seventeenth century may be said to represent the triumph of middle-class values. More difficult to explain is the abandoning of the non-reciprocal pattern of power-relationships. In general, this pattern persists in societies where rank and status are relatively fixed and transparent. When social relations become more fluid, however, specific relationships are liable to be re-interpreted, and reciprocal pronouns used instead. In many European languages, relationships involving social class or rank, such as customer/waiter, officer/soldier, employer/employee, have been resolved by the use of the plural pronoun of distance and respect; whereas differences of status in the family, as between parent and child, for example, have been interpreted as meriting the mutual use of the intimate singular. And recent research among younger speakers of French, Italian, and German shows that the system is still changing. In more and more relationships, in some countries more than others, solidarity is winning out over power, and the equivalent to *thou* in those languages is being extended. In short, people are rejecting a linguistic expression of inequality, and at the same time excluding the reciprocal expression of respectful distance. The pronouns of intimate equality are felt by young people in Europe today to be the best means of expressing democratic sentiments.

We do not have the evidence to reconstruct such a shift in sixteenth-century England. We do not know whether it was parents and children, or masters and servants, who initiated the rejection of power-coding. But it is interesting that while the merchants, tradespeople, and professions were aping upper-class manners, they abandoned the means of marking power relationships with those below them. It has been suggested that this was motivated by an egalitarian ethic. More likely was it a reflex of middle-class insecurity. In sixteenth-century urban society, particularly that of London, social relations were not fixed, which perhaps explains the Elizabethan obsession with them. With power and influence increasingly identified with the entrepreneur, there was no means of knowing who was entitled to *you*, and who to *thou*. The best solution was to stick to *you*, which would not offend, and rely on the more open-ended set of address terms discussed in the last chapter. For such terms can be avoided altogether, whereas pronouns cannot be. This, after all, is the way we handle the issue in contemporary English. Although we can still upset people by being over-familiar when they are unable, or do not wish, to respond in the same way, we at least are able to avoid committing ourselves in address by choosing not to use names, titles, and Christian names, or expressions of hail-fellow-well-met familiarity at all, at least until we are sure of our ground.

The retention of *thou* in dialect may have been motivated by covert prestige. It is noteworthy that it is still heard in northern England where the desire to maintain a regional identity is strong. Whatever the reason, dialect speakers who use the pronoun enjoy a clear advantage over speakers of the standard variety. For the former, *thou* can be the norm; *you* can be a special pronoun to establish social distance with outsiders (thus inverting the sixteenth-century middle-class pattern). Or *thou* can be used to signal extra intimacy. The gamekeeper in *Lady Chatterley's Lover* takes full advantage of these possibilities.

Finally, it is worth commenting on the selection of *thou* as the mutual pronoun of address among the Quakers. In that they chose the pronoun of lower-class solidarity, the Quakers of the seventeenth century could be said to have anticipated the future development in the other European languages. *You* was apparently too loaded with connotations of class superiority: English people had managed with mutual *thou* for centuries, and why should they not continue to do so? Moreover, the pronoun had a long, unbroken history of use in the domain of religion (as it still does). It was perhaps this insistence of the Quakers, who were not then considered to be as respectable as they have since become, that helped to stigmatise *thou* in the minds of many people. If *thou* was the pronoun of religious fanatics, subversives, and stable-boys, sensible people might be wise to forget it!

Syntactic elaboration and social prestige

In the examples above, we have seen that changes in grammar may be introduced, or extended, by upper-, middle- or lower-class usage. The same is true for the process of syntactic elaboration, particularly in the extension of use of the auxiliary verbs. Lower-class speech, for instance, seems to have promoted *do* as a 'dummy' auxiliary (see above, p. 96). Already used as a *substitute* verb in Anglo-Saxon (as in *swa hie ær dydon*, 'as they before did', where *dydon* stands for a previously-mentioned lexical verb *ricsian*, 'rule'), *do* came to be used in questions: it is not difficult to imagine how a sequence like this could be queried with *did they*? This pattern probably spread from the south-west, where it is recorded first; and by the sixteenth century, *do*-questions were a feature of lower-class London usage. In Shakespeare, it co-exists, as a marker of popular speech, with the older, upper-class inversion pattern, as in *go you?*. At this time, also, *do* was spreading into the negative construction. Originally, *I don't go* would have been *Ic ne ga (noht)*; from this arose *I ne go not*, then *I go not*, then *I don't go*. Perhaps this use of *do* was originally emphatic, as it is used today in declarative sentences — *I DO go and see him!*; from there it may have been over-used, in the way described in the last chapter, and subsequently become the norm. Today *do* is usual in questions and negative constructions except where other auxiliaries like *have, can, are*, etc., are present; and even then one of these, *have*, is yielding to the process of extension. In the USA, *do you have a pen?*, *no, I don't* is more common than the *have you (got)...*, *no I haven't* pattern heard in England.

Another development of *do* seems to be associated with the written English of the sixteenth and seventeenth centuries. We find it used in declarative sentences, as in *she doth go*, where no special emphasis seems to have been required. But the rise of this pattern is both dramatic and short-lived, since it had begun to die out by the following century. The explanation for this may be that *do* could be used to mark the tense of verbs which had no morphological distinction between present and past, like *put* and *cast*; and also of those verbs borrowed from Latin, like *illuminate* and *imitate*, which at that time were entering literary English in enormous numbers, and at too fast a rate, it seems, to become rapidly assimilated to the English tense-system.

Other extensions in the use of auxiliaries are also associated with writing. And as we saw earlier, a great deal of writing in English has evolved in the shadow of other literary traditions, notably those of Latin and French. The earliest English writing appears to show the influence of Latin structures. While Latin had verbal inflexions which marked future tense, Anglo-Saxon had not, so scholars had to find other ways of translating Latin future tenses into English. One solution was to extend *sceal* (modern *shall*), a modal verb meaning 'be obliged', for this purpose. Similarly, the Latin pluperfect tense came to be expressed using the past tense of the verb *have*, as in *he had said*. Originally this meaning in Anglo-Saxon would have been conveyed *lexically*, using an adverb with a simple past tense; so that *he had said* would have been *he sæde ær*, 'he said previously'.

Such constructions were not only copied, or adapted, from Latin; increasingly they came to be seen as 'better' than the corresponding English ones. The prestige of Latin as a written, and above all, codified language, was projected on to its structures themselves. By the end of the eighteenth century the native English pattern of negation, as in *I don't know nothing*, where negatives are used cumulatively, had been stigmatised, since it did not conform to the Latin pattern. Further sticks were found to beat it with. The cumulative negative was declared illogical, and speakers who used it must learn to tighten up their thinking. These ideas are still influential in the educational system. In the 1960s in the USA, language programmes aimed at Black school children were trying to eradicate this construction from their speech, and replace it with the 'logical' standard one.

Such attempts to link certain grammatical structures with patterns of thinking are reminiscent of the ideas of Whorf, discussed earlier in this book. We find these ideas, conscious or otherwise, in the work of many contemporary educationalists, sociologists, and psychologists. Some linguists also have applied them, notably in connection with structures larger than any we have discussed so far in this chapter. For instance, the various ways in which sentences − and those sentences within sentences that are usually called clauses − are joined, have been differently evaluated.

In Anglo-Saxon, the joining of clauses and sentences relied less on specific conjunctions like *when, before, although, while*, etc., than on *then (þa)*, and *and*; and often, such units were not linked at all, but merely juxtaposed. We can demonstrate this by using different ways of presenting much the same information:

(a) *I was tired: I went to bed.*
(b) *I was tired, and I went to bed.*
(c) *Because I was tired, I went to bed.*

Of these, (c) is sometimes described as being more explicit, in that the relationship between the two ideas — tiredness and going to bed — is made logically dependent: the first idea is subordinated to the second. *Because I was tired* can thus be called a subordinate clause, and this kind of structure is much more typical of Latin-based style than the other two examples. Of these (a) leaves the readers or listeners to work out the relationship between the juxtaposed clauses for themselves: it is less explicit. This kind of construction, called *parataxis*, is very typical of Anglo-Saxon, as is also the second, which can be called simple co-ordination.

We can use all three models today, but it is the last one, (c), that is often more highly valued than the others, because of the notion of explicitness alluded to above. Thus, the ability to use subordinate clauses has been related to more abstract, more sophisticated kinds of thinking. Parataxis has sometimes been dismissed as vague or even naive. But the prestige attaching to subordination really derives from its association with writing. This kind of sentence-linking is much less common in speech: we are back to the second misconception on our list, that grammar is something applicable to the written word rather than the spoken.

Failure to recognise this has contributed to the wide currency enjoyed by recent hypotheses relating language and educational success. Subordination is one of the features associated by Basil Bernstein with the so-called elaborated code — the kind of language capable of conveying individual perceptions to a universal audience. In Bernstein's works of the late 1960s and early 1970s, syntactical subordination, or more properly, the capacity to use syntactical subordination, is considered to reflect logical thought; therefore working-class children are disadvantaged at school because their speech makes small use of this kind of grammatical pattern. When we inspect the other grammatical habits that working-class children are alleged to use — short, simple, often unfinished sentences, simple repetitive use of conjunctions (*and, then,* etc.), rigid, limited use of adverbs and adjectives, use of the active rather than passive voice (see p. 96 above) — we find a list of features characteristic of all speech, irrespective of education or class. Speech is necessarily less 'discriminative' than writing, since the ear can best process a much less 'dense' kind of language than the eye. The ability to command the elaborated code — in the sense of being able to use the features Bernstein lists for it — is really the ability to use the structures of written English in your speech.

Even now our argument is in danger of forgetting that written English, like speech, varies. We are more likely to find the passive used in reports of chemistry experiments than in narratives. And since subordination is typical of formal, expository prose, we often find that twentieth-century novelists, like Hemingway, try to cultivate a style which avoids it. By being less explicit, a paratactic style also can be said to respect its readers by demanding that they themselves share the burden of interpretation. In the traditional ballad, for instance, we find the paratactic principle extended, so that line and stanza, narrative and dialogue, action and scene, are juxtaposed without comment. Moreover, the proverb, with its simple structure (*more haste, less speed*) is no less capable of expressing complex, even abstract thoughts than more explicit, less elliptical language. The tendency for subordination to replace parataxis as a dominant style should be seen for what it is: a matter of style, not linguistic progress, whatever that might be.

Chapter five

Pronunciation

The extent of regional variation in the pronunciation of English is universally acknowledged and often remarked on. In this chapter, we shall see how an awareness of such variation can help us understand the process of change. First, however, we need to examine some general misunderstandings about the nature of pronunciation; in particular, its relationship with spelling, and the ways in which notions about correctness, and the view that some forms of pronunciation are slovenly, have been influenced by the prestigious Received Pronunciation (RP) accent. Then we shall look at sounds themselves, and see how they can be described independently of our spelling system, by describing first some of the RP consonants, and then the vowels. RP itself will be seen to vary, according to the level of formality of context, and also with respect to the age, sex, and even social attitude of its speakers: and we shall see how such variations reflect changes in the recent past. We shall then see how three consonant pronunciations, formerly common in upper- and lower-class speech, have subsequently been stigmatised, especially in urban accents. Three widely-known regional pronunciations will then be described, and their origins traced; and we shall see how in two cases they preserve sounds that were once more generally used. Finally, we shall examine the evidence for the series of momentous vowel changes known as the Great Vowel Shift, and assess the role of social factors in the adoption of the new pronunciations that resulted.

Contrary to what many people think, regional pronunciations in England are not dying out. Although in some respects they have changed quite dramatically within living memory, the direction of change has by no means always been towards RP; the accents of the big cities – London, Liverpool, Birmingham, Newcastle – have if anything intensified certain phonetic differences across the generations. Moreover, we cannot speak of the existence of a national standard pronunciation; some regional features are so deeply embedded in the speech of all but the most privileged social classes, that it is possible to speak of *regional* standards in areas of England that are well away from London and the south-east. And although RP still provides an important point of reference in matters of pronunciation, it has lost a great deal of its prestige in recent years.

Contemporary variations in pronunciation provide us with the best introduction to changes which have taken place in the sounds of English since Anglo-Saxon times. Unlike words and meanings, and grammatical forms and constructions, the sounds of the past cannot be fully reconstructed by examining written texts. Anything we say on the subject can only be guesswork. In the past, however, historians of English have been most concerned with the interpretation of rhymes, the so-called phonetic spellings of handwritten manuscripts, and the comments of codifiers and other observers. Present-day regional pronunciations at least have the virtue of attestability, even though we can never be sure how far they may throw light on the usage of the past.

It is possible that the changes in pronunciation that have occurred during the last 1500 years are no greater than the range of regional variants that can still be heard today. But although it is likely that regional pronunciations have diverged increasingly over the centuries, it is not necessary to assume they derive from a single source. About the Anglo-Saxon dialects we know little, but it is at least conceivable that in some respects they had distinctive systems of pronunciation. By the fourteenth century, as we have seen, differences among the written manifestations of the dialects are so radical that it would be surprising if significant variations did not exist also at the phonetic level.

The history of English sounds has much to do with the spread of features from one region to another. But geography is not the only source of variation. Everybody's pronunciation varies according to the formality of a situation; and a variant developing in, say, casual style, may spread to other styles as well. Finally, new variants may arise from contexts where emphatic, or forceful, styles of speech are used. Pronunciation is infinitely variable and constantly evolving.

The spread of new variants is often dependent on social factors. For example, we must take account of the prestige enjoyed by the group with which a particular pronunciation is associated. This is especially relevant in towns and cities, where dialects of many areas are brought into contact. Often this results in the erosion of sharp differences; but new patterns are often created as different social groups strive to maintain their linguistic identity, or distance themselves from others.

The spread of prestigious pronunciations throughout the countryside may be attributed to middle-class speakers in the towns. Recent dialect surveys, and investigations of urban speech, suggest moreover that it is women who most actively try to identify with prestigious pronunciations. Men who work in traditional rural occupations preserve dialect pronunciations to mark membership of the male peer-group, while in the towns those variants stigmatised by the education system enjoy a *covert* prestige among working-class men for the very reason that they are considered incorrect.

It is not easy to perceive general trends in the history of English pronunciation. It seems likely, however, that the consonant system has remained relatively stable for the past 1500 years. As we shall see, this has much to do with the nature of consonant sounds themselves. Vowels, on the other hand, seem particularly subject to change. While the short vowel system may in many respects resemble that used by the Anglo-Saxons, the long vowels and diphthongs exhibit immense changes, just as they can be seen to be especially variable in contemporary regional pronunciation. In this chapter, we shall see the significance of three trends, involving the lengthening, raising, and diphthongising of vowels.

Changes in pronunciation cannot be attributed to a general carelessness on the part of speakers. While such a notion might recommend itself to those who take an apocalyptic view of linguistic change, it is only in some cases that economy of effort, making short-cuts in the articulation of sounds, can be specified as an important factor. Neither is it appropriate to explain the adoption of new pronunciations on the grounds that they are 'easier to say' than other variants. In general, what we find easy to say is what we are used to saying, just as we have difficulty in mastering the sounds of a strange language. We shall see the relevance of these observations in the next few paragraphs.

Popular ideas about pronunciation

Since spelling is the only widely-known system of representing sounds, it is not surprising that people often refer to letters, not sounds, when they are discussing pronunciation. The extent of this spelling-consciousness can be seen in the common misconception that English has five vowels — *a, e, i, o* and *u* (whereas most varieties of the language have at least four times that number). We find constantly that spellings are cited in support of various pronunciations: the *h* should be sounded, because it is there in the spelling, and people should avoid saying *lawr and order* because there is no *r* in *law*. Such ideas are so firmly held among certain social groups that in 1979 the BBC set up a panel to monitor the pronunciations (and also, incidentally, the grammar, words, and meanings as well) of its broadcasters, so persistent had been the letters of complaint.

There is a related misconception that not only should each letter be given a pronunciation, but it should also be given one pronunciation only. In other words, the fallacy that letters 'have pronunciations' is given a further twist, in that each letter is supposed to have a correct pronunciation. Thus, the *t* sound in *later* should be pronounced by touching the tongue-tip against the teeth-ridge behind the upper front teeth; the glottal stop, which involves a closure in the area of the throat known as the glottis, will not do. Such arguments express the relationship between sounds and spelling the wrong way round: we speak with sounds, not letters, and linguists must therefore find a way of categorising sounds independently of their written representation.

It is often thought that RP conforms most closely to such spelling-based models of pronunciation. But while it may be true that an RP pronunciation of a word like *later* respects the arguments expressed in the last two paragraphs, in other ways that accent does not match up to spelling. Both *t*'s are not sounded in a word like *hotter*, for instance, and neither is the *r*, which is also preserved in the spelling of innumerable words, such as *car*, *card*, *starter*, where it is given no realisation in sound. Thus, RP does not distinguish between pairs of words like *fort* and *fought*, unlike those accents which pronounce *r* in all positions in the word. For this reason, there is no substance in those arguments that seek to justify RP as a superior accent on the grounds that it can make more distinctions in the pronunciation of words than other accents. Thus, while it may be true that an accent that pronounces *h* can distinguish between, say, *arm* and *harm*, other accents can differentiate *meet* from *meat*, *horse* from *hoarse*, or *no* from *know*, which RP, for one, does not.

Pronunciations which do not seem to conform to either the canons of spelling or RP are often referred to as careless or even slovenly. The essential point here is that every single speaker of English uses such pronunciations, for the simple reason that we can only be 'correct' when we are conscious of how we are sounding. Recent research has shown that when people are immersed in the telling of a story, for instance, their pronunciation is not the same as when they are reading aloud from a list of individual words. In certain situations, for instance formal ones, we tend to adjust our pronunciation towards some norm of correctness; but in casual speech, where communicative intent is more relevant than form, we regularly make even those sounds that in conscious moments we would stigmatise. And if many people find this argument hard to accept, it is because they automatically turn to the carefully controlled, or monitored pronunciations they would use in formal contexts whenever they are asked to consider their own speech. But it is a fact that can be demonstrated if people are tape-recorded in unguarded moments. Not only will readers say *I'm going to go and pick some raspberries* differently from the way they would say it in casual style, but they will probably find it very difficult to tell how they would say it if they did not have the words in front of them.

The point made in the last paragraph will become clear if we remember that sounds, like words, do not occur in isolation. They are produced in conjunction with other sounds: and the articulation of one sound may affect that of another. Thus, the *d* consonant of *bread* is usually pronounced further back in the mouth than in *breadth*, where the dental articulation of *th* often influences the position of the preceding consonant. The sound represented by the letter *d* is not, therefore, always made in the same way: and we shall find this is true of all other sounds as well. Just as the pronunciation of consonants is affected by neighbouring consonants, so are they by neighbouring vowels; and vowels are often conditioned by the consonants that immediately precede or follow them. In other words, we must learn to look at sounds as part of a sequence; which is, after all, how we hear them in connected speech.

The analysis of sounds

Sounds do not occur in isolation, but a scientific description of the ways in which they are produced in the mouth requires us to take them one at a time. And since sounds are subject to such widespread regional variation, we can also only describe one accent at a time. It is customary for linguists to start with RP, and this is what we shall do here: not because it is in any way superior or even desirable, but because it is widely understood. Moreover, since we have said that the sounds of any accent vary according to situation, we must specify that it is the formal style of RP that provides the basis of the following account.

The study of pronunciation involves more than just the accurate analysis of articulatory movements. For we ought to be able to explain why most speakers of English do not need to be aware that the *d* sounds in *bread* and *breadth* are different. One reason for this is that these sounds can never bring about a change of meaning; they are therefore felt to be the same sound. To use another example: the initial sounds in *car* and *key* are different, articulated in slightly different places in the mouth, but many speakers of English may not be able to perceive this. If we substitute a *b* sound for the initial sound of *car* we get *bar*, which clearly not only involves a different sound but also creates another word with an entirely different meaning. The initial sounds of *car* and *bar* are therefore to be called different phonemes, a term we have already met, and defined, in chapter two. The different kinds of *k* sound in *car* and *key* can be called *allophones*, or different realisations, of the same phoneme.

The phoneme can be seen either as a family of sounds, or as an abstract concept encompassing a number of phonetic realisations. While these may be very large, the number of phonemes in most varieties of all languages is fixed and relatively small: many accents of English have about forty-four. Central to the notion of the phoneme is that it is a sound capable of bringing about a change of meaning. As such, it contrasts with all other phonemes in a particular accent: and together they constitute a system. A system is a structure of interdependent units, and if a change occurs with respect to one unit (phoneme), it is likely that some re-structuring of other parts of the system will occur.

This rather theoretical exposition will become clearer as more examples are cited. Many people will have direct experience of the kinds of misunderstanding that occur among speakers with different accents, where someone fails to locate the specific place of a sound in the system of another speaker. For instance, the Cockney vowel in *but* makes that word sound like *bat* to a northerner: in isolation, the vowels in both words may sometimes be considered to be the same. But though the vowels may be phonetically similar, it is quite clear that they have different places in the systems of different accents. To simplify, the vowel in Cockney *but* occurs in many words spelt with *u*, as in *cut*, *fun*, and *numb*, with *oo* as in *blood* and *flood*, *ou* as in *country* and *young*, and sometimes with *o*, as in *son*, *nothing*, and *London*. In many northern accents, a similar vowel occurs in words spelt with *a*, as in *cat*, *fan*, and *land*. Each accent, however, has its own way of making distinctions among words, distinguishing, for instance, between *but* and *bat*, *but* and *bet*, *bat* and *bet*, and so on. Every accent has its own system, and the functioning of the parts must be established before adequate comparisons can be made among them.

There is a final point to make about the patterning of sounds. Some phonemes — like the medial consonant in *measure* adopted from French — occur much less frequently than others in speech. This is partly because the number of positions in which they occur is limited: some consonants, for instance, do not occur in initial position; others may be restricted to that position. Such sounds may be said to occupy a less central place in the system than others.

The consonants of RP

Consonants, unlike vowels, can be broadly characterised as sounds which involve contact or near-contact between the organs of speech — the tongue, lips, teeth — and parts of the roof of the mouth — soft palate, hard palate, and teeth-ridge. Because such contact can be felt or sensed by the speaker, consonant sounds are more likely to remain stabler than vowels, their variants more amenable to codification and stigmatisation.

The RP system has twenty-four consonant phonemes. These can be subdivided into groups according to *how* they are produced; in other words, the kind of contact involved. We shall concentrate here on only three major groups, the plosives, fricatives, and nasals, the members of which together comprise eighteen of the total number of consonants. The first class is that known as *plosives*. These consonants are made when certain organs of speech are brought into short, sharp contact, and then smartly released. There are six plosive consonants in RP, and they can be shown to distinguish the following words, all of which have the termination -*ill*:

| pill | till | kill |
| bill | dill (the herb) | gill (of a fish) |

All English-born speakers of English will recognise that this sub-system of sounds constitutes a meaningful way of distinguishing the words listed. The arrangement of the words in pairs introduces another dimension of description: the *place* of articulation. We need to specify which speech organs are involved. /p/ and /b/ — the slanting brackets indicate that we are talking about *phonemes* — are made by bringing the lips together and then quickly emitting the build-up of air-pressure from the lungs by opening the lips. /t/ and /d/ are made by bringing the tongue-tip against the ridge behind the upper front teeth — the *alveolar* ridge — and then releasing it; and in the case of the final pair, the back of the tongue makes a similar kind of contact with the soft palate at the rear part of the roof of the mouth, the *velum*. Thus, the vital positions for the plosives are bilabial, alveolar, and velar. All native speakers of English, regardless of their accent, make these distinctions, although they sound, or realise them, in many different ways. And readers can check the accuracy of the foregoing by conscious observation of their own articulation.

It remains to explain how the members of each pair — /p/ and /b/, for instance — are distinguished. All the plosives are articulated in the manner described, but accompanying the production of the bottom series /b d g/ is a vibration of the vocal cords, folds of tissue situated in the larynx which we are capable of opening and closing. Such vibration is called *voicing*. We now have a system of description for the consonants: we can speak of the initial sound in *bill*, for example, as a voiced bilabial plosive; that in *kill*, as a voiceless velar plosive. These labels can be used in the description of any language, and their immediate value for us is that sounds can be discussed independently of the spelling system.

With its three well-spaced places of articulation, and the paired oppositions between voiced and voiceless, the system of plosives seems symmetrical and neat. It is presented quite simply in Table 5.1.

Table 5.1   System of plosives in RP

LIPS	ALVEOLAR RIDGE	VELUM	
p	t	k	Voiceless
b	d	g	Voiced

With the next group of consonants, the *fricatives*, a similar pattern can be detected. These consonants depend on a different kind of contact, one producing turbulent air. The air from the lungs passes through a narrow passage as the speech organs almost, but not quite, close the oral cavity at some point. These hissing and buzzing sounds can be maintained as long as breath lasts, in a way that is not possible for the plosive sounds. We find a different series of articulatory positions for the fricatives, but there is among all but one the same contrast between voiced and voiceless. Teeth and lips are involved in *feel* and *veal*; teeth and tongue in *thigh* and *thy*; teeth-ridge, hard palate, and tongue with *Confucian* and *confusion*; and glottis, that part of the vocal tract where the vocal cords are situated, with *heat*. Finally, the alveolar ridge, where the initial sounds of *seal* and *zeal* may be distinguished from their plosive counterparts /t/ and /d/ by virtue of the friction that occurs between tongue and teeth-ridge. Table 5.2 shows the positions.

Table 5.2   Articulatory positions for fricatives

TEETH + LIPS	TEETH + TONGUE	ALVEOLAR RIDGE	PALATO- ALVEOLAR	GLOTTAL	
*f*eel	*th*igh	*s*eal	Confu*c*ian	*h*eat	Voiceless
*v*eal	*th*y	*z*eal	confu*s*ion		Voiced

As the table indicates, /h/ has no voiced counterpart that can bring about a change in meaning.

The third group of consonants we shall examine are the *nasals*. These are articulated in the same way as the voiced plosives /b d g/ except that the oral cavity is kept closed at some point and the air passes out through the nose: thus *rib* is distinguished from *rim*, *red* from *wren*, and *rig* from *ring* by the feature of nasality associated with the last sound in the second word in each pair. The nasals therefore have the same places of articulation as the plosives, but there is no significant contrast between voiced and voiceless. They are symbolised as /m/, /n/, and /ŋ/.

The latter sound, the velar nasal in *ring*, calls for further comment. Such is the influence of spelling that many people regard this not as a single sound, but as a sequence of the sounds /n/ and /g/. But it is only in some accents — notably those of the west midlands and north-west — that a /g/ is sounded in words like *ring*. In RP, however, and many other accents, *ring* is pronounced /rɪŋ/; the back of the tongue comes into contact with the velum or soft palate, as for /g/, but air escapes through the nose rather than the mouth.

So far, we have described two-thirds of the consonants in the RP system. The other six — the initial sounds of *chore, jaw, roar, law, war,* and *yore* — will be dealt with when and if the occasion arises (see Table 5.3). Space prevents us from analysing all the consonants in detail, neither can we do justice to the wealth of phonetic variants for each phoneme. But we need now to look a little more closely at that part of the system we have described. As we inspect it, we shall find that it is a little less watertight and elegant than at first appears.

We saw above that /h/ stands out from the other fricatives in that there is no significant voiced fricative in the glottal place of articulation, as there are in the other places. /h/ stands out in other ways as well. Whereas we can usually put other fricatives in initial, medial, and final position in a word — /f/ as in *fish, heifer, off*; /v/ in *veal, ever, give,* — there are no words in any accent of English where /h/ is in final position; and the only time it occurs medially, in words like *behind* and *adhere*, it is at the onset of a syllable that is stressed.

Part of the description of a sound, then, is the range of positions it can occupy. This is known as its incidence. To take another example, the velar nasal /ŋ/ likewise has incidental peculiarities. This occurs, as we have seen, in final position, where it is frequent in the verbal termination *-ing*, as in *walking*. We also find it before the positionally-related velar plosives /k/ and /g/ in *think* and *finger*, and medially between vowels, as in *singer* (which in RP, and most southern accents, does not rhyme with *finger*). But the sound virtually never occurs in initial position, and certainly not in formal styles of pronunciation. We shall see the relevance of these observations later in the chapter.

RP vowels

Vowels are in general more difficult to describe than consonants since we often cannot feel the movements of speech-organs involved in their articulation. Of paramount importance in the description of vowels is the shape of the tongue as it moves or stays momentarily in a fixed position in the mouth. In particular, we need to know which part of the tongue — front, centre, or back — is raised towards the roof of the mouth. Also important is the shape of the lips: whether they are rounded or spread. Finally, we shall need to distinguish those vowel sounds where the tongue moves during the process of articulation — these are called diphthongs — from those where the tongue stays still; and within the latter class, we need to be aware of the *duration* of the

Table 5.3   *The consonants of RP*

			Voiceless						Voiced		
			Initial	Medial	Final				Initial	Medial	Final
A *Plosives*											
bilabial	1/p/	as in	pin	dipper	lip	2/b/	as in	bin	rubber	rib
alveolar	3/t/	as in	tin	bitter	bit	4/d/	as in	din	rider	rid
velar	5/k/	as in	kin	pocket	sick	6/g/	as in	gate	bigger	big
B *Fricatives*											
labiodental	7/f/	as in	fin	leafy	leaf	8/v/	as in	vine	never	leave
dental	9/θ/	as in	thin	ether	wreath	10/ð/	as in	this	worthy	seethe
alveolar	11/s/	as in	sin	fussy	fuss	12/z/	as in	zoo	razor	gaze
palato-alveolar	13/ʃ/	as in	shin	fishy	rush	14/ʒ/	as in	gigolo	measure	rouge
glottal	15/h/	as in	hen	behave	—					
C *Affricates*											
palato-alveolar	16/tʃ/	as in	chin	kitchen	rich	17/dʒ/	as in	gin	rigid	ridge

In the consonants below, the voiced/voiceless contrast is not significant:

D *Nasals*

		Initial	Medial	Final
bilabial	18/m/	man	gammon	ram
alveolar	19/n/	nose	sinner	sin
velar	20/ŋ/	–	singer	sing

E *Lateral*

		Initial	Medial	Final
	21/l/	love	colour	fill

F *Frictionless*
continuant 22/r/

		Initial	Medial	Final
	22/r/	run	hurry	far away

G *Semi-vowels*

		Initial	Medial	Final
palatal	23/j/	yes	–	–
bilabial	24/w/	win	away	–

vowel, whether it is long or short. We can now move on to describe the
RP vowel system.

There are seven short vowels in RP, seen in *pit, pet, pat, pot, put,
putt*, and the final vowel of *patter*. *Pit, pet*, and *pat* have front vowels:
the front of the tongue is raised towards the palate; higher for *pit*,
lower for *pat*, between the two for *pet*. Thus we can distinguish between the vowels in those words by referring to the height of the front
of the tongue in the mouth. With these sounds also, the lips are spread:
they adopt a 'smiling' position. The vowels of *pot* and *put* are *back*
vowels: the back of the tongue is raised, higher for *put* than *pot* (it is
difficult for us to feel this, but X-rays show this is so). With these two
vowels, the lips are rounded, or slightly pursed.

The vowels of *putt* and pat*ter* require careful explanation. In RP the
vowel in *putt, nut*, and *cut* is different from that in *put, good*, and
bush, a distinction not made in some accents, especially in the north
and midlands. Like *pot* and *put, putt* has a back vowel, but one that is
unrounded, and therefore made with spread lips. The social significance of this vowel − symbolised as /ʌ/ − will be discussed below.
Lastly, the final vowel in *patter* is unlike the other vowels in this series,
in that it is the centre of the tongue that is raised when the vowel is
articulated. It is also distinguished by the fact that it never occurs − in
formal style, at any rate − in syllables that are stressed. Thus, the first
syllable of *about*, and the second of *opportunity* have the same vowel
as the last syllable of *patter*; hence, as the commonest vowel of unstressed syllables, this sound is the most frequently occurring vowel in any
variety of English. If this comes as a surprise to many people, it is because the sound in question − called *schwa* by linguists, and symbolised as /ə/ − is represented by many different spellings.

We can sum up this account of the short vowels with the aid of a
simple diagram, which represents a schematised side-view of tongue-
positions within the mouth (see Figure 5.1). We have italicised *putt* because it is outside the front-spread versus back-rounded symmetry of
the RP short vowel system.

The five long vowels in RP are heard if we choose words beginning
with /b/: *bee, bar, bore, boo*, and *burr*. Only one of these, that of *bee*,
is a front vowel; it is made with spread lips, with the front of the
tongue high in the mouth. The vowel in *bar* is also made with spread
lips, but in RP it is an open back vowel. *Bore* and *boo* both have back-
rounded vowels; the back of the tongue is higher in *boo* than in *bore*.
Finally, the vowel of *burr* is a long central vowel, with a similar tongue-

Figure 5.1   Positions of tongue in pronunciation of RP short vowels

position to /ə/. It will be noticed that many of the words cited have an *r* in the spelling, which has no realisation in RP pronunciation. We shall see the significance of this below. Our system of long vowels can be summarised as in Figure 5.2.

The diphthongs, of which RP has eight (but sometimes nine) are more difficult to describe than the vowels so far introduced. Many people are surprised to be told that the RP vowel in *bait*, for instance, is a diphthong; but we have to be able to specify how that word is distinguished from *bet*, *bit*, and *beat*. In the RP pronunciation of *bait*, the tongue moves from a position similar to that of the vowel in *bet*, to one like that of the vowel in *bit*. In other words, the tongue is progressively raised in the course of articulation, and this can actually be felt if the pronunciation of *bait* is slowed right down, so that the glide from /e/ to /ɪ/ can be appreciated. A glide in the same direction also occurs in *buy* and *boy*, from the low-front-spread, and low-back-rounded starting-points respectively. These diphthongs can be shown as in Figure 5.3. The diphthongs in *bough* and *bow* (as in bow and arrow), and in *beer*, *bear*, and (sometimes) *boor*, move in different directions. *Bough* and *bow* move towards the /ʊ/ of *bush*, the last three towards /ə/. Figures 5.4 and 5.5 will make the starting-points of the diphthongs clear.

Figure 5.2   Tongue-positions for RP long vowels

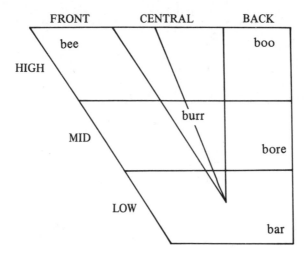

Figure 5.3   Tongue-positions for diphthongs gliding towards /ɪ/

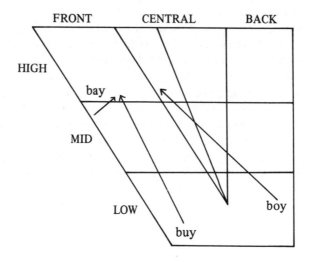

Figure 5.4   Tongue-positions for diphthongs gliding towards /ʊ/

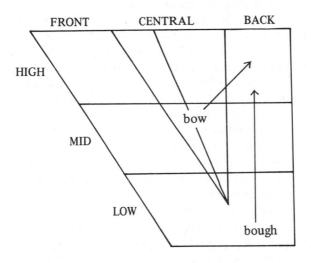

Figure 5.5   Tongue-positions for diphthongs gliding towards /ə/

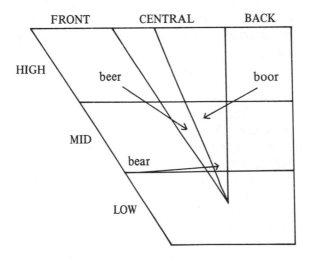

There are two points to be made about our description of the RP vowel system. The division drawn between long and short vowels, although traditional, is not meant to be absolute, since there are many grades of length. In fact, those vowels we have described as long are distinguished from the short vowels as much by quality as length. And within the long vowels, length is conditioned by the nature of following consonants. For instance, the long vowel in *leaf* is even longer in *leave*, and longer still in *leaves*. It is the voiced consonants immediately following the vowel, and combinations of them, that appear to have exerted a lengthening influence. Voiced consonants also affect the character of one of the short vowels. In RP, and in other southern accents, the /æ/ vowel before voiced plosives, as in *bad* and *bag*, for instance, is longer than in *bat*, and *back*. These examples show the importance of phonetic environment in the study of pronunciation.

The other point concerns the vowel of *boor*. Although we have described it as a diphthong, this pronunciation of the word is actually rather uncommon. Many speakers of RP do not distinguish between *boor* and *bore* (and, for that matter, *boar*); they use a long vowel in all three. What is happening here is that one diphthong is gradually being eradicated from the system. That diphthong, /ʊə/, is only used in words of rather infrequent occurrence, such as *tour* and *moor* and occasionally *sure*; and in those words, especially *tour*, it is often replaced by the vowel of *tor*. In sum, the *distribution* of the diphthong – its occurrence in particular words – is contracting: it is becoming marginal to the system. If it is lost altogether, there will be one phoneme less in the system (see Table 5.4).

Variation and style

It is when we examine connected speech that we see just how fluid our pronunciation is. This is particularly apparent in speech that is rapid and casual, and is as true of RP as any other accent. Whole words are reduced to what seems to be a minimal form, or changed almost beyond recognition. And even in RP, variants are regularly used that are commonly castigated as 'slovenly'.

In our discussion of /ə/, we noted the relevance of stress. Not all syllables in a word are given equal weight: in *hotter*, for instance, the *hot* part is pronounced with more stress. In connected speech, moreover, whole words are given less stress than others. Frequently-occurring

Table 5.4   The vowels of RP

I   *Simple Vowels*

A   Short vowels. These do not occur in stressed syllables unless before a consonant in final position.

1	/ɪ/	as in pit	
2	/e/	as in pet	Front vowels, lips spread
3	/æ/	as in pat	
4	/ɒ/	as in pot	
5	/ʊ/	as in put	Back vowels, lips rounded
6	/ʌ/	as in putt	Back vowel, lips spread
7	/ə/	as in pat*ter*	Central vowel, lips neutral

B   Long vowels

8	/iː/	as in bee	Front vowel, lips spread
9	/aː/	as in bar	Back vowel, lips spread
10	/ɔː/	as in bore	
11	/uː/	as in boo	Back vowels, lips rounded
12	/ɜː/	as in burr	Central vowel, lips neutral

II *Diphthongs*

13	/eɪ/	as in bay	
14	/aɪ/	as in buy	Front-closing
15	/ɔɪ/	as in boy	
16	/aʊ/	as in bough	
17	/əʊ/	as in bow	Back-closing
18	/ɪə/	as in beer	
19	/ɛə/	as in bear	Centring
20	/ʊə/	as in boor	

'grammatical' words like *and, but, from, for, shall, must*, have an un-stressed pronunciation with /ə/, so that *what's for dinner?* becomes /wɒts fə dɪnə/. And in the most rapid and casual styles the vowel /ə/ is a common realisation of some of these words such as *are, her, or,* and *of,* as in *what are you thinking?, he left her stranded, more or less,* and *one of the best.* Consequently, in those grammatical words like *he, him, his, her,* and *had,* where /h/ is pronounced in formal styles, or when these words are strongly stressed, it is dropped in rapid speech.

Other kinds of reduction, known as elisions, are made in casual style.

Consonant-clusters are simplified when they occur at word boundaries. Thus, in *last night*, an RP speaker is unlikely to pronounce the /t/ in *last*. Moreover, the final consonant of a word like *gone* may change in anticipation of the initial consonant of the following word. Thus, it may be /n/ in *gone riding*, but /m/ in *gone bicycling*, and /ŋ/ in *gone gliding*. This process is known as assimilation, since the articulation of one consonant is assimilated to another. Thus, the /b/ in *bicycling* is made with the lips, so the /n/ in *gone*, an alveolar nasal, is replaced by a nasal also made with the lips. Similarly, the velar position of /g/ in *gliding* determines the same position in the preceding nasal. In sum, the number of articulatory movements is minimised, and the process can be described as one that seeks 'economy of effort'.

Another kind of assimilation involves consonants that we have not yet introduced. One of these is the vowel-like palatal consonant that occurs initially in *yore, yet, yeast*, etc. Its phonetic symbol is /j/. In sequences such as *miss you*, this palatal consonant combines, in effect, with the consonant immediately before it. A new sound is created in the process. Out of *miss you* comes /mɪʃuː/, in which the medial consonant is the voiceless fricative in *shin, shoe*, etc. (The transition to the 'sh' sound can be felt if the sequence from /s/ to /j/ is speeded up.) Similarly, the sequence *got you* becomes /gɒtʃə/ (spelt *gotcher*, or *gotcha* in comics, etc.). This 'tch' sound belongs to a class of consonants, two in number, known as the *affricates*. The initial sound of words like *chin* and *chore* combines the characteristics of both plosive and fricative consonants, by starting like /t/, and ending like the /ʃ/ sound in *shoe*. The /tʃ/ sound has a voiced counterpart, the initial sound in *jaw*, or the final sound in *edge*, with the symbol /dʒ/.

So far, we have seen how the phonemic structure of a word may change in accordance with the words that occur with it. We must now consider how the pronunciation of an individual phoneme may vary in different phonetic environments. The phoneme we shall choose in illustration is the voiceless alveolar plosive /t/. In rapid, informal pronunciation, this sound is not always articulated in the manner we have described above. When in final position, as in *right*, the sound is usually accompanied by a closure in the glottis, which produces the well-known glottal stop or plosive. This is known as glottal reinforcement. And when /t/ is followed by certain consonants, as in *sit down, football*, the glottal closure becomes dominant, and there is either only very weak contact between tongue and alveolar ridge, or none at all.

Two other variants of /t/ will be discussed here. In the speech of many RP users, and of others as well, the tongue does not come away sharply from the alveolar ridge, but tends to vibrate after contact is made. Thus, a plosive articulation is immediately followed by a fricative one, and a 'ts' sound is produced. *Great*, then, has a slight /s/ at the end of the word. /t/ can therefore be said to have an *affricated* variant in certain positions. The other variant only occurs between vowels. In words like *butter*, but more particularly, perhaps, across word boundaries, as in *got away*, the /t/ often has a voiced variant, so that we hear *budder*, *god away*. The voicing occurs because vowels are usually accompanied by vibration of the vocal cords; and in these instances, the vibration carries across the intervening consonant, and includes it.

It is as pointless to condemn as 'slovenly' these glottal, affricated, and voiced variants of /t/ as it is to say that weak forms, simplified consonant-clusters, and assimilations are the marks of incorrect pronunciation. There are so many involuntary articulatory movements involved in speech that we can never be conscious of how we sound on all occasions, especially when our speech is at its most rapid and relaxed. And as we shall see, some of the phonetic tendencies we have described have been operating in the language for centuries, and may even be as old as English itself.

Variation and change

Our description of RP is by no means yet complete. No accent is monolithic: and RP, as well as varying according to situation, also has variants associated with age. We have already noted that some speakers differentiate *tour* and *tor*, while others do not; and in general, it is older speakers who keep them apart. Some older people make a further distinction: certain words, like *shore*, used to be pronounced with a diphthong, to sound like *shawə*, so that a three-way distinction could be made between *shore*, *Shaw*, and *sure* (with /ʊə/). This diphthongal pronunciation of *shore* (arising, as we shall see, from the loss of *r*) is now so rare that we can speak of a systemic difference between those types of RP that use the diphthong, and those that do not.

It might be thought that a further systemic change is under way, in that /ʊə/ is gradually being eliminated from the system. But that process has been checked, it seems, in those words which have the palatal consonant /j/ immediately preceding the diphthong. In words like *lure* (pronounced /ljʊə/) *curious*, *pure*, etc., the high tongue-position needed for the /j/ sound influences that of the following diphthong, which also has a high, though back, tongue-position. The distribution of /ʊə/, therefore, is to a large extent conditioned by the nature of the preceding consonant. It is not easy to specify the reasons for these changes. One suggestion is that there are not enough oppositions of the *shore/Shaw* type to make the diphthongal pronunciation of words like *shore* seem worth preserving. In other words, a rare diphthong gives way to a common one. Similarly, the infrequency of /ʊə/ tends to undermine its position in the system. While systemic pressures of this kind are of great importance, we must not forget that a social value often attaches to particular variants. We can illustrate this with a recent change of a different type. Younger RP speakers often pronounce the vowel in words like *cat* and *back* with a lower vowel than their elders. The older pronunciation, often heard in British films of the 1940s and epitomised today in the speech of the tennis commentator Dan Maskell, sounds to many ears more like /e/ than /æ/ (*metch* rather than *match*). In contrast, the younger RP sound is much closer to the lower vowel common in the north and midlands, and it is conceivable that this is its origin. Northern pronunciations have recently enjoyed a temporary prestige, and perhaps the older realisation of /æ/ had become a stereotype of an RP that was felt to be archaic and even quaint. Social attitude, then, may underpin this example of a *realisational* change.

RP, of course, is not the only variety of pronunciation that is changing. Any accent, at any point in its history, is in process of change, as variants associated with age, sex, or style, become either dominant or recessive. Our examples so far, however, have been changes that are only recent. Changes in the more distant past can be explained when we turn to the processes we have described for informal style. A development as significant as the rise of new phonemes depended to some extent on the voicing of consonants between vowels. It seems likely that the voiced fricatives in *love* and *thousand* were not phonemes in Anglo-Saxon, but were merely phonetic realisations of their corresponding voiceless fricatives, /f/ and /s/, when these occurred in medial positions between vowels. There were no pairs of words like *razor* and *racer*, *waver* and *wafer*, the meanings of which are dependent on the voiced/voiceless contrast in medial position; so the Anglo-Saxon scribes did not need to mark the fact that *s* in, say, *þusend* (thousand) was voiced, any more than we indicate the different articulations of /k/ in *key* and *car*. Contact with French, however, increased the incidence of the voiced sounds. A great many French words had /v/, for instance, in both initial and final position, so that oppositions like *vine* and *fine*, *serf* and *serve*, arose. In words of French origin, /z/ occurred finally (so *cause* could be kept apart from *course* after loss of /r/); and to a lesser extent, in initial position, hence *zeal* beside *seal*. Thus, a phonetic tendency within the language was reinforced from outside, enabling the French sounds to be absorbed into the English consonant system.

Many pronunciations also derive from assimilations that took place in the past. Modern *fetch* arises from Anglo-Saxon *fetian*, and the place-name Stamford originally had *stan* (stone) as its initial element. Most people today say *samwich*, not *sandwich*, but both assimilated and un-assimilated pronunciations co-exist in words like *Tuesday*. Many people may avoid /tʃuːzdeɪ/ as 'incorrect', and there is evidence that some assimilated pronunciations were once quite common in educated speech, but have since been stigmatised. Three centuries ago, *injun* for *Indian*, *shewer* for *sewer* (deriving from /sjʊə/) seem to have been quite common, but survive only in non-standard speech. Even today, some people think it more correct to avoid pronouncing *racial* as /reɪʃəl/.

In *fetch*, *injun*, and *shewer*, the consonants arising from assimilation are not new additions to the inventory of phonemes: /tʃ/ occurred in Anglo-Saxon *ceorl* (churl), /dʒ/ in *ecg* (edge) and /ʃ/ in *scip* (ship). In other words, the frequency of occurrence of these sounds was increased by assimilation. Another consonant, however, virtually owes its place in the English sound-system to this process. The medial voiced fricative /ʒ/ in words like *treasure*, *occasion*, and *usual* derives from assimilation of /z/ + /j/: *treasure* would once have been /trezjər/. The significant fact about these words is that they are all of French or Latin origin; and when we inspect the incidence of the sound in other positions, we find it only occurs – and very rarely – in words of similar source. In initial position, the sound is limited to *gigolo*; and in this word, it is likely to be replaced by the native affricate /dʒ/, as it is when it occurs in final position, in the French words *beige*, *prestige*, and *garage*. But people with pretensions to refinement are more likely to retain the 'French' pronunciation, and this is most noticeable, perhaps, in the pronunciation /gəraːʒ/, with the fricative, beside the Anglicised /gærɪdʒ/. In sum, the sound in question occupies a marginal place in the English consonant system, especially outside RP; and even within that accent it is the least common of the consonants, its occurrence in initial and final positions conditioned historically by the desire to display the refinement attaching to the sounds of a foreign, and prestigious, language.

Three stigmatised consonant pronunciations

We saw above that certain assimilated forms that are now dialectal were
once also used by upper- and middle-class speakers. Similarly, these
social groups used pronunciations that are now quite heavily stigmatised. One of these involves /h/, which we have seen is often dropped in
words like *he, him,* and *her* in unstressed position in rapid, informal
style. Like the medial /ʒ/ sound in *treasure* discussed above, /h/ has a
restricted incidence; but unlike /ʒ/, its position in the consonant system
is much less strong than it was 1500 years ago.

In Anglo-Saxon, /h/ could occur in initial position as it can today,
but it could also occur in medial position, as in *hliehhan* (laugh) and
finally, as in *heah* (high). In these latter positions, the phoneme probably had a variant similar to the final sound of the Scottish word *loch*,
the velar fricative /x/. /h/ also occurred in consonant-clusters, its realisation again being dependent on the position of such clusters in the word.
hn, hl, hr, and *hw* occurred initially, as in *hnappian* (to nap), *hlaf* (loaf),
hring (ring) and *hwæt* (what). *ht* was found medially and finally, as in
ahte (owned) and *niht* (night); and in some post-Conquest texts, like
Sir Gawain and the Green Knight, it is spelt with the symbol ʒ.

By the fourteenth century, it seems that the sound had been largely
eliminated from initial clusters: at least, this is what spellings suggest.
This process of simplification may have been motivated by systemic
pressures, as in the case of *Shaw, shore* discussed above: there were not
enough words depending on the opposition *hn* versus *n*, etc. Since simplification of consonant-clusters is common today in contact varieties of
English, however, it may be plausible to attribute the source of the process to Anglo-French bilinguals, for whom clusters of this kind were
strange. But one of them, *hw*, still survives in the speech of some older,
principally female, RP users in words like *what* and *which*. These pronunciations, whose existence today has probably been reinforced by
the spelling, are also found in Scots and in the speech of some New
Zealanders.

The *loch* variant of the sound, which is articulated in the velar – or
sometimes uvular – region of the throat, survives also in Scots, as the
popular stereotype *bricht moonlicht nicht* suggests. In Scotland, its
presence has perhaps been reinforced by the occurrence of a similar
sound in Gaelic. But the sound has also been recorded recently in *light*
and *night* along the border of Yorkshire and Lancashire; and in final
position, in *thigh*, in the Pennine village of Heptonstall. In these positions,

however, the sound has otherwise been lost entirely, or replaced by another fricative, as in *cough* and *enough*. In some dialects, this tendency can also be found in other words (*pluff* for plough is recorded in parts of Yorkshire) and may be viewed as the replacement by a common sound of one that is becoming infrequent – as in the case of *beige*, etc., discussed above.

Today /h/ is firm only in initial position, so it is not surprising that it is often eliminated in regional pronunciation. It seems that this was also true throughout English society up to the eighteenth cenury, when the influence of spelling reinforced its use, and it is now the most famous shibboleth in English pronunciation. But in dialectal pronunciation, it is sometimes retained as a marker of emphasis, so we might hear *honions* for *onions*; and similar pronunciations are heard, but for different reasons, by those anxious to avoid the shibboleth, but who are unaware of the distribution of the sound. This phenomenon is known as *hypercorrection*.

The presence of the velar nasal /ŋ/ in the *-ing* of *going*, *seeing*, etc., also owes more to the recommendations of the codifiers than to the natural preference of speakers of English. Originally, this consonant was probably no more than a phonetic variant of /n/ before velar plosives, as in *panc* (thank) and *tunge* (tongue). Gradually in words like *tongue* the /g/ was lost in many accents (but not those of the west midlands and north-west) so that the velar nasal itself became phonemic, enabling words like *sin* and *sing* to be contrasted by the final nasal consonant alone. The incidence of the sound had increased by the fourteenth century as the verbal terminal *-ing* developed, displacing earlier *-inde*, *-ande*, etc.; but in this, the /g/ was often lost, and the velar nasal replaced by the more frequently occurring /n/. Pronunciations like *goin'* and *seein'* have been dialectal, it seems, for at least 500 years. During the sixteenth and seventeenth centuries this pronunciation was also in use among the upper class, and has remained so in the speech of the aristocracy at least until the 1930s. *Huntin'*, *shootin'*, and *fishin'* is the linguistic stereotype of a class whose status has been secure enough for it to remain unmoved by the eighteenth-century doctrines of correctness.

Our third stigmatised pronunciation is the glottal variant of /t/. The phenomenon of glottal reinforcement, which we have seen is associated with informal RP style, is found in many English dialects; and outright replacement of the alveolar articulation by the glottal one is not uncommon in the eastern counties, especially those directly to the west of London. What is just a tendency in RP, then, has become a well-established variant in the dialects. And in the working-class pronunciation of many big cities, notably London and Glasgow, it has become the norm in final and medial position between vowels. It is in the latter position that the sound is most strongly disparaged. A glottal plosive in *butter* stands out more than in *late*, and we find that in London, Cockney women often try to avoid it in this position (preferring the affricated variant 'ts').

Since the glottal stop in English is only a variant of /t/, and not a separate phoneme, we should not be surprised if little explicit reference was made to it by observers in the past. We do not know how long the sound has been a common feature in the speech of London, for example. But it is difficult to resist the impression that stigmatisation actually promoted the use of the glottal plosive. What all the pronunciations discussed here have in common is that they seem to be spreading, especially among working-class men. In Norwich, for instance, the dropping of *h* is regular among this group, although Norfolk is an area where /h/ is traditionally sounded. And the glottal plosive is now found in many big cities, although it may be resisted in those which, like Liverpool with its heavily affricated /t/, /k/, and /g/, already have a clear regional variant. Moreover, the use of glottal pronunciations among young middle-class speakers is often cause for comment. Not only is it for this group a marker of informality, but it is also, perhaps, an emblem of values which they identify with the working class.

Three regional indicators

Many readers, particularly those from the north of England and the midlands, will have noticed at once that the system of pronunciation described for RP is different, in some important respects, from their own. We shall look at just three sounds that arouse regional sensitivities: the vowels of words like *nut* and *fun*, *pass* and *path*, and the consonant *r*. Of these, the vowels are indicators of social class as well, in that they fallaciously epitomise 'northern' pronunciation, part of a stereotype of ignorance, backwardness, and poverty still dominant in many southern minds, not least those of journalists on so-called national newspapers.

In much of the north and midlands, there is no distinction between the vowels of *put* and *putt*, *could* and *cud*. All four have the short, high, back-rounded vowel that characterises only *put* and *could* in RP.

We can therefore speak of a systemic difference between accents: RP has one more short vowel-phoneme. It is worth pointing out, however, that in some accents, distinctions are made that are unknown in RP: much of Lancashire, for instance, distinguishes *look* from *luck* by having a long vowel, that of *soon*, in the first word of the pair.

From observations made by scholars during the seventeenth century, it seems likely that the current northern pattern was once much more general than it is today. Shakespeare's London audience would probably have said *nut* like a northerner. In the south, the vowel has subsequently been lowered and unrounded, not only in RP, but in other southern dialects as well. Thus over much of southern and eastern England, we find the possibility of a *put/putt* contrast; but the /ʌ/ vowel is, not surprisingly, realised in different ways. In Cockney, as we have seen, it is often no longer a back vowel at all, but a front one, so that *nut* sounds like *gnat* to a northerner.

We do not know how, or where, the change began. But the first thing we can establish is that there was, as it were, space in the vowel area involving the back of the tongue. We assume that the short vowel system in Shakespeare's time was as shown in Figure 5.6. There are only two back vowels, with a lot of space between them compared with the front vowels, where any movement up or down might bring the vowels too close together to maintain a distinction. Apart from *putt*, then, this system is much the same shape as the contemporary RP one we have described above. The vowel /ʊ/ may have developed a lower variant after certain consonants, perhaps in rapid and informal style. Indeed, there may have been a set order of consonants exerting a lowering influence. Recent research in the USA suggests that the raising of the /æ/ vowel in words like *ham* to sound like *hem* is dependent on such an order, so that only in some regions is the vowel raised before all consonants. In RP, the change seems to have been checked in words with initial lip-consonants, as in *put*, *bull*, *full*, which keep the rounded vowel also found in northern accents. But there are exceptions: *but*, *pun*, etc., have /ʌ/, whereas *cushion* and *sugar*, which have no initial labial consonants, do not. This complicated distribution of the sounds makes it extremely difficult for northerners to learn this part of the RP system.

In the words so far listed, the new sound can be regarded as merely a phonetic variant of /ʊ/, since its occurrence is determined by the nature of preceding consonants. But the possibility of a new contrast was emerging. Words spelt with *oo* were in process of shortening, from

Figure 5.6   Short vowel system in Shakespeare's time

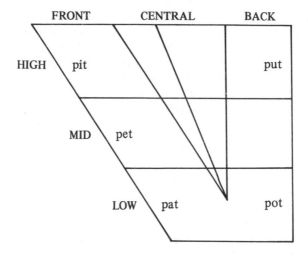

the vowel of *soon* (cf. *look* in Lancashire today) to its short counter-part /ʊ/. Thus the historically different sounds in *put* and, say, *stood*, *book*, etc., were now the same; hence *stood* versus *stud*, *book* versus *buck*. But when we examine the dialects, we find the lowering and un-rounding process has affected even the *oo* sounding words, so that *soot*, *cushion*, *put*, and *sugar* have /ʌ/. The distribution of sounds in the south-east midlands and East Anglia seems to be entirely unpredictable.

On the basis of this evidence, we may postulate the following origin and spread of the new /ʌ/ sound. It arose in a dialect contiguous to London, perhaps in informal style, and became associated in the city with immigrants from the area in question. In the mixing of dialects characteristic of London at this time, certain variants were associated with different social classes, each striving, consciously or otherwise, to maintain identity or distinctiveness from other social groups: what sociologists call the flight-pursuit mechanism. At some point, the new variant became prestigious with an influential social group. It was eventually adopted by the London elite, but in time became the norm in the capital, which in its turn began to influence the surrounding countryside.

Social prestige and dialect mixture may lie behind the adoption of the long, back vowel in words like *path* and *pass*. As in the case of /ʌ/, this is a change originating in the south-east; but unlike it, there is no systemic difference among accents involved. The reason for this is that two features are associated with the RP vowel: length, and a back quality. Most northern accents also have a long vowel, but a fronted one that contrasts with a short front vowel. Thus, in both north and south there is long-short opposition but the quality of the long vowel is different, and the *distribution* of long and short vowels is different. These differences are summarised in Table 5.5.

Table 5.5

	RP		NORTH	
LONG (+ back)	cart,	calf	cart, calf	LONG (+ front)
	path,	pass		
SHORT	cat,	map	cat, map	SHORT
			path, pass	

The lengthening of the originally short *a* sound in *cart* and *calf* in both RP and the north is associated with the loss of the following consonants, /r/ and /l/ (on which, see below). But in much of southern England, the vowel was lengthened before other consonants, notably the voiceless fricatives, as in *path*, *pass*, and *after* (and also before nasals followed by other consonants, as in *dance*). Both long and short vowels co-existed, it seems, in London speech from the seventeenth century; but their social values were still fluctuating well into the nineteenth century. In 1836, Walker wrote that the short vowel was 'polite', the long one 'vulgar', although the latter had formerly been fashionable. But Walker may have been fighting a rear-guard action, based perhaps on the spellings. For the long vowel eventually won out, developing the characteristic 'far back' quality − as some northerners aptly describe it − it shares with Cockney. Even today, fluctuation occurs in some words, such as *elastic*, while others, such as *gas* and *daffodil*, retain the short vowel. This may be why northerners who otherwise try to modify their accent in the direction of RP tend to retain the short vowel in *path*, *pass*, etc., whereas they often try to accommodate to the /ʌ/

versus /ʊ/ distinction by using an /ə/-type vowel: thus *nut* sounds like /nət/.

The situation in early nineteenth-century London concerning the vowel of *path* may have been similar to that of words like *cloth*, *cross*, and *off* in more recent times. The consonants in these words had also lengthened the preceding vowel in many southern dialects, so that *cross*, for instance rhymed with *horse*. This lengthened sound was also adopted into RP, but has since become something of a stereotype of an old-fashioned kind of RP. But the more recent preference for the short vowel may have been motivated by a desire to avoid a pronunciation that has also been a characteristic of Cockney. Or the pronunciation may have been influenced by the spelling.

We mentioned above that in many accents, the vowel in *cart* is long. The lengthening is associated with the loss of the /r/ sound before a consonant; and in many accents, including RP, /r/ is also lost in word-final position, as in *far* and *shore*. It seems likely that all varieties of English used to pronounce the /r/ in all these positions, as is suggested by the spelling. But by about the middle of the eighteenth century, scholars had recorded its decline in the speech of the prestigious, except where it occurs before a vowel. It is still pronounced in all positions, however, in the south-west of England, in parts of Lancashire, Yorkshire, the north-east, Scotland, South Wales, and Ireland; and also, of course, in North America.

The high incidence of /r/ in most of the accents listed is not a feature that attracts much social comment. But its south-western realisation, with the tongue curled right back, is often used as a regional stereotype, one that evokes the rather comfortable associations of life in a pleasant cider-drinking countryside. In the United States, however, it is more commonly a prestige feature. We see here the arbitrary way in which social values are attached to certain sounds: while dropping the *h* in a lower-class accent is stigmatised, few people notice that RP speakers regularly drop the *r* except before vowels.

Accents differ, then, with respect to the incidence of /r/. Bu the sound is also realised in many different ways in different regions. In Liverpool speech, the tongue-tip often *taps* the alveolar ridge; and in parts of Northumberland, a 'burr' is made in the back of the mouth, rather like the French /r/ we are taught in school. This sound is a uvular fricative. Moreover, 'r-pronouncing' has profound implications for the sound-system. Not only can pairs like *lore* and *law*, *sort* and *sought* be distinguished, but it seems that the sound has had, and continues to have, a marked effect on the preceding vowel. So that when /r/ is lost after vowels, we find compensatory re-alignments in the vowel system, of which the development of a diphthong in *shore*, as mentioned above, is one example. It is not unreasonable to assume that the precise phonetic character of /r/ was as variable in the past as it is today. Thus, it is difficult to know exactly how different *r*'s have affected preceding vowels. But modern pronunciations give us clues. In the north-east, the burred /r/ may be rare today, but its influence can still be heard in the back quality of many vowels in words such as *first*, which sounds a bit like *forced*. Similarly, the strongly retracted tongue-position of /r/ in many American accents has tended to obscure preceding vowels, so that in *hurry* and *very*, for instance, they sound alike. It seems probable that in Shakespeare's time, a similar obscuration of the vowel in words like *fern*, *shirt*, and *spur* was occurring. Originally, these would have had sequences of /e/ + /r/, etc., as the spellings suggest; but with the loss of /r/, the preceding /ə/-type sound was lengthened. In RP today, these words have the long central vowel, a sound unknown in accents which preserve /r/ in all positions. But in dialects which, like RP, have reduced the incidence of /r/, we find a radically different vowel-pattern in these words. Often the vowels are short. *First* is *fust* in parts of the south and East Anglia; and in Nottinghamshire, Lincolnshire, and parts of Yorkshire, we hear *bod* and *chotch* for *bird* and *church*.

Another development affecting a vowel before /r/ has acquired a social significance. The short /e/ vowel in words like *clerk* and *Derby* was lowered in some dialects to an /æ/ sound like that of *pat*, which, after loss of /r/ and lengthening, became identical with the vowel of *cart*. In sixteenth-century London, such *ar* variants co-existed with *er* ones (in one case, a variant pronunciation of *person*, *parson*, eventually became a new word). Until the eighteenth century, *ar* variants were fashionable, as in *sarve* and *varmin(t)* (vermin), but many of these were eventually stigmatised; perhaps the *er* spelling, fixed long before by the printers, was felt to match the other pronunciation better. But *clerk* and *Derby* retain *ar* in RP; and if these are often pronounced with *er* in working-class speech, it may be because many people have reacted against the stigmatised *ar* forms, and *hypercorrected* their pronunciation. Alternatively, the *er* pronunciations in those words may derive from the more usual development of the vowel before /r/, which may also explain their presence in the speech of the United States.

Space prevents us from dealing with less well-known, but otherwise

Figure 5.7   Three traditional pronunciation variants in England

more ancient features of traditional dialect pronunciation. In the area formerly known as Northumbria, for instance, an older front-type vowel in words like *stone* is preserved, as in the Yorkshire place-name Stainmore, 800 years after a rounded, back vowel had started to develop in such words in dialects of the south. It is assumed that this vowel is closer to the Anglo-Saxon one in *stan*, but it also seems likely that the northern pronunciation was reinforced by the Scandinavian form of the word (*steinr*) during the Viking Age. As we shall see, this Anglo-Scandinavian culture area preserved other sounds which help us to understand changes in the more recent past.

The Great Vowel Shift

During the fifteenth and sixteenth centuries, it seems that there were radical changes in southern pronunciation. The vowels in words such as *tide* and *house*, originally long ones, became diphthongised. Those in words like *meet* and *moot* were raised to the position formerly occupied by *tide* and *house*. Many words with *ea* spellings like *meat*, whose pronunciation had been kept separate from those spelt *ee*, were raised to the same /i:/-type vowel as in words like *meet*. And other words with *a* spellings, like *mate*, were at first raised, and then diphthongised. This generally upward movement among the vowels occurred too late for the changes to be recorded in spelling. The decisions of the printers had been made, so that our modern spellings preserve the patterns of 500 years ago.

The details of the shift are notoriously difficult to work out. We often have to contend with the puzzling, even contradictory, observations of contemporary scholars. Recent attempts to reconstruct the chronology of the changes have often, moreover, disagreed among themselves. And only in very recent times have linguists tried to suggest a motivation for the shift that is rooted in a social context. Scholars in the past have been content to attribute the changes to some inherent tendency within the language itself, as though it possessed some mysterious predisposition towards the raising and diphthongisation of front vowels. Here, however, we shall look for an explanation that takes account of social stratification and the desire to mark social identity through language.

The sixteenth- and early seventeenth-century observers whose contemporary accounts we have to interpret were men who lived and worked in the south-east of England. We shall accordingly locate the origins of the Vowel Shift in Tudor London, as different dialects mixed, and as self-consciousness about class and status intensified. As a new prestige pronunciation emerged in London as a result of the shift, it gradually spread outwards and downwards in the social scale, affecting the sound-systems of other dialects. As we shall see, regional pronunciation today often preserves sound-patterns that characterise earlier stages of the shift, or even sounds that pre-date it entirely. If we look again at dialects of the extreme north of England, we find pronunciations that may help us to understand the *phonetic* basis of the shift.

Until well into the present century, a traditional pronunciation of words like *house* and *mouse* has been preserved by speakers in rural areas north of the Humber. This vowel is not a diphthong, as in RP, but a long vowel, more like the stereotyped *hoose* of Scottish pronunciation. As such, it is closer to the vowel in RP *moon* and *soon* than *house* and *mouse*. Historians of English have assumed that a vowel of this northern type existed in words like *house* over most of England, at least up to the time of Chaucer. The *oo* vowel, then, pre-dates the Vowel Shift.

The diphthongisation of this long back vowel, /u:/, may have proceeded in the following way. Instead of the back of the tongue remaining at a constant height in the articulation of the /u:/ sound, raising began at the centre of the tongue. A glide developed, therefore, from a central vowel, /ə/, towards the /u:/ vowel. We shall call this Stage one of the process. A diphthong of this type can be heard in Cockney speech today, in words like *spoon*, which sounds a bit like *spur-oon*. Gradually the tongue movement involved in the articulation of *house* became more pronounced. The initial /ə/ element in the diphthong lost its neutral quality and took on a back vowel resonance, as in modern RP, or a front vowel quality, as in many south-eastern dialects (sounding, for instance, like *heouse*, with the initial vowel similar to *bet*). We shall call this Stage two. *The Linguistic Atlas of England* (Sanderson *et al.*, 1978) shows over a dozen distinctive pronunciations of the diphthong which have evolved in the dialects; and the sound is particularly susceptible to regional variation in the United States.

The vowel of *house* was not the only one to be diphthongised. Words like *tide* may once have sounded like /ti:d/, with a long, high front vowel similar to that found in RP *bee* and *feed*. As in *house*, a glide from the centre (but moving frontwards) may have characterised the first stage of diphthongisation. Gradually the diphthongisation has spread through all words of this class, except in certain cases. For instance, words like *night* and *right* in many northern counties retain the earlier *ee* sound, as in *it'll be reet* (right). This is because the *gh* in the spelling registers the presence of an earlier velar fricative /x/, which in these areas has been lost relatively recently, as is explained above. The fricative kept the preceding vowel short, but when it was lost, the vowel was lengthened long after other /i:/ words had been diphthongised.

We assume that a process of diphthongisation such as we have described took place in words like *house* and *tide* in southern England. The origins of the process may be sought in a casual, informal style of speech, perhaps involving the development of a 'lax' pronunciation of the diphthongs as a means of economising on articulatory energy. Alternatively, the conditioning effect of following consonants, perhaps in a set sequence (nasals, say, before fricatives, before plosives, etc.) may afford the explanation: it has been claimed that dialect maps of northern England show that in certain areas diphthongisation is still in process of occurring before certain consonants. The fortunes of *tide* and *house* are summarised in Table 5.6.

Table 5.6   Process of diphthongisation in house *and* tide

	FRONT		BACK
HIGH	/ti:d/	monophthong	/hu:s/
MID	/tərd/	Stage one: first element of diphthong is /ə/	/həʊs/
LOW	/tard/ in present RP	Stage two: first element of diphthong is a low vowel	/haʊs/ in present RP

Once the vowels of *house* and *tide* had been diphthongised, there was room for the other long vowels to move upwards. Originally, the vowel of *meet* may have been pronounced with a vowel like the *é* in the French taught in school. We can symbolise this as /e:/. The vowel in words like *moot* would have been a long back vowel of similar tongue height, /o:/. By about Shakespeare's time, it is probable that the vowels in these words were much the same in quality as they are in contemporary RP.

So far, we have described only that part of the shift where high vowels are concerned. While it is conceivable that the process began at the 'top end', it is now more usually thought that it was the raising of low vowels that triggered it. To illustrate this, we shall need to look more closely at the long front vowels, which at this time were much more numerous than is the case with contemporary RP. The vowel in *meat*, as the spelling suggests, was different from that of *meet*. It may have been like that of *met*, but with a longer vowel (/ɛ:/). Finally, there was *mate*, with a low, fairly front vowel, a bit like northern *mat*, only lengthened (/a:/). Our illustration now appears as shown in Table 5.7.

Table 5.7

		FRONT	
HIGH		*tide*	/i:/
MID-HIGH		*meet*	/e:/
MID-LOW		*meat*	/ɛ:/
LOW		*mate*	/a:/

It was the pronunciation of words like *mate* that seems to have been crucially important in sixteenth-century London. At first this was a short vowel, which was lengthened as the final *e* (a relic of the obsolescent inflexional system in the grammar) ceased to be pronounced; its phonetic quality would have differed from region to region. In some south-eastern dialects, notably those of Kent and Essex, it seems to have developed a relatively high pronunciation. Such a raising may be associated with forceful styles of speech, since it has been found that increased articulatory energy tends to raise front vowels. We do not have any knowledge of other sounds in these dialects at this time, but it is possible that if *mate* had a fairly high vowel, then either it had merged with *meat*, or *meat* had been raised to merge with *meet*. We can see here, then, the possibility that the Great Vowel Shift involved the 'pushing upward' of the long front vowels by the development of words like *mate*.

If we compare our diagram above with those representing modern

RP earlier in the chapter (Figures 5.2 and 5.3), we find that *meet* has been raised to the high front position formerly occupied by *tide*, and *meat* now has the same vowel as *meet*. The vowel in *mate* has been raised, to the position formerly occupied by *meet*, but has since (by about 1800) been diphthongised. In regional pronunciations, however, we find different patterns. Some dialects of the north midlands have a diphthongal pronunciation of *meat* (sounding like *mate* to RP ears) which keeps it distinct from *meet*. And in many regional accents of the north, the vowel in words like *mate* is not diphthongised, but retains the character of the vowel in the south before diphthongisation.

We have now outlined most of the changes involved in the shift. But we have yet to suggest the mechanism. As we have seen, a relatively high variant of the vowel in *mate* was associated with the speech of Essex and Kent, and as we saw in chapter two, Kentish was a stigmatised dialect. The London bourgeoisie, then, would want to distance its own pronunciation from that of the lower class, which was constantly being swelled by immigrants from these areas. One way of doing this was to raise the vowel of *mate* even higher than that of the lower-class variant; and raising of the lowest vowel in the system would necessitate raising all the vowels above and, ultimately, pushing the vowel of *tide* into a diphthong. It seems that in the speech of the bourgeoisie, the vowel of *mate* was raised to a height close to that of *meat*, so that some observers actually recorded a merger of the two sounds. It is arguable whether this actually occurred; but what the contemporary observers in the sixteenth century seem to have recorded is a picture of enormous complexity, with three competing systems in this area of long front vowels. The aristocracy, now no longer able to distance itself with the use of French, seems at first to have kept *mate*, *meat*, and *meet* distinct. At the other extreme, a third system had merged *meat* and *meet*. It appears that this was the lower-class pattern: and the fact that it is this that eventually formed the pattern for the future prestige accent need not surprise us. As is often the case, the unacceptable yesterday becomes the acceptable today.

Part 3
Imposition and spread

Chapter six
The imposition of English in the British Isles

In the course of the last four centuries the minority languages of the British Isles have been undermined by English political and economic power, the policies of English governments, and English attitudes, both official and unofficial. The opprobrium cast on the regional dialects of England has been visited, on a grander scale, and with far-reaching consequences, on the speech of regions diverse in language and culture, and situated far away from the metropolitan south-east. In this chapter we shall trace the long and complicated history of English as a dominant language throughout the British Isles. We shall see how a northern variety of English was developed as the national language of an independent Scotland, and how that variety was displaced in official domains by standard English after the union of parliaments in 1707. Next, we shall consider how the Celtic languages have been maintained, and even promoted, despite generations of linguistic domination. In Ireland, we see a version of English colonialism, and the only territory where a Celtic tongue has become a national, official language. We shall then consider the maintenance, first of Gaelic in the Scottish Highlands, and then of Welsh, the object of a recent and vigorous campaign of promotion. Finally, we shall discuss two cases of what has been termed language death, the abandoning of Cornish and Manx as the first languages of the local Celtic communities.

With one important exception, the languages with which we are dealing are Celtic, and therefore structurally distant from English. They represent two branches of the Celtic language-family. The Gaelic of Ireland, and its implantations in the Scottish Highlands and the Isle of Man, form one branch. Welsh and Cornish, together with the Breton of north-west France, are more closely related to the British Celtic that was displaced during the Anglo-Saxon settlement, as described in chapter one. While the two branches had diverged considerably, rather as, say, Swedish, Norwegian, and Danish have done, there was contact between the languages of each branch, at least until English domination severed the links. Such contacts ensured a degree of mutual intelligibility between Gaelic-speaking Irish and Scottish Highlander, and between Welsh and Cornish; but since the imposition of English, the absence of a centre in either branch of Celtic has precluded the cultivation of standard varieties and hastened the proliferation of regional ones. We cannot therefore speak of a standard Welsh, or a standard Scottish Gaelic, in the same way as we can speak of a standard English.

The one exception is Scots. In origin a variant of the Northumbrian dialect of the Anglo-Saxons, Scots has been spoken in southern and much of eastern Scotland for 900 years or more. But outside Scotland, it has rarely been accorded the status of a separate language, partly because purely linguistic criteria have governed attitudes to it, and partly because English people have often found it convenient to forget that Scotland was not politically united with England until 1707. This political factor inevitably complicates assessment of the current status of Scots; in fact, it constitutes one of the best examples of the difficulty of drawing the line between a dialect and a language. As we shall see, our stance on this issue will depend on the relative weight we attach to different kinds of criteria.

Whatever status we accord Scots, we must acknowledge that English has most successfully been imposed throughout the British Isles. Aggression and expansionism have emanated from England since Norman times. By the twelfth century, Norman nobles had buttressed southern and eastern Wales with great castles, and had established a presence in Ireland. The Welsh aristocracy was finally defeated in the thirteenth century; and in time, Ireland was to become the first English colony, its land confiscated for the benefit of outsiders. Scotland alone withstood military conquest; but by the early eighteenth century English domination had been achieved through political ingenuity. Thus, though their language has never figured in census returns like the Celtic ones, many speakers of Scots have felt, and still feel, that they themselves are a linguistic minority whose linguistic traditions have suffered at the hands of the English.

Unlike the imposition of Latin in Europe, the spread of English was not dependent on military victories. Nor did it confront oral vernaculars; Wales and Ireland both had developed languages and traditions of literacy as old as the English, and Scots, in the later Middle Ages, was also used for literary and legal purposes. But in other respects, the story is familiar. English in most cases has had a long time to take root; it has acted, and still acts, as a lingua franca. And, there have been obvious material advantages in learning it: industrialisation, and the consequent disruption of life in rural areas, has meant that many people have had to learn English to get employment.

As an imposed language, English has had a symbolic value clearly different from that of the minority languages. On the one hand, as the official language of a power often regarded as alien and remote, it has often been redolent of authority and high social status. It also became of course, the language of social aspiration and economic advancement. On the other hand, it has often been felt to lack those virtues of warmth, sincerity, and local dignity associated with the minority languages. We see here a replication of the symbolic values accorded to the standard variety and the regional dialects within England. Throughout the British Isles, therefore, standard English was, and still is by many, thought to be useful, but impersonal; effective, but neutral and cold.

The history of English outside England has two major strands. We must first describe how varieties of English – often non-standard ones – were established in the early Plantations of English settlers such as those in Wales and Ireland, and how those varieties developed in the relative isolation of their new locations. Second, we must trace the imposition of standard English as the language of administration, law, and education, a process which began with the Tudors. This task is impossible to do without reference to the sociolinguistic history of the minority languages themselves. Thus, we must know something about the functions of those languages in the past, how they have been maintained, and how they are being promoted, just as we needed to explore, in chapter one, the factors involved in language imposition, maintenance, and shift in the period of Anglo-Saxon settlement, and beyond. The history of *relationships* between speakers of different languages, then, cannot just involve the history of the dominant language.

So far, we have used the term *minority* in reference to the languages under discussion. Logically a minority language should be one spoken by only a minority of the population in a given area. Here we are using it differently, in the sense of a language quite widely spoken, but subordinated to a *dominant* language, in this case English. Only in Eire has the minority language become a national, official one – but there we need to distinguish between its declared status and its actual use among the mass of the population. The other surviving Celtic languages have varying functions and sociolinguistic profiles. Formerly discouraged by England, their status in recent years has been at best that of tolerated languages, although governments in London tended to ignore their existence. More recently still, they have sometimes been *promoted*, not by central government, but by local agencies often concerned to advance the cause of nationalism. Interest in the languages has been kindled, especially among the middle class, and increasingly they have been learned as second, or additional languages. The best known instance of such newly engendered language-loyalty is the recent campaign to promote Welsh, a language which has also, like Gaelic in Ireland and the Highlands of Scotland, been maintained as the first language of some small, isolated local communities. But interest in minority languages has also occurred in the absence of any native speakers at all, as in Cornwall and the Isle of Man. And it has affected the attitudes of speakers of Scots. During the past decade in particular, Scots has become a focus for language-loyalty, particularly in Scotland's universities.

The imposition of English throughout the British Isles is a process of such length and complexity that it is difficult to make generalisations that are valid for all territories. Nor is it always possible to respect national boundaries and sensitivities. Scotland, for instance, has been split culturally, ethnically, and linguistically for well over a thousand years; this means that we must deal with its Scots-speaking community quite separately from its Gaelic one, for the simple reason that linguistic history only indirectly follows the history of nations. In addition, the special relationship between English and Scots must be explored within a framework different from that of contact between English and the Celtic languages.

Two broad generalisations about the process of imposition may perhaps be made. First, we shall see the significance of the Tudors – who were, ironically enough, of Welsh descent – in implementing what we might call today a language policy towards the rest of the British Isles. This, incidentally, had profound consequences for Scots, even though the Tudors and their successors may not have counted it as one of the languages they were intent on displacing. Second, the educational system everywhere was instrumental in the spread of standard English. And after the introduction in 1870 of universal primary education, no other language was even recognised in the schools. Significantly enough, in the twentieth century it is in education that campaigns to promote the minority languages have found both a focus, and some notable successes.

Throughout this chapter we must beware, however, of assuming the existence of a unified national consciousness in the territories under discussion. Although we are dealing in part with nations and their

Figure 6.1   *The imposition of English in the British Isles*

histories, we must not be seduced by present-day nationalist ideologies that tend to obscure the fact that the interests of financiers and entre- preneurs are not necessarily the same as those of land-labourers and factory-workers. Scotland, for instance, may have been split in the ways described above: but it has also like England been fissured along a social dimension as well. It is not entirely fortuitous that the social class most active in espousing the cause of Scottish Nationalism is the modern equivalent of the class that in the sixteenth and seventeenth centuries probably felt its financial interests would best be served by union with England.

The development of Scots

The split in the cultural traditions of Scotland goes back at least as far as the seventh century AD. By then, the Anglo-Saxons of Northumbria had extended their kingdom to roughly where Edinburgh now stands, absorbing the original Celtic population. From the west, Gaels from Ire- land had established a kingdom over most of Scotland north of the Forth. By the eleventh century, Scotland had a Gaelic dynasty, its king- dom stretching from the north-west Highlands to the area of the present border with England, although the Outer Isles and parts of the extreme north-east had yet to be wrested from the Norwegians. But Northumbrian dialect of south-east Scotland was still spoken; and links with England were strengthened by the arrival of refugees from the Norman Conquest. The court and church were Anglicised; land was granted to men from England (some of whom spoke Norman-French) and many English-speaking people settled in Scottish towns. Gradually the influence of Gaelic contracted to the Highland area while southern Scotland developed a culture that was not Celtic, but Germanic, deriv- ing primarily from the Anglo-Saxons.

Scotland was at first successful in resisting the territorial ambitions of the English kings. After Bannockburn in 1314, Scotland enjoyed some form of independence from its aggressive neighbour for nearly 400 years. During this period, the Scottish court cultivated contacts with France, and developed its own educational institutions, parliament, law, and literature. And in the opinion of many, the Scottish variant of the Northumbrian dialect was developed as the language of these insti- tutions, to the point where we can speak of Scots as a language separate from, though related to, English.

The centuries of independence saw Scots emerge as a developed vernacular. We see a process of functional elaboration, similar to that described for standard English in chapter two, except that it was Latin, not French that was replaced in official domains. In 1390, Scots was first used for parliamentary records; and the laws were translated into it in 1425. Moreover, an impressive literature was written from the fourteenth century onwards. The relationship between the literary Scots of this period and that of English can be judged from lines like these, taken from William Dunbar (? 1460-1521):

> lut schulderis and luttard bak,
> Quhilk natur maid to beir a pak,

where *lut* means 'bent', *luttard* 'stooping', *quhilk* is a Scots spelling of 'which', *beir* of 'bear'. Interestingly enough, we witness during the sixteenth century the same kind of agonising about the suitability of Scots for literary purposes as we saw in our discussion of standard English.

The cultivation of Scots was not, it seems, accompanied by a consciousness that it was, or should be, different from English. Neither were ideas of nationhood particularly strong; unlike the English, the Scots had no French-speaking ruling class to grouse about. Sections of the Scottish bourgeoisie probably also favoured greater contact with England for economic reasons. The replacement of Latin by Scots was probably seen as a question of vernacularisation rather than of the explicit promotion of a national language. Although contemporary observations are almost entirely lacking, the process of standardisation is most clearly seen, perhaps, in literature: a literary standard was emerging, for poetry, and more crucially, for prose. To sum up: by the end of the sixteenth century, Scots may be seen as a national language in embryo, whose subsequent development was dominated by the imposition of English.

The undermining of Scots was not the result of decrees and proscriptions, but of the gradual weakening of independent Scottish institutions. The Reformation, which played such a key part in Tudor policy, had its strong adherents among sections of the Scottish bourgeoisie, so there was no need for the English to impose it. Elsewhere in the British Isles, the language of religion has often proved an important factor in language maintenance; but in southern Scotland, it does not seem to have been an issue. Scots accordingly never became the language of prayer books and Bible in Scotland, and this seems to have been vital in exposing Scottish people to the standard language of England. This variety was also disseminated in a great deal of printed literature at this time. Other Scottish institutions were soon to be eroded. In 1603, the Union of Crowns meant that a Scottish king was on the throne of England; but it was at London that he held his court. Gradually the most privileged and powerful class in Scotland adopted the language of England.

Finally, the Act of Union in 1707 ensured that Scotland's laws and administrative arrangements were determined in London, and therefore in English. By the eighteenth century Scots had become the Low language, and standard English was now the medium of law, administration, education, and religion. And in language, as well as politically, it was 'the end of an auld sang', as was said in Scotland at the time.

From the eighteenth century onwards, the gentry of Scotland tended to receive an English education. This meant that all ideas about the best or most correct usage were articulated with respect to English; no variety of Scots was codified. Scots, therefore, came to be seen as a dialect, to be disparaged; there was a proliferation of books listing Scotticisms to be avoided in polite company. The first Scottish Members of Parliament, finding their accents derided in the English parliament, strove to sound like Englishmen. Like the dialects of England, Scots lost all social status, and its use in school was punished after the 1872 Education Act.

Unlike the dialects of England, however, Scots was never reduced to a patois. A literary tradition was maintained, by people such as Burns; and in the nineteenth century Scots was used to record versions of ballads and folk-songs as they were found by assiduous Scottish collectors. In the twentieth century, attempts have been made by poets like Hugh MacDiarmid to promote Scots as the medium for a serious and tough-minded poetry that was international in character without losing its Scottishness, but which was unencumbered by the traditional associations of Burns. The maintenance or re-creation of a prose tradition has been more problematic, since continuity was interrupted in the sixteenth century. There are few models for serious, expository prose, and even in the novel, Scots has gone the way of English dialects in that writers have tended to use it in depictions of regional or lower-class dialogue only. Modern Scottish novelists must cultivate their own literary language, as MacDiarmid had to do for poetry; but it is worth noting that one writer, Lewis Grassic Gibbon, achieved this in the 1930s with *A Scots Quair*.

The notion that Scots is at most a dialect of English has been communicated to most Scottish people. With no census returns to remind them of the number of speakers of Scots, and no classical texts to give them a sense of historicity, many Scottish people, like some speakers of English-based creoles, may feel that their tongue is not different enough from English to justify calling it a separate language. In other words, it is linguistic criteria that are uppermost in their minds (as they are in the minds of most English people in their attitude to Scots): Scots sounds, grammar, and vocabulary are close to those of English in a way that those of Gaelic, say, are not. But purely linguistic criteria are not enough in settling demarcation disputes of this kind. Speakers of Dutch dialects, say, on the border with Germany, may understand speakers of neighbouring German dialects better than they can the speakers of Dutch dialects on the other side of Holland; but everyone agrees that people who live in Holland speak Dutch, and that Germans speak German. To call Scots a dialect of English is to ignore its development during Scottish independence, and to reduce its status to that of the regional dialects of England, unless we use the term *dialect* in a more specialised sense, to refer to regional varieties with their own traditions of writing (as we speak of the dialects of English in medieval times). In sum, the terms *dialect* and *language* are not fine enough to apply unequivocally to Scots.

Opponents of the view that Scots and English are separate languages are likely to argue that many alleged Scots usages can be found in northern dialects of English. Boundaries between usages, for instance, do not by any means always run parallel with the border. Even if they do at present, it can be shown that certain usages alleged to be Scots, like *gaed* (went) and bellies being *sair* (sore) instead of aching, used to be heard either in Northumberland or Cumbria and have only recently been replaced by a standard English form. Geographical patterns of usage are often complex: sometimes areas on each side of the border share a form unknown in standard English, such as the Anglo-Saxon word *heck* (hay-rack), and occasionally the border divides forms that are also dialectal, like Scots *pook* (to pluck) beside northern English *ploat*. Relationships of this kind are typical of the border areas between dialects; but so they are between different though related languages.

Differences between Scots and English are often therefore not absolute, but may be expressed in terms of general tendencies and frequencies of items. But we can still point to some items that seem characteristic Scots usages. We find a different selection of loan-words north of the border: *gar* (make), *gowk* (cuckoo) from Scandinavian, *dote* (endow), *vivers* (victuals), *howtowdie* (young hen) from French. Some Gaelic words, such as *tocher* (dowry) and *clarsach* (harp) are not well-known in England. Modal verbs are sometimes used differently: *will I push it?* instead of the usual English use of *shall*.

Differences in pronunciation are striking. Above all, they are often of a clearly systemic kind. Not only is there a different system of vowels before /r/ — *fern, fir,* and *fur* often have /e/, /ɪ/, and /ʌ/ respectively — but there is a significant point of divergence from all varieties of English in that vowel *length* is a contrastive feature of much less importance. It has been suggested that Scots vowels are to be regarded as short except in certain positions: finally (as in *see*), before /r/ (*seer*), and before voiced fricatives (*seethe*). Elsewhere (in *seat* and *seed*, for instance) the vowel would be short. We find a similar pattern with diphthongs. /aɪ/ is longer in *drive* than *ride*, and each diphthong may be regarded as a separate phoneme. Distinctions are also conditioned by morphology: *tied*, the past tense of *tie*, is pronounced differently from *tide*. These patterns of length are so pervasive that the pronunciation of most Scottish people must be described independently of any English sound-system. Even those who adopt an accent that is close to RP will tend to merge distinctions usually made in England: *pull, pool,* and *boot* often have the same, short vowel, as do *cot* and *caught*.

Other, more well-known features of Scots pronunciation we have already noted in our description of northern dialect sounds in chapter five. The stereotypes *there's a moose loose aboot the hoose* and *it's a braw bricht moonlicht nicht the nicht* testify to the retention of the undiphthongised vowel in words like *house*, and of the fricative in *night*. Other pronunciations, such as the unrounded, 'Scandinavianised' vowel in words like *hame* (home) are reflected in traditional Scots spellings. But within Scotland, many of these pronunciations are regarded as broad, and often stigmatised, just as other features (including words and grammatical patterns) are marked regionally, and stylistically. It is for this reason that the study of Scots in many Scottish universities has tended to promote the idea that it is a language separate from English, with its own history, its own dimensions of regional, social, and stylistic variation, and to some extent its own norms.

Recent studies of sociolinguistic variation in southern Scotland tend to suggest, however, that in many respects local speech is *exonormative*: English norms are highly influential. As we have seen, Scotland's upper class had begun to adopt the standards of the London elite during the eighteenth century; more recently, the middle class has moved in the same direction. This is partly a means of avoiding the heavily stigmatised speech of the working class in the big cities, such as the Edinburgh use of tags like *ken*? (do you know?) and the Glasgow use of the glottal plosive. Many middle-class speakers are over-anxious to adopt an accent similar to RP: the somewhat archaic stereotypes known as the Kelvinside and Morningside accents (after certain districts in Glasgow and Edinburgh) may be regarded as attempts to preserve a kind of RP similar to 'refayned' pronunciation used by people – older women, especially – in various cities of England. The diphthongs in these accents appear to be hypercorrect: in words like *side*, the first element of the diphthong is raised almost to the /e/ of *set*, so that it sounds like *sade*. In pronunciation, therefore, it is helpful to distinguish between Scots, which itself exists in regional dialectal variety in different parts of Scotland, and which is characterised by those features, among others, listed earlier, and a so-called educated Scottish accent, which is much closer to RP. The latter is one of the most prestigious regional accents of English.

Scots usages are most consistently found among working-class speakers. While a middle-class Scot may say *I'll not be going home* – a construction not uncommon in the north of England also – a farmworker might say *I'll no be gaun hame*. But in the big industrial cities, usage is changing, just as it is in England: and sometimes it may be described as moving away from a base in Scots. Thus, while a recent recording of an Edinburgh schoolboy shows the retention of the traditional vowel in *house*, research in the same city shows that a pronunciation that may be described as *r*-less may be developing among the working class, associated at the moment with young men.

Whatever linguistic changes are under way in Scotland, commitment to Scots has increased in recent years. In part this is a reflection of growing nationalism, seen in the electoral successes of the Scottish National Party (although that party has shown little interest in Scots, as distinct from Gaelic). Language-loyalty has also been inspired by the example of the Welsh Language Society's vigorous campaign. Nationalism, however, tends to obscure divisions of class and ethnic group but those issues surface, in rather subtle ways, when commitment to a particular language is espoused. Many younger, middle-class Scots resent what they see as the Anglicisation of their culture, and their loyalty to Scots may be a belated assertion of ethnicity. They want to see themselves as Scots, not citizens of the United Kingdom; ethnic distinctiveness is the issue rather than political autonomy. But since it has in general been the lower class that has maintained the minority languages, commitment to those languages is also, in part, a commitment to the values of that class. Similar motivations, incidentally, may underlie attitudes to Welsh. It has been persuasively argued that the group most loyal to that language are the heirs to the Welsh tradition of political radicalism that earlier in this century manifested itself in trade unionism and Labour Party politics. University- and college-educated sons and daughters of miners and steelworkers see their national identity as an emblem of class, and of the older, co-operative and collective values of the community.

Feelings of language-loyalty must be taken into account in any consideration of the sociolinguistic profile of Scots today. Many Scottish people feel justifiably bitter at finding their linguistic inheritance relegated to a paragraph or two in histories of English, and dismissed as just another dialect of English. Nationalist feeling, on the other hand, is often apt to inspire arguments that are clearly manipulative. Scotland deserves independence: independent nations have their own language: therefore Scots must be a different language from English. What we do need to respect is the Scots literary tradition: markedly different in language from the standard English one, it has survived the Middle Ages, as has no other regional variety of English. The current status of Scots may accordingly be defined in two different ways. If we accept the view that English is an international language, the property of no single nation, then we can view Scots as the first *national* variety of English outside England, just as American English is a later one. This view respects national sensitivities, and also the linguistic similarities between all varieties of English. Alternatively, we can see Scots as a *deposed* language, which would have enjoyed the kind of relationship to English as, say, Portuguese to Spanish, if the dominant language had not been imposed in Scotland. Our choice between these alternatives may depend to a large extent on which side of the border we happen to live!

Language imposition in the Celtic territories: some general considerations

We have mentioned the importance of the Tudors in the formulation of policy towards England's neighbours. It was they who took the first steps towards formal unification with other territories, and therefore towards the imposition of English as the official language throughout the British Isles. Religious uniformity was one instrument of hegemony, and this meant carrying the Reformation to the linguistic minorities. But the aim of linguistic suppression could be at variance with that of religious proselytisation: an effective way of achieving the latter was to make translations of the Prayer Book and Bible into the minority languages, and populate the Church in those lands with priests who could preach in them. Ironically enough, the survival of Scottish Gaelic and Welsh may have depended, to a large extent, on this 'historic blunder': those languages gained prestige by remaining the parlance of the Church.

The ambitions of the Tudors, and of subsequent rulers, may be compared in this respect with those of the other centralising European monarchies, particularly France and Spain. It is noteworthy that nations where power is devolved on a federal basis generally have a more tolerant attitude to linguistic minorities, as in Switzerland. But in France, the Celtic-speaking Bretons have been subjected to centuries of oppression; and in Spain, the Catalans in the east of the country have suffered under the dominant Castilians. Wherever we find this linguistic imperialism, we find a similar ideology expressed by the dominant power: bi- or multi-lingualism is incompatible with a unified nation and a free people, therefore the minority languages must be rooted out. They are languages associated with 'the enemy' — either secular, or religious: therefore to use them is to identify with the opponents of the State. Spuriously benign arguments are often advanced to justify the process of suppression. Gaelic in Scotland, after all, was in the eighteenth century the language of 'savages'; English was therefore a civilising force. And in Wales, it was even suggested that the use of Welsh was a *cause* of poverty: if people would only learn the right language, they could better themselves.

A number of techniques, of varying degrees of subtlety, were used by the English to impose their language. The various Celtic communities have therefore felt different effects at different times. The Cornish were an early casualty of Tudor policy: their language ceased to function as a community medium by the end of the eighteenth century. In Wales Anglicisation was begun in the sixteenth century by weaning the sons of noblemen away from their subjects by educating them in England. This removed the source of patronage for vernacular poetry and song, which subsequently became a culture of the folk. Furthermore, the introduction of English as the language of government and law broke local traditions of prose. By the early seventeenth century, a similar

process of weaning had begun among the Gaels of the Scottish Highlands; and by then, the Irish chieftains had been defeated. This broke
the cultural and linguistic links between Gaelic speakers in Scotland and
Ireland, just as contacts between speakers of Welsh, Cornish, and
Breton had already been destroyed. In the case of the Scottish Highlands, however, the full force of linguistic oppression was not felt until
after the middle of the eighteenth century.

In Ireland, the picture is more complicated. The Tudors encountered
great difficulties in extending the Reformation to Ireland, and the Irish
chieftains proved resilient in defence of their lands. Since England was
at war with Catholic Spain, it could not afford to have an unreformed
Church on its doorstep. Treatment of Ireland and the Irish, therefore,
was characterised by brutality and paranoia. Ireland became England's
first colony, its ancient local culture overlaid by a Protestant English-
speaking one. Settlers from England and Scotland were planted on land
confiscated from the Irish, and merchant companies in London were
given a free hand to plunder its resources. Like Wales, Ireland had been
colonised by small numbers of English-speakers during the twelfth century; but unlike Wales, Ireland was to endure a further, much more
significant plantation under the Tudors and Stuarts. Irish Gaelic has
therefore had eight centuries of contact with English of one kind or
another; yet alone of the Celtic languages, it has become the national
language of an independent nation-state. We shall accordingly be treating Ireland in more detail than the other Celtic communities.

Throughout the Celtic British Isles, the education system was a
powerful agent in the imposition of English. One result of the processes
discussed above was that standardisation in any Celtic language had
been difficult to maintain, and the breaking of links among Celtic
peoples had undermined the sense of historicity that plays such an important part in forming people's attitudes to their own language. Even
if opportunities had been given, the use of the Celtic languages even as
media of instruction would have been accompanied by great problems.
But the education system had no intention of focusing attention on any
language other than English. Even before the Education Acts of the
1870s, schools in Ireland had been used to coerce children to speak
English, although Wales had maintained traditions of Welsh teaching in
the Circulating Schools of the eighteenth century. But after the introduction of compulsory schooling in the last quarter of the nineteenth
century, teachers punished children if they spoke their native language,
and denied them opportunities of reading and writing in them. Older,

first-language speakers of Welsh, for instance, today often cannot write a letter in their own language. Not only was education punitive from a linguistic point of view, it was also Anglocentric, in that children learned about the history and culture, not of their own societies, but of the English and their empire, in the English language. The role of the education system was summed up very well in the nineteenth century by the MP who said: 'a band of efficient schoolmasters is kept up at much less expense than a body of police or soldiery'.

The survival of the Celtic languages was also threatened by economic factors. In general, the Celtic communities are situated well away from the centres of economic development: for this reason they are often in-sultingly referred to as the Celtic fringe. They have tended to be over-dependent on a small number of traditional industries, such as farming, crofting, and fishing, and therefore offer limited opportunities for employment today. In the past, the local economy in two areas has been especially vulnerable to upheavals which have had profound and lasting effects on demographic structure. In the Scottish Highlands, massive depopulation followed the unsuccessful Rising of 1745. By the early nineteenth century, the Highland lairds had been so successfully weaned away from their subjects that they preferred the profits from sheep, and later, deer, to the overseeing of the local communities. Gaelic speakers were evicted in their thousands, many emigrating to the industrialised cities of southern Scotland and also to Canada (where to-day, in places like Cape Breton Island, Gaelic is still spoken). Land once cultivated yielded to the wilderness. In Ireland, the potato famines of the 1840s hit hardest the Gaelic speakers of the west: death or emigra-tion reduced Ireland's population by one-quarter. Such population movements have tended to unbalance many communities with regard to sex and age: it was often the young, able-bodied men who were lost to the large towns. And where urbanisation has occurred, such as in south Wales, the Celtic tongues have failed to compete as first languages with English, the language of commerce, and of the employing class.

The psychological effects of centuries of cultural and linguistic im-perialism on speakers of the minority languages have been severe. The processes of government and law, enshrined in an alien language, have often been disorientating, if not totally mystifying, to the community. A sense of powerlessness undermined the feeling of local identity. This has often been exacerbated by the education system, where success at first was equated with proficiency in English, and later with working far away; discouraged and demoralised, those who remained in the local community awaited and expected initiative and leadership from 'in-comers'. At the more personal level, speakers of all the minority languages have been made to feel ashamed of their native speech. Lin-guistically insecure, and therefore nervous, if not sullenly defiant in their use of English, children in the schools of Scotland and Wales were often judged 'inarticulate', like their Black counterparts in the USA.

It is not surprising that there has been a substantial language shift to-wards English in the Celtic areas over the last century and a half. Indeed, some pessimistic observers have predicted extinction for some Celtic languages by the end of the next century. The census returns to some extent speak for themselves. First-language speakers of Scottish Gaelic amounted to about 5 per cent of Scotland's population ninety years ago; today, that figure has been halved. In Ireland, native speakers of Gaelic were estimated at about 23 per cent in 1851; forty years on, the figure was 14 per cent. Welsh proved more durable: the period of lan-guage shift is the present century. But in 1900 perhaps half of the pop-ulation of Wales could speak Welsh, whereas in 1971 the number was put at one-fifth. And in the course of the present century, Manx has been abandoned as a first language altogether.

Yet in some important respects, these figures do not speak for them-selves. How do they relate to different social functions, differences of age and sex, and of town and country? Can people read and write in the minority languages? Data on these issues is often lacking for the past. Today, however, we know that the figures quoted for Scottish Gaelic need to be balanced against the fact that in Harris, in the Outer Isles, 80 per cent of the population can speak the minority language. We need to know about the users of these languages, since the symbolic value of a language derives in part from its association with certain social groups and contexts. Such knowledge can also help explain how languages are maintained and promoted and how, why, and where English is learned.

The census figures also obscure another important fact. At first, native speakers of Celtic languages would have learned English as a second language. Such bilingualism would be diglossic, with English as the High language. Since the end of the nineteenth century, however, campaigns have been mounted in Ireland, the Scottish Highlands, and later Wales to arrest the decline of the Celtic languages by teaching them as second languages. In the course of the present century, there-fore, English has become the first language of increasing numbers of people in Celtic areas, while it is the Celtic tongues that have been learned as second languages. So more Scots now know some Scottish

Gaelic than a decade ago; and in the Republic of Ireland, Gaelic is generally taught in school. But there, first-language speakers are outnumbered by ten to one; and as we shall see, the second-language speakers of all the Celtic tongues tend to be different kinds of people from those who maintain Celtic as first languages in the more remote, less fertile areas.

A minority language can be maintained as the first language of the local community if there is little incentive to replace it with the dominant one. In the Outer Hebrides, and parts of the west of Ireland, isolated communities that are dependent on traditional industries, such as crofting, have maintained Gaelic as a community language. While emigration from these areas has been constant, it has still been possible for a small number of people to continue living much as their ancestors did. But since job opportunities for young people remain scarce in such a limited economy, the pull of English has been strong. In such an environment Gaelic has been maintained among the crofting class despite the absence of overt expressions of language-loyalty on the part of its speakers. All the same, Gaelic is seen by them as a symbol of group identity, even if it is rarely articulated in these terms. The language binds the community together in defiance of the values associated with the wider, urban, commercial world where English is spoken.

While the towns and cities have generally been the bastions of the English language, they have also been the only refuge for people unable to find subsistence in the countryside. In what often seem inhospitable and alien surroundings, immigrants from the Celtic-speaking areas have sometimes retained and subsequently promoted the minority language, as a symbol of their identity and their past. It has been said that Glasgow — which had 12,000 Gaelic speakers in 1971 — is the place to hear Gaelic spoken in Scotland, and in Ireland, Belfast. Thus, it is among such emigrés that the potential for feelings of language-loyalty, of expressions of commitment to the minority language, have normally developed.

It is in the towns and cities too, that people have been stimulated to learn minority tongues as second or additional languages. This trend is most noticeable among younger people, often from middle-class backgrounds. The most vociferous expressions of language-loyalty have perhaps been those of the Welsh Language Society; but such activism has also spread to Scotland in more recent years. The campaign on behalf of Gaelic has intensified, and as we have seen, Scots has also been involved. The intellectual origins of such campaigns are complex, but stem in part from the notion that language is a crucial symbol of nationality. From the end of the eighteenth century, but especially after the 1840s, struggles for independence in Europe and beyond have often been inspired, or justified, by the fact that a particular group speaks a language different from that of a dominant or conquering power.

The long-term survival of the minority languages will depend on more than just the declarations of language-loyalty among college-educated activists. Such attitudes are not uncommon when a language is under threat, even among monolingual speakers of English. Neither are these languages likely to survive if their only speakers are situated on the depopulated, infertile peripheries. The decisive factor may be their ability to function as community languages in the towns and cities, where most people live and work. And at the very least, sustained and active support in a number of official institutions may be necessary. Experience has shown that it is one thing to pass laws to promote a minority language, and quite another to implement them.

A great problem for minority languages everywhere is that of standardisation. Standard varieties usually exist only in the written mode, and these are often based on too narrow, and too archaic a range of texts. In particular, these languages must be cultivated as media for serious prose. Another problem concerns the lack of any kind of spoken standard. If, say, Gaelic is to be taught in Highland schools, which variety is to be taught? None of these problems, however, are insuperable. They were overcome in Belgium, Switzerland, Finland, and many other European nations.

Many people in England may feel doubtful about the usefulness of such language-promotion. If English is widely available, why not just let people learn it, and save the effort and expense? It is unlikely that any minority language could compete with English in the domain, say, of commerce, so why bother with them when jobs might be at stake? These arguments are powerful, but they forget, or ignore, at least three issues. First, people will learn a language if communal experience has shown that it can guarantee a job, or at least offer the possibility of getting one. But in a period of increasing unemployment, knowledge of English will no more secure a job, of any kind, than will the acquisition of the standard variety by speakers of regional types of English. Second, language means other things to people than mere utility. Different languages in a bilingual society have different social values, and these are of great personal importance to the people who speak them. Third, there is no reason why people should not be competent in both languages, as we have argued elsewhere. We may conclude this section with a few general remarks about English as it is spoken in the Celtic territories. We must not forget that some form of English has been spoken in parts of those areas for many generations; this kind of English will accordingly differ in character from that more recently acquired. Some of the more obvious features are associated with pronunciation; a salient aspect to English ears is their intonation patterns, the way in which the pitch of the voice rises and falls, or lilts, to use the popular term. Since we have not dealt with intonation in this book, we cannot define this aspect in technical terms here; but other features of accent are widespread. These varieties tend to be *r*-pronouncing, in the sense established in the last chapter. This may be because English was introduced to these areas when the pronunciation of /r/ before consonants and in word-final position was more general in English, or because contact has been maintained with *r*-pronouncing dialects of English (and, in the case of Highland English, Scots). Neither must we discount the reinforcing influence of the Celtic languages, which tend to pronounce /r/ in all positions. The latter influence may account also for the treatment of *l* after vowels and before consonants. In many varieties of English, including RP, the *l* of *lip* is pronounced differently from that of *pill*. The final consonant in the latter has a back vowel resonance, and is accordingly called 'dark *l*' whereas in *lip* it is described as 'clear'. A 'clear *l*', however, is common in all positions in many of the varieties described here. Finally, the vowels in words like *mate* and *home* are often less clearly diphthongised than in RP, and have the /e:/ and /o:/ type vowels described in chapter five.

In vocabulary, naturally, we find words of Celtic origin. Some, like *ptarmigan* (the bird) in the Scottish Highlands, refer to local objects or affairs, but others, like *shannach* (chat) in Ireland, are words for very general concepts. More striking changes have been made in grammar, in the system of tense and aspect. Often this reflects the influence of the grammars of the minority languages. In Scottish Gaelic, for example, the present tense has come to be used in reference to future time only; consequently, present time is indicated, very roughly, by using verb-groups. So in Highland English, the present continuous forms are used where English speakers use the simple present: *you put that there* becomes *you're putting that there*. Similarly, many people in south Wales use continuous forms to specify habitual aspect: *they are going to chapel every Sunday*. And in some varieties of Hiberno-English, a habitual present, as in *I do be*, has been created.

In general, the English of Wales, the Highlands, and to some extent Ireland enjoys relatively high prestige among many people in England. The prestige derives from the fact that these Englishes are often much closer to the standard variety than are many dialects of English. In other words, they still have the hallmarks of a taught, second language; and nowhere is this more true than in the speech of the Scottish Highlands, often acclaimed by English people as the home of the 'best' English. Where such local varieties bear the imprint of other dialects of English, or of the Celtic language, they are often evaluated in a rather patronising way, as quaint, disingenuous, or fresh. It is not uncommon to hear these sentiments expressed about the English of Ireland. The sources of these attitudes may be many, but one of them may have to do with an unconscious desire to atone for the imposition of English. It is characteristic of conquering powers that they only 'discover' the culture of the conquered peoples when the material basis for that culture has been destroyed, and is beginning to disappear.

Linguistic colonialism in Ireland

The first English spoken in Ireland was that of settlers of the late twelfth century. In Henry II's rather piecemeal campaign of Normanisation, a company of English (mainly, it seems, from Somerset), Welsh, and Flemings from south-west Wales was established on the coast of south-eastern Ireland under the direction of Norman knights. The variety of English they spoke became known as the Wexford or Yola dialect. Later settlements were made in the area of Dublin, which was captured from the Irish; and the dialect spoken just to the north of that city, known as Fingal, lasted until about 1800.

The native culture, however, was largely untouched by these early settlements. The Irish were heirs to a monastic tradition that had surpassed all others in Europe, and their literature was one of the richest and most ancient. It was to this culture that the Normans adapted, just as their kin in England were to become Anglicised. Thus, though they controlled two-thirds of Ireland by the middle of the thirteenth century, the area of English hegemony, known as the Pale, had contracted by the 1490s to a small part of the east coast around Dublin. The Gaelic chieftains were still in arms, and many Norman families, now Gaelic in law and language, were degenerate subjects in the eyes of the English kings. The Tudor campaigns against the ruling Irish families were long, costly, and bitter. Military victories were followed by confiscations of land, expulsions of Irish people by the planting of English settlers; the first of these colonised the south-east midland area of Ireland from the 1550s. By the beginning of the seventeenth century, the last vestige of Irish resistance − involving mainly the chieftains of Ulster − was crushed. The Gaelic nobility fled − an event known as the Flight of the Earls − and large tracts of Ireland were given over to London companies as resources to exploit.

It might be said that the Reformation in Ireland was achieved not by conversion, but by Plantation. Although by 1603 the Prayer Book and New Testament were translated into Irish Gaelic, Ireland remained a bastion of Catholicism. Protestants were accordingly planted in large numbers in the eastern half of Ireland, originating from England and, in the case of Ulster, from Scotland. The Catholic Irish, denied the right to own land, became tenants of the new Protestant owners, and many were forced to live in the infertile west. Sectarian violence was common, and Catholic rebellions were put down with the ruthlessness and arrogance that have characterised English attitudes to Ireland for the last 300 years.

By the beginning of the eighteenth century, it seems that language in Ireland had become a clear indicator of social class. Gaelic was a marker of rural, Catholic poverty; English was associated with Protestantism, ownership, and the towns (although some towns, like Galway and Drogheda, had a sizeable Gaelic-speaking working class until well into the nineteenth century). Increasingly, however, use of the English language was not synonymous with allegiance to the English crown. The Irish ruling class − known during the eighteenth century as the Protestant Ascendancy − found, like its counterpart in the American colonies, that governments in London were thwarting its attempts to exploit Ireland's economy: and many English-speaking Protestants were active in the unsuccessful independence movements of the 1790s. In 1803, an Act of Union made Ireland part of the United Kingdom; and henceforth the Ascendancy became Anglo-Irish, its sons educated in England, its horizons now determined by the dominant culture of the English.

At the time of the Act, perhaps half the population of Ireland used English as a community language. By the end of the nineteenth century, it was the language of the great majority. Gaelic had no official champions. Neither the Catholic church nor the variety of schools of the eighteenth and nineteenth centuries promoted it. On the contrary, every circumstance and condition favoured the use of English. Gaelic culture, now only kept alive by poets and priests, had no centre: regional variations had intensified, so that English could act almost as a lingua franca. Moreover, education for ordinary people meant learning to read and write English: the Irish schoolmasters themselves were the keenest to punish the speaking of Gaelic in school. And literacy in English was a necessary weapon in the growing campaign for independence – now the concern of Catholics only – and in the agitation against the abuse of absentee landlords. The enemy spoke English, and had to be fought in a language with unbroken traditions of literacy and political discussion. Finally, hundreds of thousands of Gaelic-speakers died in the potato famines of the 1840s, in which a quarter of the population was lost through death, or emigration to America, where of course English was spoken. The incentive to abandon Gaelic was now overwhelming.

A movement to promote the minority language did not emerge until 1893. The Gaelic League set up classes to teach it, and the language became a symbol for the cause of independence, though not a vehicle of it. In 1921, however, Gaelic was declared the national language of the new Free State, and it has since been promoted in the educational system. For most people in what is now the Republic of Ireland, Gaelic is a second language, learned in school; they may not speak it very well, but a majority express loyalty to the language when questioned directly. In contrast, Gaelic has been maintained as a community language in pockets of the remote west; and younger people have been encouraged to stay in some of these Gaelteacht areas by means of generous economic aid. While in the west Gaelic symbolises a traditional way of life, elsewhere it is associated with social mobility. Certain jobs, such as those in the civil service, depend on a knowledge of Gaelic, and language-loyalty is therefore stronger among professional groups than it is, say, among business people. Efforts are being made to promote the language in the capital, Dublin: all-Irish primary schools are trying to develop social contacts among Gaelic speakers, who tend to be scattered over a wide area.

Several varieties of Hiberno-English have emerged from the long and complex involvement of the English with Ireland. Usages originating in the dialect speech of the early settlers have in turn been influenced by the more recent, and more standardised English of the Irish ruling class. Patterns vary between south and north, where many Scots speakers were planted; and between east and west, where the acquisition of English is relatively recent. In general, however, Hiberno-English often preserves features that were once more common in England, as contacts with English models have weakened. *Cog* (cheat) was once fairly general in sixteenth- and seventeenth-century English, while an /eɪ/-type diphthong in *easy*, *tea*, etc. preserves a pronunciation once current among the Ascendancy in the eighteenth century, one that became a stock joke among the London literati. Such a pronunciation suggests the merger of *meat* and *mate*, discussed in chapter five, which was no longer the fashionable pattern in eighteenth-century London.

Gaelic influence on Hiberno-English can be seen in all levels of structure. Consonant-clusters unknown in Gaelic, such as *lm*, as in *film*, are pronounced in accordance with Gaelic patterns of vowel and consonant combination; hence, /fɪləm/. The grammar of tense and aspect has also been re-structured. A habitual present is realised as *I do be*, and the perfect is modelled on Gaelic: the present tense of *be* is linked to the *-ing* form of the following verb by *after*, as in *he is after writing* (instead of *he has written*). The verb-group *have been* is therefore rare: *how long are you here?* refers to past, not future time. And Gaelic-influenced structures are also found in written usage. Literal translations of idioms, such as *we were going to put the fight upon the rebels*, and of figurative expressions, such as *'tis an aise to the gate they to be married* (said of a couple who have been busy courting by a certain gate), are found in the work of writers such as Synge, Lady Gregory, and Douglas Hyde, at a time when the nationalist movement was urging the cultivation of the English of Ireland as a literary medium.

The linguistic profile of the north is strikingly complex. The sources of different groups of colonists can still be traced today. A traveller moving from the Ards peninsular, on the coast east of Belfast, towards the north-west coast of Donegal on the other side of Ireland, will first encounter what were originally Plantations of Scots; then English ones from the midlands of England; then the Gaelic community of the Tyrone area; then midland English again; then the Scots Plantation of the Laggan, now in the Republic; then the Gaelic of Donegal. To some extent the traditional speech of each community preserves its ancestry. In areas originally settled by the English, we sometimes find words known to the Anglo-Saxons, like *thole* (endure), and pronunciations like those of the seventeenth-century prestige accent of English. The vowel in words like *side* is /əɪ/, which is the kind of diphthong associated with Stage one of the Great Vowel Shift. Ulster Scots, which has many of the Scots features discussed earlier in this chapter, tends to be influenced by this Ulster English; but this sometimes results in the borrowing of a form that is non-standard. Thus, the traditional Ulster Scots *bag* for *udder* is replaced by Ulster English *elder*, a form still used in the midlands of England.

Since the early nineteenth century, industrialised Belfast has drawn immigrants from different parts of Ulster. Protestants from the north and east, with a linguistic background in Ulster Scots, have often been ghettoised in the Protestant working-class communities, while immigrants from the south and west have settled in Catholic ghettos. Recent research has revealed the heterogeneity of Belfast speech, where variations associated with class, age, and sex are complicated by religious differences. Catholic children tend to be educated in schools run by their church, while most children of Protestants attend state schools — and thus in this respect too, their communities remain separate from one another. Innovations in working-class speech show little influence from models that can be broadly described as RP. Thus, while words like *bang*, *back*, *that*, and *bad* have the same vowel in RP and in middle-class Belfast speech, they often have different vowels, conditioned by neighbouring consonants, in working-class pronunciation. Furthermore, a change in the pronunciation of these words is in process of crossing the sectarian divide. A back vowel is becoming more common among the Protestant working class in the east of the city, and it is spreading, via younger Catholic women, into the communities of the west.

Bilingualism and language maintenance in the Scottish Highlands and Wales

In the Scottish Highlands, the assault on Gaelic has been more recent than in Ireland, and in some ways more dramatic. At the Union of Crowns in 1603, Highland society was still organised in clans, each owing allegiance to a chieftain, the local economy still being dependent on cattle and the cultivation of crops where soil and climate permitted. All affairs were conducted in Gaelic, a common literary form of which was shared with Ireland. And of great concern to governments in London, and their agents in southern Scotland, was the fact that Highland society was still in arms — something they had to put up with until the middle of the eighteenth century.

In the course of the seventeenth century, attempts were made to undermine the allegiance of the clans to their religion, and to their language. One effect of the Reformation was to remove the single institution uniting southern Scotland with the Highlands, the Catholic church: so Protestant ministers were sent among the clans. Attachment to Gaelic — seen as a chief cause of 'barbaritie and incivilitie' — was weakened among the Highland nobility after the Statutes of Iona decreed in 1609 that the sons of chieftains be educated in the south. Gradually, the Scottish Society for the Propagation of Christian Knowledge established schools in the Highlands, in which Gaelic was retained for worship, but English was the medium of instruction. It seems, however, that these early attempts at Anglicisation were not successful in promoting a shift away from Gaelic.

Highland involvement with the Stuart Pretenders to the throne stimulated the most ruthless repression of clan life, customs, and language, by forces loyal to the crown. After the rising in 1745 the clans were crushed militarily, their weapons confiscated, and their language proscribed. The destruction of social organisation was followed by the erosion of its economic base, as thousands of Highlanders were evicted from their homes and forced to emigrate in the course of the nineteenth century. In the crofting communities that remained, people went to school to learn English; and since then, many achieving success at school have been educated at secondary level in schools requiring residence away from home, and consequently in an environment favouring English. All the same, Gaelic has been maintained in some of the more isolated communities; in Lewis, for instance, availability of secondary education since the beginning of the present century has meant that Gaelic has also been taught there.

The depopulation of the Highlands stimulated the expression of loyalty to the Gaelic language. In Glasgow, emigrés set up schools where Gaelic was used as a teaching medium, and books and newspapers were published in the language. An Comunn Gaidhealach was founded in 1891 to promote Gaelic, and in 1918 it succeeded in securing an Education Act that required local authorities to provide for the teaching of Gaelic wherever there was a demand. Since then, literature in Gaelic has been cultivated, the language has been taught in some schools, universities, and further education, particularly at evening classes, and there have been numerous campaigns to promote Gaelic in the mass media.

Ninety-odd years of language-activism have checked the steady decline in numbers of Gaelic speakers. It seems, moreover, that such activism is on the increase: during 1980 for instance, parents on Mull have agitated for their children to be educated in Gaelic. Furthermore, it has tended to become politicised: a Scottish Nationalist MP, Donald Stewart, has recently introduced a parliamentary bill demanding parity of treatment with Welsh. This trend contrasts with the essentially apolitical nature of An Comunn Gaidhealach's activities, which eschewed involvement in issues such as crofters' rights, and which failed to identify with any kind of nationalist movement, either cultural or political.

A recent study of language use on the island of Harris suggests that there are some grounds for optimism about the future of Gaelic. The Outer Hebrides are now officially bilingual, and it is the schools that are promoting the minority language. Now that secondary education is available on the islands, children can study Gaelic as a subject at that level, while in the primary schools they are taught in the language. Text-books have been published in Gaelic, even in scientific subjects, and it is noteworthy that bilingualism is now something that is achieved by first-language speakers of English, as well as of Gaelic.

Outside the education system, Gaelic has been introduced into business transactions, notably by the Post Office. And while the language is not used in such a wide range of functions as Welsh — political debate, for instance, tends to be in English, even when local issues are discussed — it is significant that younger people are re-interpreting the appropriateness of Gaelic in certain situations. Thus, while older, working-class crofters testify to the importance of Gaelic to the home, religious worship (the Bible had been published in Gaelic by 1801), and to the traditional dance and song session known as the ceilidh, younger islanders are more likely to use the language on the telephone, or in the bank, where their parents would tend to use English as a marker of politeness or social distance. For the older generation, Gaelic is often a symbol — albeit covert — of older, traditional values, while younger people seem to have more faith in the *vitality* of the language.

We must now turn to Welsh. To a large extent, the great tradition of Welsh literature survived Plantations of the twelfth century, and military defeats of the thirteenth. Although in 1284 the law in Wales was to be administered in English, no attempt was made to proscribe the use of Welsh in the law-courts. But in parts of south-west Wales, the language was eradicated. During the early twelfth century, pockets of English settlers were established in the fertile areas to the west of the Gower peninsula. It was from these that the Flemish farmers, woollen manufacturers, and traders, planted later in the same century in what is now south Pembrokeshire, gradually learned their English. The original Welsh inhabitants were displaced, and this part of south-west Wales retains an Anglicised character to this day.

The imposition of English was formalised by the Tudors. The Act of Union in 1536 demanded that Wales be ruled in English, and that all holders of high office use the dominant tongue. This meant that the sons of the Welsh gentry were to be educated in England, depriving Welsh culture of official patronage. Access to English, however, remained limited. The increasing use of English in law meant that for many ordinary Welsh people, justice was a mockery. They continued to use their own tongue, while legal arrangements were made for them, and argued about, in another, incomprehensible language.

The Reformation, however, gave the Welsh what it had given the English — a text which came to be regarded as classical. In 1588, the Welsh Bible was published. Throughout the next three centuries, Welsh was maintained in the religious domain; and in the dramatic rise of Nonconformism in the eighteenth century, it played an important role in symbolising the values of Methodism as opposed to those of the hieratic, and English, Anglican church. And not only did this religious revival stimulate the production of a sacred literature, it also gave rise to the Circulating Schools, which taught reading and writing to over half the indigenous population. Today, language-loyalty is strong in those remote, rural parts of Wales where Nonconformist values are still held.

It has been suggested that the language of the Welsh Bible exerted too strong an influence on the literary Welsh of succeeding centuries. As its functions in other official domains were limited, written Welsh lacked models of its own other than the Bible. Sixteenth-century written usage was also codified to some extent, in that a dictionary and grammar of Welsh were produced; and these, too, were greatly influential. While written Welsh was felt to be fixed, and certain forms and structures, even pronunciations, were taught as correct, the spoken Welsh of ordinary people continued to change and diverge. The only standard available for Welsh was therefore a sixteenth-century written one, and so the relationship between written and spoken usage may be described as potentially diglossic.

Two developments in the nineteenth century assisted the spread of English. First, much of south Wales, principally Glamorgan, was industrialised. The extraction of coal and iron ore depended on massive immigration into the industrialised Valleys, at first from surrounding Welsh counties, then from the south-west of England. After about 1850, the population increase in Glamorgan was second only to that of London. Although mining areas in the northern valleys were initially strongly Welsh in culture and language (in 1851 about 90 per cent of Merthyr Tydfil's population was Welsh-speaking, and the town was an important publishing centre in the language), the influx of English-speaking newcomers was too large to be assimilated to that culture. Since then, the trend in south Wales has been towards English monolingualism. The second development was the extension of universal education after the Acts of the 1870s. Industrialisation favoured the use of English among the working class in the south: and that process was formalised in the education system, which ignored the existence of Welsh altogether.

In the twentieth century, however, it is in education that Welsh has made most headway. Since the 1930s, Welsh has been taught in primary schools in the strongly Welsh-speaking areas, and since 1950 there have also been bilingual secondary ones. The Ministry of Education has approved a policy of bilingual education for all Welsh children, and it is as a teaching medium that the language is used in over 650 schools in both urban and rural areas. And for the language-loyalists, one of the most encouraging trends, perhaps, is the way in which many parents, including monolingual English-speaking ones, send their children to Welsh-speaking nursery schools.

Most English people cannot fail to be aware of the more newsworthy attempts by the Welsh Language Society to promote the minority language. With an ideology clearly articulated by its founder, the playwright and lecturer Saunders Lewis, the predominantly young membership of the Society has been seeking to promote Welsh, not only in education, but in other official institutions. Since the Welsh Courts Act of 1942, defendants are entitled to use their own language, and since 1975 the Post Office has submitted to the demand for bilingualism in its transactions. But perhaps the most spectacular advances have been made in the broadcast media. Very recently, in 1981, the government has been forced to restore its original pledge to establish a Welsh television channel.

The spoken English of Wales reflects not only the influence of Welsh and the standard English of the schools. In parts of the south, as we have seen, varieties of English have been spoken for centuries, and Welsh English may also reflect features originally widespread in England, but now dialectal, and from the non-standard speech of immigrants into the industrialised south. Welsh word-order underlies *saw him yesterday, I did* and *it's happy I am*, Welsh pronunciation the quality of the /r/ sound, which in many parts is made by tapping the tongue-tip rapidly against the alveolar ridge. The pronunciation of words like *blew* and *threw* may reflect earlier, or dialectal English. In parts of south Wales these words, which are often kept distinct from *blue* and *through*, belong to the class of /ju:/ words such as *Tuesday, due, duke,* and *feud* discussed in chapter five. Up to the seventeenth century these words were pronounced in the prestige accent of London with a short /ɪ/ before the /u:/ sound; gradually the /ɪ/ became more dominant, to be replaced by /j/ (to give /tju:zdeɪ/ etc., from which the assimilated variant /tʃu:zdeɪ/ derives). In contemporary RP, however, the /j/ has been lost after /l/ and /r/, so that *blew* is /blu:/, identical to *blue*; while in these parts of Wales, this loss has not occurred, and the earlier /blɪu/ pronunciation is retained. A diphthong of this kind can also be heard in parts of England such as Berkshire, so that a source in English dialects is also possible.

Language death: Cornish and Manx

Cornish and Manx have been abandoned as community languages, the former in the course of the eighteenth century, the latter in the course of the present. In Shakespeare's time, however, Cornish was quite widely spoken in much of Cornwall, while Manx was almost universally known on the Isle of Man. In each case, they seem to have survived as first languages among lower-class speakers from peripheral rural areas. These two examples of language death invite consideration of the factors involved in the successful maintenance of minority languages.

A recent study of the decline of Gaelic in a part of north-east Scotland has attributed the cause of language death to the destruction of traditional economic and social life. A minority language can therefore be said to lose vitality as its community of speakers is threatened. When we consider the language of Cornwall, we find that it survived longest in the fishing and mining communities, whose traditional forms have not survived the social and economic changes since the eighteenth century. Similarly, urbanisation in the Isle of Man has been seen as an influential factor in the demise of Manx. But such factors are not the only ones. Language-loyalty tended to surface too late, education and religion were too unsympathetic, or too powerless to maintain them, and there were too many opportunities for contact with speakers of English (unlike, say, in the Highlands of Scotland), and too few for contact with other Celtic languages. The literary traditions of both Manx and Cornish were likewise too fragile to sustain a sense of historicity. We can see the importance of these as we examine each language in turn.

Cornish derives from the British Celtic that was displaced by the Anglo-Saxons. Before its demise as a community language it had been used in certain High domains: in church services until 1678, and as the medium for oral drama, especially during the fifteenth and sixteenth centuries. The period of overt interest in the language, however, corresponds with its decline as a community language. Antiquarians translated parts of the Bible into Cornish in the course of the seventeenth century, and in recent years a revival movement has developed among sections of the middle class. Mebyon Kernow (Sons of Cornwall, founded in 1951) won seats in the 1968 local elections, and has been agitating for bilingual education in schools.

Since the Anglo-Saxon invasions, Cornwall has from time to time rebelled against English authority. Deprived of political autonomy in the tenth century, Cornwall became an earldom; and after the Norman Conquest, an English-speaking bailiff class served the needs of French-speaking landowners. When the Tudors introduced the Prayer Book in 1547, the Catholic Cornish rebelled, but were treated in much the same ruthless way as were the Irish; and the demand for a Cornish Bible and Prayer Book was refused. Bilingualism increased rapidly during the seventeenth century. There is evidence, however, that after its demise in the community Cornish was maintained by what have been termed semi-speakers — individuals who, for a variety of reasons, show interest in learning a language when it is in process of being abandoned by a community. Such speakers survived into the nineteenth century, and have provided a tenuous link with the efforts of the revivalists, where the only other source is the written language.

Manx is a variety of Gaelic, which took root on the Isle of Man when it was conquered by the Irish in the fourth century. After a period of rule by Scotland, control passed to certain English families in the fourteenth century. English has been the official language since then, although formal absorption of the island by the English monarchy did not take place until the eighteenth century. Today, Man has its own parliament, and some economic autonomy, but the language has never been identified with self-government. Manx plays only a symbolic role in government ceremony.

As a community language, Manx died out in the course of the present century. It had been maintained by speakers in the rural areas, whose populations have been declining since the growth of towns in the eighteenth century. Immigration from England at that time made the towns centres of English influence. It is only since the beginning of the seventeenth century that the language has had a written form: the Prayer Book was translated into it, as was the Bible in the eighteenth century, along with some verse. Manx continued to be used in church services until the nineteenth century, when formal education began to undermine it.

In the 1940s there were still some speakers who remembered Manx as a language they had used with parents and grandparents. And since then, there has been some interest in learning the language on the part of some islanders. While Manx flourished, its fortunes seem to have been attended with indifference; now that it no longer has a function in the community, it is a cause for revivalists. It remains to be seen whether Manx, or Cornish, are successfully revived as community languages. Before we write them off, we should remember that a number of languages around the world, like Hebrew, have been raised from the dead.

Chapter seven
English overseas

As a first language, English is now spoken by over 300 million people in North America (including Canada), Australia, New Zealand, the Caribbean, and South Africa. Hundreds of millions of others, especially in Africa and southern and south-east Asia, speak it as a second language. In this chapter we shall see how the spread of English beyond Europe is associated with four centuries of colonialism. Three different strands of colonial expansion will be distinguished. First, we shall see how the activities of trading companies brought speakers of English into contact with people in many different parts of the world, and how such contact with West Africa in the sixteenth century gave rise to the Atlantic slave trade. One result of this was the formation of English-based pidgins, some of which subsequently became the creoles of the Caribbean. Second, we shall discuss colonial settlement, and how new varieties of English were established in America, Canada, Australia, New Zealand, and South Africa. The extent to which new standards have emerged in these countries will be explored, and we shall discuss in some detail how American English developed, and its status in the world today. Third, we see how nineteenth-century imperialism institutionalised English in certain older colonies, such as India, and newly-acquired ones, principally in Africa. The spread of English in the education system in these areas will be traced, and we shall assess the development and status of second-language varieties of English, with the main focus on Africa. Finally, we shall examine some of the language planning problems of ex-colonies which have chosen English as an official language.

It need hardly be said that such a vast topic, spanning four centuries across four continents, should be the subject of a very large book, or series of books, rather than a single chapter of this length. Not only are the issues highly complex, involving a great variety of cultural settings and changing political, social, and economic circumstances, but also controversial: the terms *colonialism* and *imperialism* themselves are good examples of words whose meanings depend on the loyalties of the user. But the student of English is entitled to ask some very basic questions about the spread of the language today. How long has it been used in a certain territory? Who took it there? How did people learn it? We can sketch the answers to some of these questions, but we can also pose others of a more general sociolinguistic character. What relationships do the overseas varieties have to the standard in England? Do they show the same kinds of patterning with regard to region, social class, sex, and age as we associate with speech in England? How do English people regard them? What problems do they pose for those wishing to write literature? The answers to these questions must at the moment be fragmentary, since research on particular varieties is often not only very recent, but unevenly spread. But it is essential for any student of English today to be aware of them.

We can deal with only a few examples, and offer only a few insights, in the course of this chapter. But some rather crude generalisations may help the historian of language. In dealing with English involvement with the world beyond Europe, we do not see a concerted, systematic policy during the last 400 years. Different types of colony were established, for different reasons, in different areas, at various times. We are dealing moreover with a number of impulses and movements, with a focus that is at times more economic than political, or vice versa. It has been said with justification that the flag often followed trade: commercial exploitation, as in India, preceded any kind of co-ordinated attempt by government to lay claim to a territory and then administer it. When governments tried to do this their policies were often ignorant of local conditions, their functionaries having to work from hand to mouth. As we shall see, colonial policies and practices may at times have worked in opposite directions. Finally, England was not the only adventurer into the New World, still less the first. Its exploits were often governed by political rivalries, at first with Spain, later with the Dutch, later still the French and Germans. European wars were fought on colonial territories in different parts of the world, and colonies subsequently changed hands often; they became like the commodities – spices, oils, or sugar – they were often plundered for, to be bought, stolen, or tricked from other European powers.

English came into contact with an enormously wide range of languages and cultures during this period. Moreover, it was virtually always in a position of dominance. In general, this was as true of the languages of other European colonists – Spanish, French, Dutch – as it was of the previously unencountered languages of American Indians, Africans,

Mogul princes, Australian bushmen. Some of these were oral vernaculars; some had long traditions of literacy; others, like Hindi and Arabic, were the languages of great religions. English gradually came to symbolise Christianity, military and administrative power, and modern technology. But because it was introduced over areas of great linguistic heterogeneity, English was widely adopted as a lingua franca, like Latin during the Roman Empire.

Throughout the period of colonisation, English has had a reference point in the standard variety of England. The early colonists were of diverse social and regional origins, yet their speech continued to be influenced by the prestige norms of their country of origin. It was standard English that was taught in and by the schools and colleges of the old colonies, and that was spoken by the administrators of these territories. But while attachment to the norms of England was strong, new standards have eventually emerged. The best example is that of the United States of America, which not only has the most speakers of English in the world today, but whose variety has also been increasingly influential in many parts of the world, like the Caribbean, Canada, and Australia. We shall accordingly be treating the English of the USA in more detail than other national or areal varieties of the language.

Early trade in the Atlantic, and its linguistic consequences

By 1600, England had made trading contacts in three continents. Fishing expeditions off Newfoundland were to open up a trade in fur; the quest for ivory and gold established contact with parts of the west coast of Africa, which led to the trade in African slaves; and one of the most famous trading companies of all − the East India Company − had gained a foothold in India, from which it continued to enjoy a monopoly on India's wealth for over two centuries. The trading companies were run by bourgeois entrepreneurs, who were granted concessions to exploit certain areas by the government in return for the right to tax profits. The activities of these companies lasted throughout the colonial period, and their importance for the history of English is that they brought speakers of English into contact with people throughout the world.

A more immediate linguistic consequence can be seen in certain areas. Contact with people in parts of West Africa, for instance, sometimes gave rise to English-based pidgins. These simplified varieties of

English, learned through intermittent and unsystematic contact, and bearing the heavy imprint of African languages, were at first used for only marginal purposes such as trade. But by the eighteenth century it seems that such pidginised varieties of English were the dominant trade languages on Africa's west coast, having displaced pidgins based on the languages of other European colonial nations. West African pidgins could therefore function as a kind of lingua franca in an area of spectacular multilingualism; and even today substantial numbers of speakers in West African nations, such as Cameroon and Sierra Leone, speak them.

During the slave trade, however, pidgins were often the only means of communication among the African people who were shipped off to work in colonies elsewhere. What is more, they were to become the *first* languages of the slaves' children, or grandchildren, since there was no other lingua franca available. To operate as first languages, the functions of pidgins had to be elaborated, their structures amplified: they became *creoles*. Creoles of various origins are still spoken in many islands of the West Indies, and it has recently been argued that the speech of Blacks in the United States should be analysed not as a dialect of American English, but as a variety that has evolved from a creole.

The Caribbean is a good example of an area dominated by the trading and political rivalries of European colonial powers. The first of these were the Spanish. Having either killed, driven out, or passed on fatal diseases to the native Carib populations, the Spanish needed people to work in their mines and on their plantations. West Africans had the requisite skills, and were accordingly shipped over in vast numbers, an enterprise in which the English played no small part. Gradually the English acquired their own possessions, usually by dismembering the empires of others. From Spain were gained St Kitts and Barbados in the 1620s, and, more important, Jamaica in 1660. Gradually African slave labour was brought in to work on the tobacco and sugar plantations of the English possessions, displacing white convict labour, and creole speech was established on those islands.

An account of Jamaica speech in the middle of the eighteenth century shows a continuum between the African speech of newly-imported slaves and the standard English speech of trading company officials. There was the creole of those Blacks who had been settled on the island for some time, the less strongly creolised speech of freed slaves, the speech of poor whites, the English dialect speech of newly-arrived servants from the British Isles, and the 'Jamaica accent' of some planters and merchants. Since the abolition of slavery in the 1830s this continuum

has been preserved, in that standard English has been taught in the education system. Jamaicans have been taught to see themselves as speakers
of English, and their creole has been dismissed as dialectal, or at worst,
inadequate. Thus, many Jamaicans have turned away from what they
call their 'patois'. We can therefore describe the linguistic situation in
contemporary Jamaica as a post-creole continuum, in which several varieties of local speech have emerged as speakers have oriented themselves
towards standard English.

Arguments about the status of creole are similar to those we have encountered for Scots. Creole forms and structures are often felt to be
too close to English to warrant a designation as a separate language; but
unlike Scots, creoles have no traditions of literacy and standardisation.
All the same, many educators have recently insisted that creoles should
be regarded as separate languages, and their arguments are partly based
on historical factors, partly on social ones, and partly on psychological
grounds. Creoles should be seen as languages with their own histories,
and their role as media for tales and proverbs recognised and if possible
extended. Creoles have been developed as standard languages with written forms in different parts of the world; therefore, the argument goes,
there is no reason why the same should not be done for those whose
structure is ultimately based on English.

Jamaica speech shows its hybrid history: English dialect words,
such as *maliflaking* (beating), borrowed from either convicts or servants;
Hindi ones, like *roti* (bread), from contact with traders from the East
Indies; words from African languages, like *jook* (pierce), and common
English items with new meanings, such as *look for* (visit). In grammar,
we find the kinds of morphological simplification we have described
with respect to pidgins and creoles in chapter four. Plural inflexions are
often absent, as are distinctive past tense forms; the latter because consonant-clusters, such as /st/, are often reduced, so that *pass* and *passed*
sound alike. Such features — which are also found in the Black speech
of the United States — are often adopted by British-born children of
West Indian background as they reach adolescence, as a means of identifying themselves with Caribbean culture. The fact that they are
usually regarded as incorrect by their teachers raises a crucial issue in
the teaching of English around the world. Are such deviations from
standard English to be regarded as incorrect, or as instances of a local
variety distinct from, but related to, English? We shall pose this question again, in a sharper form, when we come to consider the 'second-
language English' of Africa.

Colonial settlement

The transplanting of English-speaking communities in different parts of the world was an intermittent process that lasted over 300 years. The motives for settlement were various, as political, social, and economic climates changed: the search for new lands to farm, or to grow a newly-discovered crop, tobacco; for new seas to fish, or for gold, which the Spanish had found in the Americas. Overseas possessions were also useful for getting rid of what was thought of as surplus population, or for encouraging religious or political radicals to emigrate. Colonies were also established simply to stop other European nations from getting to certain areas first, or to furnish the English navy with depots. And as we have seen above, they were also handy dumping grounds for people convicted under English law to deportation.

The origins of the settlers were likewise diverse. Some of the first were gentry, as in the abortive attempts to colonise Virginia in the 1580s. Later, they were sometimes bourgeois, like the religious dissenters of Massachusetts in the 1620s; or lower class, like the convicts of the West Indies in the early seventeenth century, or of Australia after 1788. Others were just ordinary land-labourers, evicted during the Enclosures of various periods. And some were not English at all, but Irish displaced by the Plantations, or Scottish people emigrating to Canada as a result of the Clearances. These latter examples show the interconnection of events in the Celtic British Isles with those beyond Europe.

In many colonies the indigenous inhabitants were often treated in much the same way as the Caribs of the West Indies. Their languages were not widely learned by the white settlers, although the latter were not averse to borrowing individual words from them. Often these had references specific to the new locale, or to the practices of its inhabitants. In the course of three centuries of contact, Americans borrowed words like *raccoon* and *tapioca* from the American Indians; more specific to Canada are *mocock* (a birch-bark container) and *kamik* (a seal-skin boot). In Australia, *dingo* and *budgerigar* were similarly adopted, and in New Zealand English, *pa* (fortified village) was borrowed from the Maoris. Although local conditions and circumstances varied in all these areas, the white settler populations eventually not only dominated the indigenous inhabitants, but came to greatly outnumber them.

In some colonies, however, speakers of English co-existed with those of other European languages. Some of the early Americans, for instance, were Dutch, French, and German: and some of their words, like *winkle-hawk* (right-hand tear in a garment, from Dutch) and *smearcase* (cottage cheese, from German) are still used in some eastern states just as their languages in some instances have also been maintained. While early European linguistic minorities have generally been assimilated to the dominant English-speaking culture of the United States, their presence in other colonies has been the source of long-standing language conflicts. The early French settlements in Canada, for example, were taken over by the English in 1763, and parts of eastern Canada settled by speakers of English. The first of these were Americans who had stayed loyal to the English crown during the American War of Independence; after 1812 they were joined by emigrants from the British Isles. Ever since, the predominantly agrarian French-speaking community has felt beleaguered, and today Canada's population is still one-fifth monoglot French-speaking. Language activism eventually secured a policy of bilingualism in 1969. In South Africa likewise, an English-speaking community has co-existed with a larger one of Dutch origin, dating from 1652, and speaking Afrikaans. English settlement began in 1814, and until dominion status was granted in 1910 the English community and its language were dominant in South African society. By the 1930s, however, the newly urbanised Afrikaans community had developed a strong sense of its own identity, and its language had become a political issue. We shall see how the history of English in South Africa has been affected by the Afrikaans consciousness later in this chapter.

Contact with Dutch colonists had at least one interesting linguistic consequence. The process of settlement, as we saw in chapter one, is invariably accompanied by the adoption of new words, or the adaptation of old ones to denote the topographical features typical of a strange environment. It seems that wherever English-speaking colonists settled, their use of the term *bush*, a Scandinavian borrowing first recorded in the thirteenth century, was influenced by the meaning of the related Dutch word *bosch*. Already in England by the sixteenth century *bush* had developed extended meanings, to refer to nettles, heather, ferns, or clumps of shrubs; and this extension was carried further in the colonies. The words *wood* and *forest* were subsequently used less: by the end of the eighteenth century the word meant 'forest' in both the United States and Canada. But the forest was also the wilderness: so the term eventually denoted land that was uncleared or uncultivated and, by extension, anywhere that was beyond or opposed to the 'civilising' atmosphere and values of urban settlement. We find such meanings in

Australia, where *bush* denotes the outback, in contrast to the town and city. In New Zealand and South Africa, however, the term usually refers to a *type* of landscape: dense forest in the former, grassland and scrub in the latter.

The rise of new standards

The written standard of England is international. It is used in the areas of colonial settlement we have described with hardly any modifications. Among the most well-known of these are American variations in spelling, such as *tire* for *tyre*, *honor* for *honour*. Differences in grammar and vocabulary are also minor, and again American examples will serve: the past participle form *gotten* (cf. *forgotten* in England) is used as well as *got* (in a slightly different way); and instead of *autumn*, *fall* is used, a word originating in English dialect and still used in some south-western counties.

Divergence is most noticeable at the level of pronunciation. The United States, Canada, South Africa, Australia, and New Zealand are sometimes said to have their own national standards; and most people in the British Isles can probably recognise the accents of the United States and Australia, although many might have difficulty in distinguishing Canadians from Americans, New Zealanders from Australians, and either of the latter from South Africans. National standards in pronunciation, however, are very difficult to define, as are the regional accents of England. It might be more accurate to say that each area has its own norms of pronunciation, at times formulated with an ear to the standard in England, at other times responding to local circumstances. Even then, there are sometimes considerable variations in pronunciation within these areas, as we shall see.

The sound-systems in each of these areas are closest to those of the south-east of England. This reflects the origins of the earliest settlers in East Anglia, London, and what are now known as the Home Counties. It was the early colonists who set the pattern, and although they came from many areas the south-eastern influence was dominant. Theirs was the voice of the new colony; and each second and subsequent generation of immigrants − drawn from the most diverse sources − tried to assimilate to the local voice. Thus, speakers of many different European languages learned to sound like Americans, while on the other side of the world large numbers of Irish people, and later immigrants from

Germany and Italy, were to Australianise themselves in the course of the nineteenth century.

When people settle in a new area their children generally try to identify with the new-found norms of language and culture. This was as true of settlement in the colonies as it is of movement today between, say, the towns and cities of England. But when people emigrate, they also often cling tenaciously to some vestige of their past. For many early settlers from the British Isles, the Bible was a precious link with the past, its language an enduring point of reference. Minority languages, such as the German of Pennsylvania, have also been maintained for centuries; and we find therefore that conflicts of identity can often be traced in the histories of each colonial variety. They help to explain, for instance, the developmeent of some variations and changes in the speech of the early American colonists. Their first settlements were on, or near, the ocean, which they or their ancestors crossed; and this meant that they could stay in touch with developments, linguistic or otherwise, that occurred in England. Thus, when 'r-pronouncing' ceased to be prestigious in south-east England, cities like Boston, New York, Jamestown, and Charleston followed suit: 3,000 miles is no distance when a prestige feature is at stake. In England, however, the hundred-odd miles between Bristol and London have been enough to resist it.

The prevalence of south-eastern features in the speech of colonial settlers may account for the frequent assertions of English visitors that such speech was more 'correct' than could be generally heard among ordinary people in England. This was said of American English until the last quarter of the eighteenth century, and of Australian in the nineteenth. Observations like these, however, must be treated with caution. We generally do not know what the observers were used to hearing, and what their expectations were when they sailed, perhaps with some trepidation, to the new lands. If their experience was of the immense dialectal variety in England, and their expectation to find something wild or exotic, they may well have been agreeably surprised.

Another comment made by observers at this time was that colonial speech was more uniform than speech in England. And this is something that has been said ever since. It is important to remember, however, that such statements can only be relative: we must not see the new varieties of English as monolithic. What they lack is the extent of regional variation that is found in England. The reasons for this are clear. Colonial society has in most cases been mobile, especially since the introduction of railways in the nineteenth century. It was often relatively urbanised, or semi-urbanised, from the start: we do not find the kind of village structure so characteristic of England. Education, furthermore, often took root early: we shall see the consequences of this below. Only in the eastern parts of the United States, where there was substantial early settlement, can we speak of regional dialects in the sense understood in Europe, but here, as in other former colonies, the English language has not had long enough in a stable environment for strong regional varieties to develop, at least to the extent known in England.

The absence of marked dialectal variation has meant that there were few of the social problems associated with the selection of a standard variety that we have seen in England and other European societies. In a sense, the standards selected themselves. This is not to say that the early colonial societies were egalitarian; but there was less social stratification, in general, among the settler populations, than in Europe, and at times they were strongly anti-elitist. It has been suggested that in early Australian society, for instance, the elite were actually the ex-convicts who had completed their sentence, and had subsequently become expert in sheep-shearing and cattle-herding. And in newly-independent America, some argued that questions of a standard in the language would be settled by the nature of American society — for instance its mobility — rather than any kind of academy of intellectuals: many Americans wanted to get away from the identification of correctness, or standardisation, with a wealthy, powerful elite. Instead, they concerned themselves with elaborating the functions of American English, by encouraging the writing of scientific and imaginative prose; and they also concentrated, to the point of obsession, on the process of codification.

Standardisation has inevitably been less of an issue in those areas which were to become Dominions in the course of the nineteenth and early twentieth centuries. In Canada, South Africa, Australia, and New Zealand linguistic usage was for a long time exonormative: speech as well as writing was oriented towards the standard in England. In Australia today, however, there is a strong sense of a local standard in matters of vocabulary and pronunciation, a development hastened perhaps by the growing dominance of the USA and its variety of English. Such influence is not surprisingly felt most acutely in Canada, where usage reflects the conflicting models: *tap* is more common than the American *faucet*, but the northern United States merged pronunciation of *cot* and *caught* is commonly heard there. It seems likely that Canadian usage will be increasingly Americanised. In South Africa, the development of a local standard has corresponded, very roughly, with the gradual rise of Afrikaaner political power in the course of the twentieth century. Declared the only official language in 1822, English was widely learned by an often resentful Afrikaans-speaking community; and the RP norms of the Victorian middle class were reinforced when English entrepreneurs came to dominate economic life after the discovery of minerals in the 1870s led to industrialisation. Now that the power of the English-speaking community in both political and economic life has been challenged, a variant of South African English, often showing traces of Afrikaans influence, has acquired the status of a local standard of pronunciation.

It seems that the absence of rigid social stratification in the early English-speaking colonial communities has meant that a clear relationship between variants of pronunciation and social class has been relatively slow to emerge. An interesting feature of both Australian and South African pronunciation, for instance, is that neither has the stigmatised consonant pronunciations so common in the south-east of England, especially London. Initial /h/ is sounded, and neither the glottal plosive nor the Cockney substitution of /f/ for the initial sound in *thin*, and of /v/ for the medial consonant in words like *other*, is widely heard. There may be several explanations for this. The stigmatised pronunciations are most characteristic of Cockney today, but we do not know how common they were in London speech at the end of the eighteenth century when people were moving, or being taken, to these colonies. Although some of them were recorded by Walker (1836), they may have been relatively infrequent variants which have since spread in London; Australian and South African speech may therefore preserve an earlier set of patterns. Alternatively, non-Cockney variants in south-eastern pronunciation may have been dominant: elderly people in rural parts of East Anglia and Kent, at least until very recently, have been largely '*h*-pronouncing'. Finally, the desiderata of so-called educated pronunciation in the nineteenth century may have been easier to disseminate in the more fluid social conditions of the early colonies.

Other variations in the speech of south-eastern England can be traced in some of these areas. Both South African and Australian Englishes have 'Cockneyfied' diphthongs in words like *mate* (starting with a vowel more like that of *mat* than *met*) and *might* (starting with a vowel like that of *mock*). In Australia these diphthongs have often been modified by educated people in the direction of RP. The vowel in words

Figure 7.1 The Atlantic trade and colonial settlement

like *dance*, *plant*, and *sample* also fluctuates according to the patterns we have described in chapter five. In South Africa and New Zealand the vowel in these words is a long back one, as it is in RP; but in Australian pronunciation a front vowel is common in these words, although a back one is used in *path*, *pass*, etc. These examples suggest that the back vowel was first introduced before voiceless fricatives, as in *path* and *pass*, in the south-east of England, and Australian pronunciation preserves this early stage. Later, the backing spread before nasals, as in *dance*, in time for it to be used by the later immigrants to New Zealand and South Africa. Most Americans, however, tend to use the long front vowel, which is also of course found in parts of south-east England, and which is the earlier pattern.

American English

Only in America, it seems, have there been attempts to elevate the status of the colonial variety to that of a language separate from the English of England. Not surprisingly it was during the early years of independence that the issue was raised. For Webster, the lexicographer, a national language was 'a national tie', and what country wanted it more than America? Many Americans thought that now they had won independence (in 1783) their usage would diverge increasingly from that of England; and that this would be a good thing. Webster himself contrived to make it different by changing spellings; and his *Dictionary* of 1806, which, with subsequent additions and revisions is still the standard one in America, was inspired by the feeling that differences between the two varieties would multiply, necessitating the writing of a separate dictionary.

Some Americans also wanted to establish an Academy to regulate their new variety. An American Academy would be one in the eye for the English, who had demonstrated their inferiority by failing to set up one of their own. The American Academy of Language and Belles Lettres was accordingly established in 1821. But there was a great deal of argument about what it should do. Some members championed the cause of linguistic separatism; others were more conscious of England's literary tradition, and felt that America's best interests would be served by keeping cultural links open. Gradually, interest in the Academy waned. Some had seen the dangers of elitism, and in 1828 Webster himself argued that dictionaries and grammars should guide Americans on matters of usage, rather than the usages of a particular clique, or the recommendations of an Academy. To a large extent his wish was granted. Nationalist feelings during this period were often expressed through partisan statements about language. A great deal of the acrimony came from the English side of the Atlantic. All the previously rather commendatory remarks about the correctness and uniformity of American English were replaced by hostility to American addiction to 'innovation', 'new-fangled words', and bombast. A sole neologism was enough for one observer in 1803 to condemn American English as 'wholly unintelligible', like a teacher with a child who utters a single non-standardism. Not only did some Americans use new words, like *crass*, they also made free with morphemes like *-ise*, and wrote *utilise*. And they were even guilty, like Shakespeare, of functional shift: *spade* was used as a verb as well as a noun. The much-praised uniformity was now a stick to beat them with. The American intellectuals of the eastern cities had no business talking like the people in the backwoods: they should cultivate elegant and correct speech, to show their class.

To some extent the acrimony continues. It is not unusual to hear English spoken of as though it were a national commodity; neither is it rare to hear America blamed for every new word, every disliked usage, and every non-standardism heard on the British side of the Atlantic. Sometimes this has bizarre results: a long-standing feature of southeastern English dialect, *ain't*, has often been attributed to the influence of American films. (In fact, it is a variant of both *aren't* and *haven't*; in the latter, a /vnt/ consonant-cluster has been simplified, and the preceding vowel lengthened, raised, and subsequently diphthongised.) Examples like this show the difficulty of drawing clear-cut distinctions between the English of America and that spoken in the British Isles. It is difficult to find 'Americanisms' that are not used by some people, in some context, on this side of the ocean. Many Americans may say (but tend not to write) *mad* instead of *angry*, but this usage is also known in some English dialects. And sometimes the difference is more subtle. Americans see *hogs* in fields, but tend to *pig* their food; in England, the opposite pattern is more common.

It is not usual to hear people today insist that American English is a separate language. But like Scots, it is another example to expose the coarseness of our terminology: American English can best be called a national variety of English, with its own norms. The closer we look, however, we find that those norms are partly regional – not surprisingly, in a country of such vast size – but are also, more importantly, social ones as well. Social variation in American English, which has been the subject of a vast amount of research, has a great deal to do with the presence of ethnic minorities, who together form a significant proportion of the population in the United States.

As we have seen, other language groups had settled in America from the earliest times. Some of the intellectuals who steered America to independence saw these languages as cultural assets: people would learn English if they felt they needed to, and it was not up to the government to tell them what to do. Bilingual schooling was quite common in parts of the country until the early twentieth century. But in many ways these liberal ideals were crushed in the entrepreneurial climate of the nineteenth century. As the frontier moved west, those Indians that remained were to be taught English, and Americanised, according to a statute of 1868. And speakers of Spanish in the south-west came in for similar treatment. Only about 30 per cent of the population of New Mexico could speak English in 1874 (most of these were bilingual), but a statute of 1891 demanded schooling in English, and eighty years later some Texan schools were discouraging the use of Spanish even in the playground.

In the course of the nineteenth century immigrants from Russia, Germany, Italy, Scandinavia, Ireland, and other European nations settled in the United States, many of them in the cities which mushroomed in the otherwise empty West. Unlike the early European colonists the later immigrants were often working class, and were keen to Americanise themselves in the hope of economic improvement. We can see the results of such adaptive behaviour in the speech of some New Yorkers of Italian descent. Immigration from Italy continued into the twentieth century, and second-generation speakers from this background tend to try to avoid the 'Italian' vowel in words like *bad*, and *bag*. This is a low vowel, not unlike the 'north country' vowel in England; but for these descent groups, it sounds too Italian. They therefore avoid it by adopting a raised vowel, but tend also to over-compensate, so *bad* sounds like *beard* (without the *r*). Such processes introduce new variants into city speech; they subsequently often acquire a social value, in turn promoting changes in the pronunciation of other social groups.

Other ethnic minorities have a more ambivalent attitude to the local variety of American English. Mexican-Americans in California and the south-west suffer discrimination in jobs, and are generally low-status. Accordingly, some are loyal to Spanish, while others, indifferent to language affiliation, speak a variety of Spanish heavily influenced by English: *birria* and *ganga* in Spanish mean 'a meat dish' and 'bargain' respectively, but in this group — known as *pachucos* — they often mean 'beer' and 'gang'. Rapid urbanisation during the last thirty years may mean the abandoning of Spanish by Mexican-Americans, and many of them have already shown the desire to Americanise themselves. Upwardly mobile bilingual speakers in San Antonio, Texas, tend to use two pronunciations of unavoidable Spanish words in the local vocabulary, such as *corral* and *plaza*: a Spanish one with other bilinguals, and an Americanised one with monoglot *Anglos*. And in California, they tend to avoid using *sofa* (beside *couch*, and the more regionally marked *chesterfield*) because it sounds like a word from Spanish.

Black speech in the United States has attracted a great deal of research in the last decade. This variety — which nonetheless has variations within it — is spoken in many northern cities such as New York, Chicago, and Detroit, and has many of the features associated with creoles, which we have also seen in the discussion of Jamaican English. Thus, the consonant-cluster /st/ is simplified, even before vowels, so that *testing* sounds like *tessin'*; and in common with many languages around the world, the verb *be* is often not expressed, so that we hear *he mad, she gone*. But one of the most important features of the Black English Vernacular, as this variety has been called, is that in many respects it is like that of whites in the Deep South — whence many Blacks migrated after the Civil War in the 1860s. The direction of linguistic influence — Black to white, or white to Black — has been the source of much speculation in recent years.

Southern speech, with its distinctive vowels — such as that of *die*, *dive*, etc., which sounds like a lengthened /æ/ — and forms, such as *you-all* as a plural of *you* — is an important reminder that there have been long-standing variations in the speech of the earliest colonies. The southern plantation economy, based on tobacco and cotton, led to a more stratified society than was to be found in the north-eastern colonies of, say, New England. It seems also to have been more receptive to new prestigious pronunciations emanating from England. Thus, southern speech is, broadly speaking, not 'r-pronouncing'; and this marks a significant divergence from usage in many other parts of the USA.

'R-pronouncing' is associated with the speech of the mid-west of the United States. This variety tends to be the one that is broadcast; and since it is also spoken over a very large area (corresponding, very roughly, to that developed and settled during the last century) it has been termed General American. Most people outside the United States tend to think of this pronunciation as constituting some kind of spoken standard; it has never, however, enjoyed the prestige of RP in England. Since the Second World War many of its features have been spreading geographically, a notable example being the introduction of *r*-pronunciation in eastern cities like New York. Here, upper-middle-class speakers have generally adopted it, though many working-class speakers have not; while lower-middle-class people, anxious to identify with the prestige feature, register the highest incidence of all when they are conscious of how they are sounding. In the United States, therefore, *r* has almost become to Americans what *h* is to the English.

Despite the prestige of General American, different regions of the USA still preserve to a large extent their own norms of usage. Southern speakers, for example, tend to be socially stereotyped, and their speech in, say, the mid-west gives rise to comment and even hilarity. But throughout the USA it seems also that certain pronunciations and morphological items are widely stigmatised. The pronunciation of *pen* to sound like *pin*, the insertion of an *r* in *wash* (so that it sounds like *worsh*), and the past tense form *drownded* tend to be regarded as the marks of low social status.

The language of imperial rule

Despite the misgivings of many politicians, the activities of the trading companies intensified in the course of the nineteenth century. By 1900, Britain had come to control five times the area it possessed in 1860. The most spectacular gains were in Africa, the greater part of which was shared out among the European powers between 1880 and 1900. Increasing awareness of the role of colonies in the industrialising economies of Europe led to more and more government intervention in their administration. Exploitation by trading companies slowly gave way to exploitation by government. In this era of colonial expansion, which we shall call imperialism, Britain was the most successful among the nation-states of Europe.

Developments in India to some extent foreshadowed events elsewhere. In 1813 the trading monopoly of the East India Company was abolished; new territories were subsequently seized, railways were built, and local economic activity shaped to fit the needs of British capital. India became the keystone of the Empire, and the British took steps to protect their access to the sub-continent. The opening of the Suez canal brought British armies and influence to Egypt; and a British presence was established in Burma and in what is now Malaysia to protect its most prized possession against encroachment from the south-east. India came to be ruled by a white English-speaking administrative caste, imbued with a belief in European superiority. Unlike their predecessors of the East India Company, who had been happy to assimilate in many respects to Indian life and customs, the new ruling class sought to distance itself from the local populations.

Colonial settlement was not a feature of the nineteenth-century British imperial possessions. Although there was some white settlement in Africa (for example in Southern Rhodesia, now Zimbabwe, and Kenya), the newcomers, like the earlier colonists in South Africa, constituted only a small minority of the population. They tended not to exterminate the indigenous inhabitants, but to exploit their labour in farming the most fertile land. Power was therefore vested in a small, white, landowning and employing caste, living by a code similar to that adopted by the imperial administration in India. Africans, like Indians, were felt to be backward and untrustworthy, and incapable of looking after their own lives.

In many areas, however, imperial rule necessitated the cultivation of local leaders or tribes to act as its agents. Conquered peoples fought in British armies in campaigns to secure new possessions and to consolidate older ones. Often the British ruled indirectly through local puppet rulers; and certain sections of the population were increasingly educated into the role of administrators, although they invariably constituted only a lower stratum in the imperial hierarchy. It is to this process that we can trace the origins of new varieties of English among the native populations of areas ruled by Britain.

Like Latin during the Roman Empire, English was imposed over an enormous area as the language of law, administration, and commerce. English enjoyed the sanction of military superiority, but two other factors helped it to spread. Like the territories ruled by Rome, the colonies seized by Britain were areas of striking social, cultural, and linguistic diversity. Territorial boundaries imposed by European powers cut across tribes, polities, empires, culture-areas, and language-groups. In Nigeria alone, it has been estimated that over 200 languages are spoken. English therefore has often been invaluable as a lingua franca (although there were local ones, too: Hausa in northern Nigeria, Swahili in much of East Africa, and Bazaar Malay in Malaysia). In addition,

Key

C   = Cameroon
E   = Egypt
G   = Gambia
Gh = Ghana (formerly the Gold Coast)
K   = Kenya (formerly British East Africa)
M   = Malawi (formerly Nyasaland)
N   = Nigeria
S   = Sudan
SL = Sierra Leone
T   = Tanzania (formerly Tanganyika)
U   = Uganda
Za = Zambia (formerly N. Rhodesia)
Z   = Zimbabwe (formerly S. Rhodesia)

Figure 7.2   The legacy of British imperialism

knowledge of English could lead to a prestigious job: there were clear economic advantages in learning it.

Many British administrators, however, did not view the spread of English as an end in itself. Provision of education was often on an *ad hoc* basis; and in some areas such as northern Nigeria the spread of English may actually have been discouraged. It was more useful for Britain to deny access to a lingua franca in certain areas, since divided populations might be easier to rule: English opened up the possibility of unity among diverse peoples, and subsequently ideas about independence and nationalism. Also, some missionary societies favoured use of major vernaculars as vehicles of evangelism and of education. Thus, local languages were sometimes encouraged and even taught in some areas, reinforcing the distinction between ruling elites and subject populations. These practices contrast markedly with those of the French, which tended to promote the idea that to speak French implied citizenship of the French nation. The French language — specifically, its standard variety — was accordingly promoted in education, administration, and the army, as the Romans had promoted Latin; and the populations of French colonies were encouraged to think of themselves as French, and to place their ethnic or ancestral identities second.

It is as a second language, therefore, that we must trace the history of English in India, Malaysia and Singapore, and Africa. But the term 'second language' tends to obscure its wide range of functions and the varying motives for learning it. Not only is English a major lingua franca, but it has functioned as the medium of independence movements and, more recently, of a considerable literature. And from the first, demands for the language have had a clear political significance. Bengal Hindus wanted to learn it in the first decades of the nineteenth century, not only because they thought it was the key to Western thought and science, but also because it was a means of checking the influence of Arabic, the language of Islam. Today, many Black Africans in South Africa bitterly resent the denial of access to English education since it deprives them of the opportunity of participation in political life, as well as underlining the doctrine of separate development that lies at the heart of South African society.

English has also symbolised many different and even contradictory states and processes in the areas of imperial rule. As the language of the colonial era it symbolised dominance and exploitation and therefore collusion with the white master; it has often since become the dividing line between privileged and poor. But it also symbolises education and literacy, since in many areas these were virtually synonymous with English. It has also been an emblem of Christianity, of material and technological development, and of urbanisation and western capitalism; and since the Second World War in particular it has been seen as a key to nationhood, and the means of access to international diplomacy and commerce. Not surprisingly, different territories responded differently to this legacy of associations when they won their independence.

English and education

The earliest educational institutions were the mission schools. In Sierra Leone, for instance, they were soon to follow the establishment of that West African colony in 1787, and others were founded in the colonies of Malaya in the first decades of the nineteenth century. In some places, such as South Africa, the mission schools at first appear to have done a competent job, and in southern Nigeria they have been accused of removing all African characteristics from their charges.

In general, the medium of education was English. Pupils were encouraged to use English as often as possible, and sometimes there were sanctions against speaking local languages in school. Above all, English was the language of literacy: in future years it was to become identified with education itself. But Protestant mission schools in some areas tended to use local languages in religious instruction, as befitted the ideals of the Reformation. Thus, Yoruba was developed in southern Nigeria as the language of Scripture.

As well as the mission schools there were other kinds of institutions such as the Free Schools of the Malayan colonies. But the existence of all these early schools depended on local initiatives, enthusiasm, and the availability of resources; we cannot yet speak of an educational policy. Something like this developed as British administration was extended and consolidated. But although local people began to acquire English as a means of employment in administration, education, and therefore English, reached only a very small proportion of the population. Since the expansion of state education, enrolment in African schools, for instance, has seldom reached half of the school-age population.

British educational policy can be seen in all its complexity in India. In 1835, the famous Minute associated with T.B. Macaulay, member of the Supreme Council of India and later author of the *History of England*, called for the creation of a class of 'Indians in blood and colour, but

English in taste, in opinions, in morals, and in intellect' who would be able to act as 'interpreters' between English-speaking rulers and the governed. They were to 'refine' the vernacular languages of India as vehicles for conveying the alleged benefits of Western civilisation to the indigenous 'masses'. An education in English, then, was for an elite only; education for the mass, as and when it might exist, could only take place in the vernaculars, and these were also used widely for administration at regional level. At the same time, English was used for many official purposes, and it was an important academic language in five universities that were founded in the course of the nineteenth century. After 1918 the establishment of more schools and colleges made English more widely available, and a survey of publications in 1928 found an influential amount of writing in the language.

In parts of tropical West Africa, the spread of English in education had been complicated by other factors. In 1807, the British slave trade was abolished; and one of its consequences was the re-settling of slaves, or potential slaves captured from slaving expeditions conducted by other powers, in the colony of Sierra Leone. A community of creole speakers receptive to English influence and education was established; and as early as 1827 Fourah Bay College had been set up as an institution of higher education, from which Africans preached Christianity and spread education in English in many parts of western Africa. It was here that the first Westernised, English-speaking Black intelligentsia emerged, and its influence spilled over into other British colonies of West Africa. During the latter half of the nineteenth century there was a vigorous tradition of political journalism in English, some of it openly critical of British colonialism.

It was after the Second World War that education expanded most dramatically in Africa. Again, this was more true of West Africa than the colonies in the south and east, where the racist attitudes of white settlers inhibited the development of schools for Africans. In Rhodesia in 1965, for instance, roughly the same amount of money was spent on education for Africans as for whites, although the latter were outnumbered by ten to one. As in other parts of Africa, such education was at the primary rather than secondary or tertiary level. The imperialist attitude remained what it had been in the previous century: the highest positions in all jobs and professions were to be open only to whites. Thus, although in the Gold Coast (now Ghana) in 1949 there were about 10,000 Africans employed in the elite professions, one-third of this number in the civil service, no African held a job at the top. This remained the case throughout Africa until independence was won in the late 1950s and early 1960s, even though by that time Africans had been able to study at universities in Britain and the United States.

The emergence of second-language varieties of English

Since we are dealing here with English primarily as the product of the educational system, we need to take account of levels of education, the origins, both ethnic and linguistic, of the teachers of English themselves, and their teaching strategies. We must bear in mind that these factors vary enormously and that access to education is extremely uneven: it is much more open in towns and cities, for instance, than in the country. Another factor is the language or languages also used by speakers of English as a second language: we need to allow for the possibility of those languages influencing the English of particular areas. We must also know how English functions in the communities where it is widely spoken. Is it a medium of everyday conversation, and what kinds of writing are undertaken? Finally, we must consider the status of these new varieties of English. To what extent should they be judged against the norms of standard English in England? Should they be considered as varieties, even standards, in their own right? Do the attitudes of their speakers towards them differ from the attitudes of speakers of English as a first language? And are the new varieties felt to have different styles, and perhaps different levels of acceptability?

Several attempts have been made to describe varieties of English in former colonies by referring to the level of education of different groups of users. In Africa, for instance, it has been argued that changing social conditions brought about by urbanisation, availability of higher education, and opportunities of high status jobs in the professions, have enabled some Africans to develop a competence in English which exceeds that of their native or ancestral language. Thus, the terms first language and second language lose much of their value when the speech of this group is considered. An African language such as Twi or Wolof may be learned first in life, but English may be spoken in many more contexts, particularly within households where husband and wife speak mutually unintelligible languages. Among this small elite of Africans a local variety of English has emerged, and attachment to the African language(s) in an individual's repertoire will not be strong. A closely related variety of English is used, again in a wide range of contexts, as a second language by Africans who also have more occasion to use an African language to which they may express feelings of loyalty. This group will have been taught English at least as far as secondary school level. Finally, there is a variety of English imperfectly acquired, by those whose teaching in English has perhaps been limited to primary level, for whom English is a foreign rather than a second language. This variety must be distinguished from pidgins and creoles which evolved outside the education system and which, most importantly, Africans themselves do not consider to be English.

In most former colonies, English has rarely been taught by native speakers except in the early days of education in the colonial period itself. Latterly, although senior teaching positions may have been held by British-born speakers of standard English, the bulk of teachers have themselves usually been second-language speakers. Opportunities for contact with native speakers have therefore been limited; where this has occurred the effects are often obvious, as in the case recently reported of mission school pupils speaking with the Scottish accents of their expatriate teachers. Since speakers of many different languages may turn out to be teachers of English to pupils whose range of languages is also very wide, the possibilities of influence from those languages on the local variety of English are likely to be immense. Not only is this true of Africa; in Malaysia and Singapore, many teachers of English have actually been from India, the source of much indentured labour on rubber plantations since the early twentieth century.

Limited contact with native speakers of English, and insufficient attention paid to spoken English, help to account for the flavour of literariness that is often found by native English speakers in the English of both Africa and India. Most Indians, for example, would have encountered the written English of administration and learning more than any other variety: hence, it has been said that Indians are over-fond of polysyllabic vocabulary, and are likely to say *demise* rather than *death*. They are also said to be prone to empty verbosity in their use of phrases such as *each and every* and to favour formal variants such as the uncontracted *do not*, *cannot* rather than *don't* and *can't* in their speech. Similar tendencies have been found in African usage: the use of *witness* rather than *see* has been noted, as have some spelling pronunciations arising from unfamiliarity with native models. *Plumber*, for instance, has been heard with the /b/ pronounced.

Influence from African and Asian languages can be readily identified. Well-known examples include the phonetic realisations of certain phonemes, such as the Indian retroflex pronunciation of /t/ and /d/, made with the tongue curled back, as in the pronunciation of /r/ in the south-west of England. An African grammatical pattern underlies *he values his car than his wife*, where there is no word corresponding to *more*. Local vocabulary is also used: in the English of Malaysia and Singapore, the Malay word *(h)ulu* (upstream) has come to refer to a place where not much is going on, so that people speak of an *ulu area*.

Other tendencies, with greater structural consequences, are more widespread. Many Asian languages do not have the range of fricatives that are found in English, so we often find them substituted by plosives. This is particularly the case with the initial consonants of *thin* and *then*, replaced by /t/ and /d/ respectively (as they are in many non-standard urban varieties of England and the United States). Consonant-clusters similarly are reduced or re-structured. In Hindi, /sp/ does not occur in initial position, so Hindi speakers often insert a vowel before the cluster, giving *ispeak*. In Malaysia and Singapore, a vowel is sometimes inserted *between* the consonants, producing *setem* for stamp. In the same area, clusters in final position are often simplified: *recent* becomes *recen*.

Another general tendency concerns the system of tense and aspect. Many Indian speakers, like the Celtic language speakers of the British Isles, use continuous forms for habitual actions: *I am doing* for *I do*. Neither Malay nor Chinese, as spoken in Malaysia or Singapore, have tense systems of the kind associated with western European languages, although they have ways of marking aspect: thus, a perfect is often signalled with the use of an adverb, such as *already*. *My father already pass away* means 'my father has passed away'. In parts of West Africa *I am having a cold* is used instead of *I have (got) a cold*: this reflects the aspect system of the Kwa languages, where temporary states, such as having a cold, are distinguished in the grammar from permanent ones, such as having a body.

A significant point about many of the features listed is that they are found among speakers whose native languages do not themselves have the structures that have influenced the development of the feature in question. *I am having a cold* is also heard in East Africa, where the aspect distinction characteristic of Kwa is not made among local languages. It seems therefore that certain local variations in English have spread widely among speakers of many different native languages. It has recently been argued that both West and East African Englishes share many features, but that those features are also essentially African, rather than Caribbean, Black American, etc. Similarly, different varieties of English in India, Sri Lanka, Pakistan, Nepal, and Bangla Desh influence each other; and some of these in turn have influenced the English of Malaysia and Singapore through the teaching of English in the schools.

In each broad area under discussion, therefore, we can speak of a local variety of English, within which there is a range of variants. These variants are partly determined by geography, but more importantly perhaps by the level of education and social position of the speaker. There is a continuum, therefore, between the broader, most local usages of the less educated to the less markedly local varieties of educated elites. At first the usage of this latter group would have been orientated towards the English of England: usage was exonormative. Gradually, however, local norms have developed; even the most educated speakers are aware of these. Attempts to speak English with an RP accent are often greeted with ridicule in these areas. English-speaking Africans, for instance, want to sound like Africans. And while the broader local variants are stigmatised, many Africans resist changing their linguistic habits, either because they want to assert their ethnic identity, or because they sense that there is no immediate or automatic prospect of economic advancement if they do change them.

Some scholars have used the term standard to refer to these local varieties. A 'South Asian Standard' is said to exist in the area of the Indian sub-continent; similarly, people speak of a West Indian one, although there we need to take account of a different historical development. The English of Singapore and Malaysia is distinctive, as is the English of Africa, where it has been claimed that a West African and East African standard will in time emerge. The vital point about all these varieties is that they have their own norms. The fact that these are not the norms of people in England or America is of no consequence; nor does it matter that these varieties are in origin second language ones. They are increasingly used as media of communication among educated people; in addition, they are used in writing, for a number of purposes. They are legitimate Englishes in their own right: not yet national standards, but at least areal ones.

Many English speakers in the United Kingdom and America will not agree with these arguments. Attitudes to such overseas varieties are still often rooted in the colonial era when Indian English, for instance, was referred to derogatively as 'Babu' or 'Cheechee' English. The 'literariness' of Indian English is thought to be evidence of an inadequate grasp of levels of style; other aspects are dismissed as quaint, pompous, or the hallmarks of a deferential, even grovelling disposition. Empty verbosity, however, is by no means limited to South Asian speakers of English: and these attitudes also forget that there are many different users and uses of English. If a feature becomes general among a group of users of a language, then that feature may be described as characteristic of the local variety, whatever its origins. Thus, in parts of Africa where many children learn only a little English, it is in principle impossible to know where to draw the line   between a 'mistake' and a usage that enjoys local currency. Standard English is not the only norm in English today, just as the Classical Latin of Rome was not the norm in the Gaul of the fifth century.

It is in the writing of fiction and poetry that the status of local varieties assumes crucial importance. While the standard variety of England is an international one where functional writing is concerned (although the South Asian Standard has developed some local features in such writing) many novelists and poets from these areas have tried to find a personal voice in the local variety of English. For such writers the question of audience is a vital consideration. To be taken seriously throughout the English-speaking world their English must not be too marked for localisms; but how else can local feelings, ideas, and identities be expressed? Indian writers have spoken about the difficulties involved in representing Eastern modes of address and greeting among characters in novels, and in referring to systems of kinship and authority in an alien language. For West Indian writers, the problem concerns the status of creole, the language of many central characters in their novels. In Africa, many Black writers have unashamedly appropriated the language of their colonial past, and found an African voice by drawing on images, metaphors, and allusions current in African languages. In this, the lead was given in West Africa in the 1950s; since then more and more writing has come out of Africa, including East Africa, where Nairobi has emerged as an important centre for the publication of African writing in English.

Independence and language planning

Britain's colonies generally achieved independence after the Second World War: India in 1947, others in the 50s and early 60s. New governments had to come to terms with the multicultural and multilingual character of their territories, their borders arbitrarily defined, their economies unbalanced by European imperialism. Nationhood, in the

European sense, was thrust upon them; and as in all nations, their leaders felt the need for a national language. The processes associated with standardisation discussed in chapter two — selection, acceptance, elaboration, codification — had to be telescoped within a time-scale unknown elsewhere. In short, the new nations had to evolve a language-plan, with a degree of engineering far more conscious than that we have described in the context of England.

The language problems of the new nations are akin to those of many Central and Eastern European states of the nineteenth century, which had newly emerged within the empires of the Austro-Hungarians and the Turks. The choice of a national language in all cases is partly governed by the desire to establish distinctiveness from neighbouring states, and partly by the need to promote cohesiveness among many different languages and cultures within a single territory. But the choice has often been extremely difficult. Internal rivalries, themselves often exacerbated by imperial practices; shortage of educational resources; and the influence of super-power politics have complicated the issue. Today, many problems remain unsolved, and language-policies are often incoherent and riddled with contradictions.

In choosing a national language, symbolism plays a large part. Many governments have wanted to choose a local one, as the emblem of an indigenous culture. One problem is, which one? Many local languages are not spoken by a majority of the population in a given area; nor do they have traditions of literacy and use within the specialised domains required by a national government. Some governments have eschewed such a nationalistic, or *authenticist* course, and opted instead for a language which they feel answers to the needs of a modern nation-state. Efficiency, rather than symbolism, is the keynote of such a *modernist* course.

In many former colonies, especially in Africa, the language chosen has been English. Although in many African territories it had less than a century to take root, its usefulness as a lingua franca and as an international language of commerce has ensured its survival and continued use. While it may have been the language of the colonial master, it was also the language of nationalism, of independence movements; and it is also the language of America, the most powerful nation in the world. Conditions both internal and external have therefore favoured its retention, and it is worth noting that for many of the same reasons it is also in great demand among nations that were never part of the British or any other European empire.

Those nations which have chosen an indigenous tongue as the national language have usually retained English as an official language. Thus, while the national language of India is Hindi, English is retained as a subsidiary language. A great deal of writing is undertaken in it, and it is also a lingua franca among peoples who have been estimated to use as many as 800 different languages. From the linguistic point of view, Hindi is actually closer to English than to, say, the southern Indian language Telugu. India has a bilingual education policy: English is taught in schools, as are those languages which have been designated the official languages of different Indian states, so that some Indian children need to learn four languages: Hindi, English, the state language if it is not Hindi, and sometimes their own native language if it is not one of these.

The choice of language will inevitably affect the character of the local variety of English. Malaysia has developed Bahasa Malaysia as its national language, although Singapore retains English: we can expect the latter to develop a more local variety of English than the former, which also uses English in commerce and teaches it in schools. But now that Bahasa Malaysia is being developed in domains previously associated with English, the latter's functions will contract, and it will take on more of the features of a taught language rather than of a medium of inter-ethnic communication.

English is also used extensively in Africa. But although it is an official language for over 160 million Africans, it is almost always a second language only, and many have little knowledge of it. Many nations, such as Nigeria, Kenya, and Uganda, have adopted it as a national language, but bilingual education programmes are of necessity also quite common. In one former colony, Tanzania, the national language is the East African lingua franca, Swahili. This choice may be seen as an assertion of authenticist values: English is the language of Western capitalism, and Tanzania is striving to build an egalitarian, African nation. The decision was helped, however, by the fact that Swahili was the language of the nationalist movement there. English has also been retained in Tanzania as an official language; as in most African nations it has had a head-start in the education system in a continent too poor to develop rapidly the necessary resources in the local languages.

Notes and suggested reading

(I have tried to draw attention to the most accessible books and articles. For full details of all works cited, see the Bibliography.) Most general histories of English have been consulted. Baugh (1978, 3rd ed.) is a standard work by an American scholar; it has been valuably up-dated on contemporary varieties. A very readable introduction is Barber (1972, 5th ed.); Bolton (1967) is short and very clear. More difficult, but infinitely rewarding are Strang (1970) and Samuels (1972). Partridge (1969), Barber (1976), and Blake (1977) are invaluable studies of particular periods. A very useful collection of essays is edited by Lass (1969).

I have used the standard sociolinguistics introductions. A recent and clear one is by Hudson (1980), but the beginner might best start with Trudgill (1974b). Bell (1976) is a handy reference book. Two collections of essays are now regarded as classics: Giglioli, and Pride and Holmes (both 1972). An excellent introduction to English as a world language is a collection edited by Bailey and Robinson (1973); for studies of British English varieties see the collection edited by Trudgill (1978). The journals *International Journal of the Sociology of Language* and *English World-Wide* have proved invaluable.

Introduction

The notion of 're-tribalisation' is taken from Khlief (1979). For multilingualism in contemporary England, see Edwards (1979) and Rosen and Burgess (1980); for the study of linguistic history, see Bynon (1977).

Chapter one   Languages in contact

A great many insights and even formulations of points depend on an indispensable article by Haugen (1966). See also Stewart (1968). For diglossia, see Ferguson (1959); for bilingualism, Hornby (1977); pidgins and creoles, Todd (1974).

On Latin see Elcock (1975); for its imposition, see Brosnahan (1963). For the multilingual heritage of the British Isles, see Jackson (1953) and Lockwood (1975). The Anglo-Saxons are the subject of Whitelock (1965), Loyn (1962), and to some extent Finberg (1976).

Place-names are a subject of inexhaustible fascination, but the student requires knowledge of their early forms. See Ekwall (1947) and for recent research, Cameron and Gelling (1976). On the Vikings, see Loyn (1977). Norman-French relations with English are discussed by Berndt (1965). An interesting study of English in the fourteenth century is by Cottle (1969).

Chapter two   Standardisation and writing

The four stages of standardisation are proposed by Haugen (1966). A great deal of the data in this chapter is from Dobson (1955). Williams (1961) offers a clear social and political perspective.

On spellings, see Scragg (1975); alphabets and literacy in general, Goody and Watt (1962), and Oxenham (1980). Medieval English is discussed by Blake (1977) who elsewhere (1976) provided the basis for the discussion of Kentish. A very useful study of literary representations of non-standard speech is by Page (1973). On Cockney see Matthews (1938) and Sivertsen (1960).

For sixteenth-century attitudes to English see Jones (1953). A very good introduction to Shakespeare's language is by Quirk (1974). On prose, see Gordon (1966). For contemporary attitudes to usage, Mittins *et al.* (1970) is excellent; it discusses the history of certain shibboleths. On the middle-class 'market' for correctness, see Wyld (1936) and Labov (1972a).

Chapter three   Words and meanings

A good general history of English vocabulary is by Sheard (1954). The discussion of Anglo-Saxon topographical terms is based on Strang (1970); that of euphemism, and of emphatic variants, on Samuels (1972). Williams (1976) has proved indispensable in writing this chapter.

An excellent chapter, 'Lexis', in Strang (1968) provided the basis for the discussion of dictionaries. The categories of meaning are those of Leech (1974), who has a good chapter called 'Semantics and Society'. For other examples and insights see Waldron (1967); for detailed studies of individual words, see Lewis (1968) and Tucker (1967, 1972).

Letters of complaint to the press about usage are reproduced in Strang (1970, pp. 3-5). Status terms are discussed in Barber (1976), and the section on Elizabethan terms of address is based on Salmon (1967). Schulz (1975) provided the basis for the discussion on words denoting women.

Chapter four   Grammar

The list of misconceptions about grammar is taken from Palmer (1971), an excellent introduction to the subject of grammar. On the grammar of speech and contemporary varieties of English, see Quirk (1968) and Crystal and Davy (1969). On standard grammar, see Quirk and Greenbaum (1973); on non-standard, see Trudgill and Hughes (1979).

On the loss of inflexions, and sixteenth-century hypercorrection, see Samuels (1972). For sociolinguistic study of forms of address, see Brown and Gilman (1960) and Ervin-Tripp (1969); on the history of *thou* and *you*, see Byrne (1936). For Bernstein's early ideas, see his 1970 article; those of Whorf can be found in Carroll (ed., 1956).

Chapter five   Pronunciation

Indispensable for the study of English sounds, present and past, is Gimson (1980, 3rd ed.). The sociolinguistic framework derives from Labov (1972a). On dialect pronunciations, see Sanderson *et al.*, *The Linguistic Atlas of England* (1978); on regional sounds, both rural and urban, see the works and editions of Trudgill (1974, 1975, 1978) and Trudgill and Hughes (1979). On the conditioning effect of consonants on vowels, see C.-J. Bailey (1973). The section on the Great Vowel Shift is based on Labov (1974).

Chapter six   The imposition of English in the British Isles

Most standard histories of English do not deal in any detail with the linguistic minorities of the British Isles. An accessible place to start is Lockwood (1975). Stephens (1976) has proved invaluable. See also Trudgill (1974b) and Trudgill and Hughes (1979). On Scots, the collection of essays edited by Aitken and McArthur (1979) is indispensable. The discussion of border usage is based on Glauser (1974), Mather and Speitel (1975/7), and Speitel (1978). On recent research in Edinburgh, see essays by Reid and Romaine in Trudgill (1978).

A helpful introduction to languages of Ireland is edited by Ó'Muirithe (1977). See also Bliss (1979). The section on Gaelic in contemporary Ireland is based on Turvey (1978) and Ó'Riagáin and Ó'Gliasáin (1979). On usage in Ulster, see Gregg (1972), and in Belfast, J. and L. Milroy in Trudgill (1978).

A recent sociolinguistic study of Gaelic in Scotland is Mackinnon (1977). See also Thomson (1976). On Welsh, see Lewis (1978), R.M. Jones (1979), and Khlief (1979); on Cornish, Berresford Ellis (n.d.). The phenomenon of the semi-speaker is discussed by Dorian (1980).

Chapter seven   English overseas

There are few general introductions to English as a world language. Treatments of overseas varieties are scattered and uneven. Other than Baugh (1978) and Bailey and Robinson (1973) the student must rely on more specialised books and articles.

On Caribbean varieties, see Cassidy (1961), Ramchand (1970), Craig (1976), and Edwards (1979). Not surprisingly, there is no dearth of books on American English. A good, short introduction is by Strevens (1972). On varieties of American English, see Reed (1967), Kurath (1972), McDavid (1980). On contemporary sociolinguistic variation, see Labov (1972a and 1972b). There are two fascinating chapters on relations between American and British English by Quirk (1972). On standardisation in American English, see Smith and Lance (1979), Heath (1976), and Švejcer (1978). For American Indian languages, see Spolski and Kari (1974) and Stoller (1976); for Chicano English, Metcalf (1974), Thompson (1974), Sawyer (1964).

On Canadian English, see Orkin (1971); for relations with Canadian French, Inglehart and Woodward (1967) and Vallée and de Vries (1978). For South African English, see Lanham and McDonald (1980) and for Australian and New Zealand English, Turner (1972).

There is a fairly extensive literature on English in Africa, much of it concerned with language planning. See Spencer (1963 and 1971a), Whiteley (1971), Ladefoged et al. (1972). The article by Angogo and Hancock (1980) is excellent. See also Mazrui (1967) and Adeniran (1979).

On English in India, see Kachru (1969) and in Singapore and Malaysia, Platt (1980).

On colonial language policies in general, see Spencer (1963, 1971b). A good introduction to problems of language planning is by Le Page (1964).

Bibliography

Below is a list of books and articles consulted in the writing of this book. Fuller bibliographies can be found in the standard histories of English.

Adeniran, A. (1979), 'Personalities and policies in the establishment of English in northern Nigeria (1900-1943)', *International Journal of the Sociology of Language*, vol. 22, pp. 55-77.

Angogo, R. and Hancock, I. (1980), 'English in Africa', *English World-Wide*, vol. 1, no. 1, pp. 67-96.

Aitken, A.J. and McArthur, T. (1979), *Languages of Scotland*, Edinburgh, Chambers.

Andrew, S.O. (1940), *Syntax and Style in Old English*, Cambridge University Press.

Bailey, C.-J.N. (1973), 'The patterning of language variation', in Bailey and Robinson (eds), pp. 156-87.

Bailey, R.W. and Robinson, J.L., eds (1973), *Varieties of Present-Day English*, New York, Macmillan.

Baldi, P. and Werth, R.N., eds (1978), *Readings in Historical Phonology*, Pennsylvania State University Press.

Barry, M. (1967), 'Yorkshire sheep-scoring numerals', *Transactions of the Yorkshire Dialect Society*, part LXVII, pp. 21-32.

Barber, C.L. (1964), *Linguistic Change in Present-Day English*, Edinburgh, Oliver & Boyd.

Barber, C.L. (1972), *The Story of Language*, 5th ed., London, Pan.

Barber, C.L. (1976), *Early Modern English*, London, Deutsch.

Baugh, A.C. and Cable, T. (1978), *A History of the English Language*, 3rd ed., London, Routledge & Kegan Paul.

Bell. R.T. (1976), *Sociolinguistics: Goals, Approaches and Problems*, London, Batsford.

Berndt, R. (1965), 'The linguistic situation in England from the Norman Conquest to the loss of Normandy (1066-1204)', *Philologica Pragensica*, 8, pp. 145-63, reprinted in Lass (1969).

Bernstein, B. (1970), 'Social class, language, and socialisation', in Bernstein, B. (1971), pp. 170-89.

Bernstein, B. (1971), *Class, Codes and Control*, vol. 1: *Theoretical Studies Towards a Sociology of Language*, London, Routledge & Kegan Paul.

Bernstein, B., ed. (1973), *Class, Codes and Control*, vol. 2: *Empirical*

Studies, London, Routledge & Kegan Paul.

Berresford Ellis, P. (n.d.), *The Story of the Cornish Language*, Truro, Tor Mer Press.

Blake, N. (1976), 'Born in Kent', *Lore and Language*, vol. 2, no. 5, pp. 5-9.

Blake, N. (1977), *The English Language in Medieval Literature*, London, Dent.

Bliss, A.J. (1979), *Spoken English In Ireland 1600-1740*, Dublin, Dolmen; Humanities Press.

Bolton, W.F. (1967), *A Short History of Literary English*, London, Arnold.

Brosnahan, L.F. (1963), 'Some historical cases of language imposition', in J. Spencer (ed.), *Language in Africa: Papers of the Leverhulme Conference on Universities and the Language Problems of Tropical Africa Held at University College Ibadan*, Cambridge University Press, pp. 7-24, reprinted in Bailey and Robinson (1973).

Brown, R. and Gilman, A. (1960), 'The pronouns of power and solidarity', in T.A. Sebeok (ed.), *Style in Language*, MIT Press, pp. 253-76; reprinted in Giglioli (1972).

Bynon, T. (1977), *Historical Linguistics*, Cambridge University Press.

Byrne, Sister St G. (1936), *Shakespeare's Use of the Pronouns of Address, its Significance in Characterisation and Motivation*, New York, Haskell House.

Cameron, K. and Gelling, M., eds (1976), *Place-name Evidence for the Anglo-Saxon Invasion and Scandinavian Settlements*, Cambridge, English Place Name Society.

Carroll, J.B., ed. (1956), *Language, Thought and Reality: Selected Writings of Benjamin Lee Whorf*, MIT Press.

Cassidy, F.G. (1961), *Jamaica Talk: Three Hundred Years of the English Language in Jamaica*, London, Macmillan.

Clark, J.W. (1957), *Early English*, London, Deutsch.

Cottle, B. (1969), *The Triumph of English 1350-1400*, London, Blandford.

Craig, D.R. (1976), 'Bi-dialectal education: creole and standard in the West Indies', *International Journal of the Sociology of Language*, vol. 8, pp. 94-105.

Crystal, D. and Davy, D. (1969), *Investigating English Style*, London, Longman.

Davidson, B. (1978), *Africa in Modern History: The Search for a New Society*, London, Allen Lane.

Dittmar, N. (1976), *Sociolinguistics*, London, Arnold.

Dobson, E.J. (1955), 'Early modern standard English', *Transactions of the Philological Society*, pp. 25-54, reprinted in Lass (1969).

Dobson, E.J. (1968), *English Pronunciation 1500-1700*, Oxford University Press.

Dorian, N.C. (1980), 'Language shift in community and individual: the phenomenon of the laggard semi-speaker', *International Journal of the Sociology of Language*, vol. 25, pp. 85-94.

Edwards, V. (1979), *The West Indian Language Issue in British Schools*, London, Routledge & Kegan Paul.

Ekwall, E., ed. (1947), *The Concise Oxford Dictionary of English Place-Names*, 3rd ed., Oxford University Press.

Ekwall, E. (1956), *Studies in the Population of Medieval London*, Lund, Lund Studies in English.

Elcock, W.D. (1975), *The Romance Languages*, London, Faber.

Ervin-Tripp, S. (1969), 'Sociolinguistic rules of address', from 'Sociolinguistics', in L. Berkowitz (ed.), *Advances in Experimental Social Psychology*, vol. 4, pp. 93-107, reprinted in Pride and Holmes (1972).

Ferguson, C.A. (1959), 'Diglossia', *Word*, 15, pp. 325-40, reprinted in Giglioli (1972).

Finberg, H.P.R. (1976), *The Formation of England*, St Albans, Paladin.

Fisher, J.H. and Bornstein, D. (1974), *In Forme of Speche is Chaunge*, Englewood Cliffs, Prentice-Hall.

Fishman, J.A. (1965), 'Who speaks what language to whom and when?', *La Linguistique*, 2, pp. 67-88, reprinted in Pride and Holmes (1972).

Fishman, J.A. (1971), *Sociolinguistics: A Brief Introduction*, Rowley, Newbury House.

Fishman, J.A. (1972), 'The sociology of language', in Giglioli (1972).

Fishman, J.A., ed. (1978), *Advances in the Study of Societal Multilingualism*, The Hague, Mouton.

Fishman, J.A., Ferguson, C.A. and Das Gupta, J., eds (1968), *Language Problems of Developing Nations*, New York, Wiley.

Fishman, J.A., Cooper, R.L. and Conrad, W., eds (1977), *The Spread of English: The Sociology of English as a Second Language*, Rowley, Mass., Newbury House.

Giglioli, P.P., ed (1972), *Language and Social Context*, Harmondsworth, Penguin.

Gimson, A.C. (1980), *An Introduction to the Pronunciation of English*, 3rd ed., London, Arnold.

Glauser, B. (1974), *The Scottish-English Linguistic Border: Lexical Aspects*, The Cooper Monographs, Berne, Francke Verlag.

Goody, J. and Watt, I. (1962), 'The consequences of literacy', *Comparative Studies in Society and History*, 5, pp. 304-26, 332-95, reprinted in Giglioli (1972).

Gordon, I.A. (1966), *The Movement of English Prose*, London, Longman.

Green, A.E. (1972), 'Folksong and dialect', *Transactions of the Yorkshire Dialect Society*, part LXXII, vol. 13, pp. 20-47.

Gregg, R.J. (1972), 'The Scottish-Irish dialect boundaries in Ulster', in M. Wakelin (ed.), *Patterns in the Folk Speech of the British Isles*, London, Athlone, pp. 109-39.

Hall, R.A. Jr (1980), 'Language, dialect and regional Italian', *International Journal of the Sociology of Language*, vol. 25, pp. 95-106.

Haugen, E. (1966), 'Dialect, language, nation', *American Anthropologist*, 68, pp. 922-35, reprinted in Pride and Holmes (1972).

Heath, S.B. (1976), 'A National language Academy? Debate in the new nation', *International Journal of the Sociology of Language*, vol. 11, pp. 9-43.

Holm, J. (1980), 'African features in white Bahama English', *English World-Wide*, vol. 1, no. 1, pp. 45-65.

Hornby, P., ed. (1977), *Bilingualism: Psychological, Social and Educational Implications*, London, Academic Press.

Hudson, R. (1980), *Sociolinguistics*, Cambridge University Press.

Huffines, M.L. (1980), 'Pennsylvania German: maintenance and shift', *International Journal of the Sociology of Language*, vol. 25, pp. 43-57.

Inglehart, R.F. and Woodward, M. (1967), 'Language conflicts and the political community', *Comparative Studies in Society and History*, 10, pp. 27-45, reprinted in Giglioli (1972).

Jackson, K. (1953), *Language and History in Early Britain*, Edinburgh University Press.

Jesperson, O. (1968), *Growth and Structure of the English Language*, 9th ed., Oxford, Blackwell.

Jones, R.F. (1953), *The Triumph of the English Language*, Oxford University Press.

Jones, R.M. (1979), 'Welsh bilingualism: four documents', in ·W.F. Mackey and J. Ornstein (eds), *Sociolinguistic Studies in Language Contact*, The Hague, Mouton, pp. 231-243.

Kachru, B. (1969), 'English in South Asia', in T.A. Sebeok (ed.), *Current Trends in Linguistics*, vol. 5, The Hague, Mouton, pp. 627-78, reprinted in Fishman (1978).

Katzner, K. (1977), *The Languages of the World*, London, Routledge & Kegan Paul.

Khlief, B. (1979), 'Language as an ethnic boundary in Welsh-English relations', *International Journal of the Sociology of Language*, vol. 20, pp. 59-74.

Kurath, H. (1972), *Studies in Area Linguistics*, Indiana University Press.

Labov, W. (1969), 'The logic of non-standard English', *Georgetown Monographs in Language and Linguistics*, vol. 22, pp. 1-22, 26-31, reprinted in Giglioli (1972).

Labov, W. (1970), 'The study of language in its social context', *Studium Generale*, vol. 23, pp. 66-84, reprinted in Giglioli (1972).

Labov, W. (1972a), *Sociolinguistic Patterns*, University of Pennsylvania Press; Oxford, Blackwell.

Labov. W. (1972b), *Language in the Inner City*, University of Pennsylvania Press; Oxford, Blackwell.

Labov, W. (1974), 'On the use of the present to explain the past', *Proceedings of the Eleventh International Congress of Linguists*, vol. 2, Bologna, pp. 825-51, reprinted in P. Baldi and R.N. Werth (1978).

Ladefoged, P., Glick, R. and Criper, C. (1972), *Language in Uganda*, Oxford University Press.

Lanham, L. and McDonald, C.A. (1980), *The Standard in South African English and its Social History*, Heidelberg, Julius Groos Verlag.

Lass, R. (1969), *Approaches to English Historical Linguistics*, New York, Holt, Rinehart & Winston.

Leech, G.N. (1974), *Semantics*, Harmondsworth, Penguin.

Leith, R. (1973), The Traditional Phonology of North London Speech, unpublished MPhil thesis, University of Leeds.

Le Page, R.B. (1964), *The National Language Question*, Oxford University Press.

Lewis, C.S. (1968), *Studies in Words*, Cambridge University Press.

Lewis, G. (1978), 'Migration and the decline of the Welsh language', in Fishman, ed. (1978), pp. 263-351.

Lockwood, W.B. (1975), *Languages of the British Isles Past and Present*, London, Deutsch.

Loyn, H.R. (1962), *Anglo-Saxon England and the Norman Conquest*, London, Longman.

Loyn, H.R. (1977), *The Vikings in Britain*, London, Batsford.

Macafee, C. (1980), review of A.J. Aitken and T. McArthur, *Languages of Scotland*, in *English World-Wide*, vol. I, no. 1, pp. 137-8.

McDavid, R. (1972), 'Go slow in ethnic attributions: geographical mobility and dialect prejudice', in Bailey and Robinson (1973), pp. 258-73.

McDavid, R. (1980), *Varieties of American English*, Stanford University Press.

Mackey, W.F. and Ornstein, J. (1979), *Sociolinguistic Studies in Language Contact*, The Hague, Mouton.

Mackinnon, K. (1977), *Language, Education and Social Processes in a Gaelic Community*, London, Routledge & Kegan Paul.

Mather, J.Y. and Speitel, H. (1975/7), *The Linguistic Atlas of Scotland: Scots Sections*, vols 1 and 2, London, Croom Helm.

Matthews, W. (1938), *Cockney Past and Present*, London, Routledge & Kegan Paul.

Mazrui. A.A. (1967), 'The English language and the origins of African nationalism', *Mawazo*, vol. I, no. 1, reprinted in Bailey and Robinson (1973), pp. 56-70.

Mazrui, A.A. (1975), *The Political Sociology of the English Language*, The Hague, Mouton.

Metcalf, A.A. (1974), 'The study of Californian Chicano English', *International Journal of the Sociology of Language*, vol. 2, pp. 53-8.

Milroy, J. and L. (1978), 'Belfast: change and variation in an urban vernacular', in P. Trudgill, ed. (1978), pp. 19-36.

Mioni, A.M. and Arnuzzo-Lanszweert, A.M. (1979), 'Sociolinguistics in Italy', *International Journal of the Sociology of Language*, vol. 21, pp. 81-107.

Mittins, W. *et al.* (1970), *Attitudes to English Usage*, Oxford University Press.

Mossé, F. (1952), *A Handbook of Middle English*, Johns Hopkins University Press; Oxford University Press.

O'Donnell, W.R. and Todd, L. (1980), *Variety in Contemporary English*, London, Allen and Unwin.

Ó'Muirithe, D. (1977), *The English Language in Ireland*, Dublin, Mercier Press.

Ó'Riagáin, P. and Ó'Gliasáin, M. (1979), *All-Irish Primary Schools in the Dublin Area*, publication 16(b), Dublin, Institiúid Teangeolaíochta Éireann.

Orkin, M. (1971), *Speaking Canadian English*, London, Routledge & Kegan Paul.

Orton, H. and Wright, N. (1974), *A Word Geography of England*, London, Seminar Press.

Oxenham, J. (1980), *Literacy: Writing, Reading and Social Organisation*, London, Routledge & Kegan Paul.

Pace, S. (1975), 'A sociolinguistic consideration of the English spoken in Grenada, British West Indies', in Mackey and Ornstein (1979), pp. 265-76.

Page, N (1973), *Speech in the English Novel*, London, Longman.

Palmer, F. (1971), *Grammar*, Harmondsworth, Penguin.

Partridge, A.C. (1969), *Tudor to Augustan English*, London, Deutsch.

Platt, J.T. (1980), 'Varieties and functions of English in Singapore and Malaysia', *English World-Wide*, vol. 1, no. 1, pp. 97-121.

Pride, J. and Holmes, J. (1972), *Sociolinguistics: Selected Readings*, Harmondsworth, Penguin.

Quirk, R. (1968), *The Use of English*, London, Longman.

Quirk, R. (1972), 'Philology, politics and American English', and 'Linguistic bonds across the Atlantic', *The English Language and Images of Matter*, Oxford University Press, pp. 1-13, 14-31.

Quirk, R. (1974), 'Shakespeare and the English language', *The Linguist and the English Language*, London, Arnold, pp. 46-64.

Quirk, R. and Greenbaum, S. (1973), *A University Grammar of English*, London, Longman.

Ramchand, K. (1970), 'The language of the master', from *The West Indian Novel and its Background*, London, Faber, reprinted in Bailey and Robinson (1973), pp. 115-46.

Rayfield, J.R. (1970), *The Languages of a Bilingual Community*, The Hague, Mouton.

Reed, C. (1967), *Dialects of American English*, New York, World Publishing Co.

Reid, E. (1978), 'Social and stylistic variation in the speech of children: some evidence from Edinburgh', in Trudgill (1978), pp. 158-71.

Romaine, S. (1978), 'Post-vocalic /r/ in Scottish English: a sound-change in progress?' in Trudgill (1978), pp. 144-57.

Rosen, H. and Burgess, T. (1980), *Languages and Dialects of London Schoolchildren*, London, Ward Lock.

Salmon, V. (1967), 'English colloquial language in the Falstaff plays', *Leeds Studies in English*, New Series, vol. 1, pp. 37-70.

Samuels, M.L. (1972), *Linguistic Evolution*, Cambridge University Press.

Sanderson, S. *et al.* (1978), *The Linguistic Atlas of England*, London, Croom Helm.

Sawyer, J.B. (1964), 'Social aspects of bilingualism in San Antonio,

Texas', *Publications of the American Dialect Society*, 41, pp. 7-15, reprinted in Bailey and Robinson (1973).
Schulz, M.R. (1975), 'The semantic derogation of women', in B. Thorne and N. Henley (eds), *Language and Sex: Difference and Dominance*, Rowley, Mass., Newbury House, pp. 64-75.
Scragg, D.G. (1975), *History of English Spelling*, Manchester University Press.
Sheard, J.A. (1954), *The Words we Use*, London, Deutsch.
Sivertsen, E. (1960), *Cockney Phonology*, Oslo, Oslo Studies in English, no. 8.
Smith, R.B. and Lance, D.M. (1979), 'Standard and disparate varieties of English in the United States: educational and sociopolitical implications', *International Journal of the Sociology of Language*, vol. 21, pp. 127-40.
Speitel, H.H. (1978), 'The word geography of the Borders', in H. Speitel (ed.), *The Scottish Literary Journal*, Supplement no. 6, Spring 1978.
Spencer, J. (1963), *Language in Africa*, Cambridge University Press.
Spencer, J. (1971a), *The English Language in West Africa*, London, Longman.
Spencer, J. (1971b), 'Colonial language policies and their legacies', in T. Sebeok (ed.), *Current Trends in Linguistics*, vol. 7, The Hague, Mouton, pp. 537-47.
Spolsky, B. and Kari, J. (1974), 'Apachean language maintenance', *International Journal of the Sociology of Language*, vol. 2, pp. 92-100.
Stephens, M. (1976), *Linguistic Minorities of Western Europe*, Llandysul, Gomer Press.
Stewart, W.A. (1968), 'A sociolinguistic typology for describing national multilingualism', in J. Fishman, ed. (1968), *Readings in the Sociology of Language*, The Hague, Mouton, pp. 531-45.
Stoller, P. (1976), 'The language planning activities of the US office of bilingual education', *International Journal of the Sociology of Language*, vol. 11, pp. 45-60.
Strang, B. (1968), *Modern English Structure*, 2nd ed., London, Arnold.
Strang, B. (1970), *A History of English*, London, Methuen.
Strevens, P. (1972), *British and American English*, London, Collier-Macmillan.
Švejcer, A.D. (1978), *Standard English in the United States and England*, The Hague, Mouton.
Thompson, R.M. (1974), 'Mexican American language loyalty and the validity of the 1970 census', *International Journal of the Sociology of Language*, vol. 2, pp. 7-17.
Thomson, D., ed. (1976), *Gaelic in Scotland: A Blueprint for Official and Private Initiatives*, Glasgow, Gairm.
Todd, L. (1974), *Pidgins and Creoles*, London, Routledge & Kegan Paul.
Traugott, E.C. (1972), *A History of English Syntax*, New York, Holt, Rinehart & Winston.
Trudgill, P. (1974a), *The Social Differentiation of English in Norwich*, Cambridge University press.

Trudgill, P. (1974b), *Sociolinguistics: An Introduction*, Harmonds-worth, Penguin.

Trudgill, P. (1975), *Accent, Dialect and the School*, London, Arnold.

Trudgill, P., ed. (1978), *Sociolinguistic Patterns in British English*, London, Arnold.

Trudgill, P. and Hughes, A. (1979), *English Accents and Dialects: An Introduction to Social and Regional Varieties of British English*, London, Arnold.

Tucker, S. (1967), *Protean Shape: A Study in Eighteenth Century Vocabulary and Usage*, London, Athlone.

Tucker, S. (1972), *Enthusiasm: A Study in Semantic Change*, Cambridge University Press.

Turner, G.W. (1972), *The English Language in Australia and New Zealand*, London, Longman.

Turner, G.W. (1973), *Stylistics*, Harmondsworth, Penguin.

Turvey, H. (1978), *Language Policy and Socioeconomic Development in Ireland*, occasional paper 4, Dublin, Institiúid Teangeolaíochta Éireann.

Underwood, G. (1974), 'American English dialectology: alternatives for the south west', *International Journal of the Sociology of Language*, vol. 2, pp. 19-40.

Vallée, F. and de Vries, J. (1978), 'Trends in bilingualism in Canada', in Fishman, ed. (1978).

Wakelin, M.F. (1972), *English Dialects: An Introduction*, London, Athlone.

Wakelin, M.F., ed. (1972), *Patterns in the Folk Speech of the British Isles*, London, Athlone.

Waldron, R.A. (1967), *Sense and Sense Development*, London, Deutsch.

Walker, J. (1836), *A Critical Pronouncing Dictionary*, Preston, Banks.

Wallwork, J.F. (1978), *Language and People*, London, Heinemann.

Whiteley, W.H. (1971), *Language Use and Social Change: Problems of Multilingualism with Special Reference to Eastern Africa*, Oxford University Press.

Whitelock, D. (1965), *The Beginnings of English Society*, revised ed., Harmondsworth, Pelican.

Williams, R. (1961), 'Standard English', *The Long Revolution*, Harmondsworth, Penguin.

Williams, R. (1976), *Keywords: A Vocabulary of Culture and Society*, Glasgow, Fontana/Croom Helm.

Williamson, R.C. and Van Eerde, J.A. (1980), 'Sub-cultural factors in the survival of secondary languages: a cross-national sample', *International Journal of the Sociology of Language*, vol. 25, pp. 59-83.

Wyld, H.C. (1936), *A History of Modern Colloquial English*, Oxford University Press.

DATE DUE

GAYLORD PRINTED IN U.S.A.